Spirit and Beauty

Spirit and Beauty

An Introduction To
Theological Aesthetics

PATRICK SHERRY

CLARENDON PRESS · OXFORD
1992

Oxford University Press, Walton Street, Oxford OX2 6DP
Oxford New York Toronto
Delhi Bombay Calcutta Madras Karachi
Petaling Jaya Singapore Hong Kong Tokyo
Nairobi Dar es Salaam Cape Town
Melbourne Auckland
and associated companies in
Berlin Ibadan

Oxford is a trade mark of Oxford University Press

Published in the United States
by Oxford University Press, New York

British Library Cataloguing in Publication Data
Data available

ISBN 0–19–826743–6

Library of Congress Cataloging in Publication Data
Spirit and beauty : an introduction to theological aesthetics
Patrick Sherry.
Includes bibliographical references and index.
1. Aesthetics—Religious aspects—Christianity.   2. Holy spirit.
I. Title.
BR115.A8S53   1991   230—dc20   91–26544
ISBN 0–19–826743–6–0

Typeset by Cambridge Composing (UK) Ltd
Printed in Great Britain by
Bookcraft (Bath) Ltd.,
Midsomer Norton, Avon

PREFACE

In recent years there has been a renewed concern with the
Holy Spirit, both among theologians and in the life of the
Church. This concern, however, rarely extends to the area of
aesthetics. Yet if we look back over the history of theology,
we find that some of the earliest Christian Fathers associated
the Holy Spirit with both natural beauty and artistic skill,
supporting their case by appeals to biblical texts about Creation or to the account in Exodus of the inspiration of the
craftsman Bezalel by the spirit of God. We find, too, that the
association is made by many later theologians, so that the
topic is like a subterranean stream which breaks out into the
open periodically throughout Christian history, in widely
different places and eras (not to mention similar beliefs in
some other religions). It is also an ecumenical topic, for those
who have touched on it include such diverse figures as St
Irenaeus, St Clement of Alexandria, Calvin, Jonathan
Edwards, Sergius Bulgakov, and Hans Urs von Balthasar,
people of very different ecclesiastical and intellectual backgrounds. But of course the topic is of interest to others besides
theologians, for many ordinary people regard outstanding
works of art as inspired by God and see natural beauty as
reflecting His glory.

This book is designed to be an introduction to theological
aesthetics which concentrates on the role of the Holy Spirit.
It will both investigate the connection between the Holy
Spirit and beauty and range more widely by considering
topics like divine glory and the nature of inspiration. In doing
so it will bring together two areas of lively interest in
contemporary Christianity, the theology of the Holy Spirit
and theological aesthetics.

Appropriately, most of the research for this work was done
in two places of great beauty, one rural and one urban. I am
grateful to Dr Patrick Henry for inviting me to be a Fellow at
the Institute for Ecumenical and Cultural Research, Collegeville, Minnesota; and likewise to Professor Peter Jones for

inviting me to be a Fellow at the Institute for Advanced Studies in the Humanities at the University of Edinburgh. I owe much to conversations with them and with other Fellows at both places. I am grateful, too, to my colleagues in Lancaster for their help and encouragement, and to Mrs Joan Chesters for her skilful typing.

P.S.

CONTENTS

I

Introduction: The Holy Spirit
and Aesthetics

IN 1956 the theologian Karl Barth published a short book of writings about Mozart, to honour the bicentenary of the composer's birth. He confessed that for years and years he had begun each day by listening to his music, and only after this (not to mention reading the newspaper) had he given attention to his *Church Dogmatics*; and that if he ever went to heaven, he would first of all seek out Mozart, and only then enquire about Augustine, Thomas, Luther, Calvin, and Schleiermacher. Barth was doing more than expressing his appreciation of his favourite composer, for he spoke of the 'parables of the kingdom of heaven' glimpsed in Mozart's music, and surmised that 'we must certainly assume that the dear Lord had a special, direct contact with *him*'.[1] Here he was touching on some themes developed a few years earlier, in volume iii of his *Church Dogmatics*, where he asked why it is possible to hold that Mozart has a place in theology, especially in the doctrine of creation and also in eschatology, although he was not a father of the Church, nor, it seems, a particularly devout Christian. Barth answered his own question:

because he knew something about creation in its total goodness that neither the real fathers of the Church . . . nor indeed any other great musicians before and after him, either know or can express and maintain as he did. . . . He had heard, and causes those who have ears to hear, even today, what we shall not see until the end of time—the whole context of providence.

Again, Barth spoke of Mozart as God's instrument: 'He simply offered himself as the agent by which little bits of

---

[1] Karl Barth, *Wolfgang Amadeus Mozart*, trans. Clarence K. Pott (Grand Rapids, 1986), 57, 26.

horn, metal and catgut could serve as the voices of creation . . .'[2]

Barth's tributes point towards the territory which I shall explore in this book; and his remarks about God's direct contact with Mozart and about the latter's offering of himself approach an idea which goes back to the earliest Christian Fathers, and indeed to the Old Testament, and which will be our main focus, the idea that through His Spirit God creates beauty which foreshadows the world to come. Curiously, Barth does not explicitly appeal to the Holy Spirit in this context; but Peter Shaffer supplies what Barth has omitted in his play *Amadeus*, where he depicts Mozart's rival Salieri as recognizing that God's spirit is blowing through Mozart and as being led by jealousy to attempt to frustrate God's work by blocking Mozart's career.[3]

The full development of this idea involves the claims that the Spirit of God communicates God's beauty to the world, both through Creation, in the case of natural beauty, and through inspiration, in the case of artistic beauty; that earthly beauty is thus a reflection of divine glory, and a sign of the way in which the Spirit is perfecting creation; and that beauty has an eschatological significance, in that it is an anticipation of the restored and transfigured world which will be the fullness of God's kingdom. We have, then, to consider both natural and artistic beauty; and hence two forms of divine agency whereby God manifests His glory in such beauties, namely creation and inspiration (both of which may be labelled as creation; but in the case of inspiration God is working through human minds). It is not simply a matter of saying that God is the cause of beauty through the Spirit, for the claim is being made that God is Himself beautiful, or indeed, some would say, beauty itself, and that earthly beauty participates in His nature or at least reflects it in some way.

If indeed the beauties of nature and art reflect God's glory, then they *show* us something of Him. This means that we are

---

[2] Karl Barth, *Church Dogmatics* (henceforth abbreviated as *CD*), iii, pt. 3, trans. G. W. Bromiley and R. J. Ehrlich, (Edinburgh, 1960), 298.

[3] For a comparison between Barth's and Shaffer's treatments of this theme, see my 'Mozart, *Amadeus* and Barth', *New Blackfriars*, 67 (1986), 233–40.

not concerned now with making inferences to God's existence and nature from beautiful things we perceive, with what has come to be called natural theology. Many philosophers and theologians have indeed used beauty as the basis for such arguments, or they have claimed that the existence of God is the best explanation of it. The fifteenth-century Neoplatonist Marsilio Ficino said 'By its utility, harmony and decorativeness, the world testifies to the skill of the divine artist and is proof that God is indeed its Maker.'[4] More recently, F. R. Tennant used the appeal to the beauty of the world as part of his re-presentation of the argument to God's existence from design, in his *Philosophical Theology*.[5] Such arguments, however, are not our present concern, for we are looking rather at the claims of those who are seeking to discern the Holy Spirit's presence and activity in the world. I am not ruling out their validity, but I suggest that however plausible the arguments of natural theology turn out to be from a philosophical point of view, they must face the religious consideration that, as Frederic Crosson puts it, 'an inferred God is an absent God'.[6]

Such claims to discern the presence of God or the workings of the Holy Spirit are made in connection with some other qualities, besides beauty. The most obvious example is holiness (which, as we shall see, some theologians regard as a kind of beauty). Tolstoy said of the *staretz* Amvrosy 'when one talks with such a man, one feels the nearness of God'.[7] In saying this, Tolstoy was not, again, making an inference, but expressing his feeling that he discerned God's presence in Amvrosy. The experiences of encountering a holy person and beholding something of great beauty might both be described as sacramental, in the sense that for many people they are

---

[4] Quoted by Wladyslaw Tatarkiewicz in his *History of Aesthetics*, iii (The Hague, 1974), 102.

[5] F. R. Tennant, *Philosophical Theology*, ii (Cambridge, 1930), 89–93. Aquinas' Fourth Way (*Summa Theologiae*, 1a. ii. 3) is an example of a different kind of argument, from degrees of perfection in the world, which might also include an appeal to beauty.

[6] In C. F. Delaney (ed.), *Religion and Rationality* (London and Notre Dame, 1979), 54. The argument of Andrew Louth's essay, *Discerning the Mystery* (Oxford, 1983) is very relevant to this point.

[7] Quoted in K. Leech, *Soul Friend* (London, 1977), 48. It is claimed that the character Fr. Zossima in Dostoevsky's *The Brothers Karamazov* is based on him.

signs of God's presence and activity, the sensible revealing the spiritual, and also occasions for wonder and awe. In both cases, too, people often appeal to the idea of inspiration. Of course, there are also significant differences: holiness in the sense of saintliness is a perfection of rational beings, whereas beauty can be possessed by inanimate nature and artefacts, and in the case of the latter the artist serves as an agent of creation.

The fascination of the idea which I have just outlined stems from the fact that it brings together two important areas of human existence, religion and aesthetics, both of which are concerned (or should be concerned) with what is profound and moving in our lives. Philosophers from Plato onwards have recognized the power of beauty, even if they have taken a dim view of some artistic creations. This power and the wonder it evokes explain why they have often listed beauty together with truth and goodness as subjects of utmost importance, rather than associating it with, say, humour— though that also is an area of human creativity. Religious people, too, have responded to natural beauty, and have recognized that art may have a moral or a religious dimension and may serve as a vehicle of a religious vision. In linking the question specifically with the theology of the Holy Spirit, I am seeking to enrich an area of theology which has received a lot of attention recently after being relatively neglected for several centuries, at least in the Western churches, both Catholic and Protestant.

The topic is also fascinating because in so far as it has been treated by theologians, they have been of very varied times and backgrounds: early Alexandria, eighteenth-century New England, and the twentieth-century Russian Orthodox emigration. It is thus a truly ecumenical topic. To see this and to get a clearer view of the ideas we are considering let us look briefly at a few treatments of the question.

A GLANCE AT HISTORY

The first Christian theologian to have dealt with the topic was, as far as I know, St Irenaeus. In Book iv of his *Against the Heresies*, written towards the end of the second century, he identifies God's Word with the Son, and Wisdom with the Spirit, and says that they were both with the Father before Creation, and that God made all things by the Word and adorned them by Wisdom (iv. 20. 1–3). This is part of Irenaeus' polemic against the Gnostics: in response to them he insists on the goodness of matter and the knowability of God, who reveals Himself through His two 'hands', the Son and the Spirit, and who made the world through them. In another work, the *Demonstration of the Apostolic Preaching*, Irenaeus quotes Ps. 33: 6, 'By the word of Yahweh the heavens were made, their whole array by the breath of his mouth', and says that the Word establishes the reality of being and the Spirit gives order and form to the diversity of powers (ch. 5; there is, of course, a play on words here, for both in Hebrew and in Greek the same word means 'breath' and 'spirit'). Two chapters later he lays down an important principle which seeks to relate the three divine Persons in the order of salvation and which will recur in several later Trinitarian discussions: he says that without the Spirit it is impossible to see the Son, and without the Son no one can approach the Father.[8]

Irenaeus' brief remarks were expanded into a formula nearly two centuries later by one of the Cappadocian Fathers, St Gregory of Nazianzus, who described the three Persons of the Trinity as, respectively, the Cause, the Maker, and the Perfecter.[9] His remarks are also echoed by some twentieth-century theologians, especially in the Russian Orthodox Church. Sergius Bulgakov, for instance, writes that 'God is glorious, and His Glory is Beauty itself'. He then says that the Father gave existence to the world through the Son, and completes it through the Holy Spirit; and that at the end of time the heavenly Jerusalem will come, and 'the whole world,

---

[8] *Demonstration*, ch. 7. The same progression is delineated in *Against the Heresies* (henceforth abbreviated as *Adv. Haer.*), v. 36. 2.

[9] *Oration* xxxiv. 8 (Migne, *Patrologia Graeca* (henceforth abbreviated as *PG*) 36: 249a); the three terms used are *aitios*, *demiurge*, and *telepoios*. Cf. *Or.* xxxviii. 9 (*PG* 36: 320c). His friend St Gregory of Nyssa says that by the will of the Father every good thing is brought to perfection in the power of the Spirit through the only-begotten God (*On Not Three Gods*, (*PG* 45: 129ab); cf. St Basil, *On the Holy Spirit*, xvi. 38 (*PG* 32: 136b). For further references to the Holy Spirit as 'Perfecter', see Yves Congar, *I Believe in the Holy Spirit*, trans. David Smith (3 vols.; London, 1983), iii. 153, n. 28.

too, the waters and the land, will be transfigured by the Holy Ghost, and will appear in their beauty'.[10] Another Russian writer, Pavel Florensky, distinguishes between the work of the Word and of the Spirit in a somewhat different way, when he says that lawfulness, good order, and *cosmos*, which he describes as the realm of science, are rooted in the Word, the Son; whereas on the Spirit rest inspiration, creativity, freedom, asceticism, and beauty, things which stand outside scientific investigation, because here there is interruptedness rather than lawfulness.[11]

Irenaeus was thinking of natural beauty. But another early Christian writer, St Clement of Alexandria, made the connection between the Holy Spirit and artistic beauty. He too quotes a text from the Old Testament, Exod. 31: 2–5, which relates how the Spirit of God came on Bezalel, so that he was endowed with wisdom, understanding, knowledge, and skill in every kind of craft; and he says that this text shows that 'artistic and skilful invention is from God'.[12] The text he uses was quoted also, as we shall see, by many later writers; it is one of the first biblical texts to describe people being filled with the Spirit of God, and notable in relating Bezalel's artistic gifts to wisdom given by the Spirit.[13] Although he was

[10] Sergius Bulgakov, 'Religion and Art', in E. L. Mascall (ed.), *The Church of God: An Anglo-Russian Symposium* (London, 1934), 175–6. See also his *Le Paraclet* (Paris, 1946), especially ch. 4, where he describes the beauty of the world as the effect of the Holy Spirit; and Charles Lee Graves, *The Holy Spirit in the Theology of Sergius Bulgakov* (Geneva, 1972), ch. 2.

[11] Pavel A. Florensky, 'On the Holy Spirit', in Alexander Schmemann (ed.), *Ultimate Questions: An Anthology of Modern Russian Religious Thought* (New York, 1965), 137–72, esp. 155. This is an excerpt from Florensky's *Pillar and Ground of Truth*. See also V. Ivanov, 'The Aesthetic Views of Fr. Pavel Florensky', *Journal of the Moscow Patriarchate* 1982, no. 9, 75–8.

[12] *Stromateis* (Miscellanies) i. 4.

[13] The Talmud parallels Bezalel's wisdom, understanding, and knowledge with the Lord's wisdom in founding the earth, His understanding in founding the heavens, and His knowledge in breaking up the depths, citing Proverbs 3: 19–20 (*Berakoth* 55a, in *The Babylonian Talmud*, i, ed. I. Epstein (London, 1948), 336). Joseph Gutmann argues that the priestly writers may have utilized and embroidered the Bezalel tradition to show that the furnishings of the Temple, e.g. the lampstand of pure gold (Exod. 37: 17 ff.), were already found in the tabernacle in the desert; thereby they would seek to justify the artistic appurtenances of the Temple. Gutmann thinks that the costly materials mentioned in Exodus would have been out of keeping in a semi-nomadic existence (*Beauty in Holiness: Studies in Jewish Customs and Ceremonial Art* (New York, 1970), 4–5).

a man of wide culture, who regarded Greek philosophy as the preparation of the pagan world for Christ, Clement himself did not pursue this theme any further; indeed, later in the same work he warns against artists claiming the divine prerogative of creation (*Strom.* vi. 16). He did, however, take two steps which influenced much subsequent discussion of the question: he says that God (or Christ) is the true beauty, and that on earth the best kind of beauty is spiritual beauty. Of Christ, Clement says, quoting John 1: 9, 'our Saviour is beautiful to be loved by those who desire true beauty, for he was "the true light"' (*Strom.* ii. 5). Hence the person in whom the Word dwells is made like God and is beautiful: 'This is the true beauty, for it is God'.[14] Such a beauty is labelled 'spiritual beauty', and it is brought about through the agency of the Holy Spirit: 'The best beauty is spiritual [*psychikon*] beauty . . . and it appears when the soul is adorned by the Holy Spirit and inspired by its lustre—righteousness, reason, courage, temperance, love of good and modesty, which is matched by nothing with pleasant colour' (*Paed.* iii. 11). Clement is not dismissing natural or artistic beauty, as his remarks about Bezalel show; but he regards them as transitory (*Paed.* ii. 8). Like Plato in the *Symposium*, he treats earthly beauty as the bottom rung of a ladder from which we ascend to beauty itself: Clement says that he who in chaste love looks on beauty sees the body as an image by whose beauty he transports himself to the Artist and to the true beauty[15] (whereas the fallen angels renounced the beauty of God for a beauty which fades[16]).

Clement's 'spiritualization' of beauty is followed by several other early Christian Fathers. St Basil, for instance, also compares God to an artist, whose workshop, the earth, shows forth His wondrous works; and he assigns the Holy Spirit a role in Creation.[17] But in his treatise *On the Holy Spirit* he is more concerned with the divine beauty and with our spiritual beauty. He says that those who have been cleansed from the

[14] *Paedagogus* (Instructor), iii. 1.
[15] *Strom.* iv. 12.
[16] *Paed.* iii. 2. See further Tatarkiewicz, *History of Aesthetics*, ii (The Hague, 1970), 18–20, 24–5.
[17] *In Hexaemeron*, iv. 33 (*PG* 29: 80b); ii. 6 (*PG* 29: 41c–44b).

shame of their evil and returned to their natural beauty can draw near to the Paraclete, who 'like the sun, with the help of your purified eye will show you in himself the image of the unseen. And in the blessed sight of the image you will see the inexpressible beauty of the archetype' (ix. 23; the image and the archetype are the Son and the Father). Souls illuminated by the indwelling Spirit are compared by Basil to bright and transparent bodies lit by a sunbeam: they send out their grace to others. Likewise, St Cyril of Alexandria makes a specific link between the Holy Spirit and beauty, but again limits his treatment to spiritual or moral beauty. Towards the end of his commentary on St Matthew's Gospel, for instance, Cyril says that when God created Adam, He gave him most perfect beauty, making him a sharer in his spirit (Gen. 2: 7), which he lost through sin; but it pleased God that everything should be recapitulated in Christ, and that our nature should be restored to its former beauty; and so when Christ after the Resurrection said 'Receive the Holy Spirit' (John 20: 22) he renewed our former beauty, and the Spirit was thereby united with us.[18] Cyril also says that the Spirit makes us partakers in the divine nature and engraves in us the divine image, imprinting the transcendent beauty in us, like a seal.[19] But as we shall see in Chapter 6, Cyril was a Dualist in his view of the relation between soul and body, and so he restricted the likeness between God and human beings to the soul.

We find similar lines of thought in the early Father who was most concerned with aesthetic matters, St Augustine (though he contributes little to our specific concern, the role of the Holy Spirit). He seems to have had a divided mind about the importance of beauty. On the one hand, he follows Clement's view of the arts when he says that God's art works through artificers who make beautiful and harmonious things.[20] He also sees the beauty of the world as created by God, quoting the text 'consider the lilies of the field' (*City of God*, x. 14). He has much to say, too, about God's beauty: in

---

[18] *In Mt.* xxiv. 51 (*PG* 72: 446c). See also *In Jn.* xiv. 20 (*PG* 74: 277b–d), and Headings of the Arguments on the Holy Spirit (*PG* 75: 1144b–c).

[19] *Dialogue 7 on the Holy Trinity* (*PG* 75: 1085a, 1088b–c).

[20] *On Eight-three Questions*, no. 78 (Migne, *Patrologia Latina* (henceforth abbreviated as *PL*) 40: 89–90).

his *Confessions* he calls on God, 'O my supreme and good Father, Beauty of all things beautiful' (iii. 6), and goes on to acknowledge Him as the source of the splendour of the heavens and earth: 'It was You, Lord, who made them: for You are beautiful, and they are beautiful' (xi. 4). Indeed, God is that beauty 'in imitation of which the rest of things are beautiful';[21] He is 'the Good and the Beautiful, in, by and through whom all good and beautiful things have these qualities' (*Soliloquia*, i. 1. 3). On the other hand, he feels that earthly beauty may prove to be a trap, which by its allure keeps people away from God and provides only a transitory satisfaction. Perhaps this suspicion of beauty arose from Augustine's own experience: in a famous passage in his *Confessions* he exclaims 'Late have I loved Thee, O Beauty so ancient and so new! For behold Thou wert within me, and I outside; and I sought Thee outside and in my unloveliness fell upon those lovely things that Thou has made' (x. 27, trans. F. Sheed). He warns us that physical beauty is the lowest grade of beauty, which is mixed up with all kinds of imperfections (*On True Religion*, xl. 74 *f.*). We should seek, rather, beauty of soul; and that incorporeal beauty, which gives form to the mind and through which we judge that all the actions of a wise man are beautiful (*Letter* 118). Moreover, the greatest beauty is God Himself, compared with whom nothing else is beautiful (*Confessions*, xi. 4).

Augustine exhorts people to go from the beautiful things which they see and admire to love the beautiful but invisible creator.[22] But evidently he did not expect that many of them would seek to go beyond beautiful things in search of their source, and so he did not trust that after all they would be led from earthly beauty to the true Beauty Himself. He thought that there is too much risk of being satisfied to remain on the bottom rungs of the ladder without mounting further, and so of being kept away from God by beautiful things. Again, autobiographical considerations are revealing here: in his *Confessions* Augustine chides his younger self for having had

---

[21] *De Ordine* ii, ch. 19 (*PL* 32: 1019); he goes on immediately to say that compared with God everything else is filthy.

[22] *Exposition on the Psalms*, lxxix. 14 (*PL* 36: 1028).

his back to the light and his face on the things on which the
light falls (iv. 16; he is describing the writing of his early
work on aesthetics, the *De Pulchro et Apto*). More generally,
he warns that the love of temporal things is an obstacle to our
reaching heavenly things (*On True Religion*, xxiv. 45).

In all of the passages in his writings which I have mentioned
Augustine is speaking of the beauty of the One God, without
bringing in any Trinitarian considerations. In so far as he
associates beauty with any particular Person, it is with the
Son: in his *On the Trinity* he mentions St Hilary's characteri-
zation of the three Persons as Father, Image, and Gift, and
then ascribes beauty to the Son, who is the exact image of the
Father and also the 'perfect Word and, so to speak, art of the
almighty and wise God'. He goes on to describe the Holy
Spirit as 'the sweetness of the begetter and of the begotten,
pouring out upon all creatures . . . His immense bounty and
the fullness of His gifts . . .' (*De Trin*. vi. 10. 11). He does
not, however, single out beauty among those gifts.

There is no reason why an orthodox Christian should not
associate beauty with *both* the Son and the Spirit, for it may
be that they have different roles in manifesting the glory of
the Father (I shall argue later that this is the correct position).
Indeed, some of the early Christian writers whom I have
already mentioned also associated beauty with the Son, and
did not seem to find any inconsistency in doing so. Clement,
as we have seen, attributes beauty to Christ, whilst Basil says
that we see the unbegotten beauty (i.e. of the Father) in the
Begotten;[23] and Cyril of Alexandria, commenting on John 17:
6, says that the Disciples were led from the natural beauty of
the Son to the beauty of the Father, and from the accurate
image perceived the archetype[24] (cf. Heb. 1: 3). Augustine,
however, mentions only the connection between beauty and
the Son; and such was his influence that his view predomi-
nated in Western theology for several centuries.

We find the classical development of the Augustinian view
in St Thomas Aquinas. In a much-quoted passage in the
Summa Theologiae he says that three conditions are required
for the ascription of beauty to anything: integrity or complete-

---

[23] *Letter* 38 (PG 32: 340b).   [24] *Thesaurus*, xxxii (PG 75: 560d–561a).

ness (*integritas sive perfectio*), right proportion or harmony (*debita proportio sive consonantia*), and radiance (*claritas*). He then goes on to say that these three characteristics make it particularly appropriate to associate beauty with the Son: wholeness, because he truly and fully possesses the nature of the Father, who is perfection itself; right proportion, because he is the express image of the Father; and radiance, because he is the Word, the resplendent light of understanding. Similarly, Aquinas finds it fitting to ascribe harmony (or connection) and joy to the Holy Spirit, for reasons to do with the procession of the Spirit in the Trinity which we shall discuss in Chapter 4 (1a. xxxix. 8; Augustine had already described the Holy Spirit as the harmony of the Trinity[25]).

It is to be noticed that Aquinas is not claiming that beauty is to be ascribed *only* to the Son. He uses a technical term 'appropriation', which was made current by an earlier medieval thinker, Alan of Lille, and explained by Aquinas in the previous article (ia. xxxix. 7). To 'appropriate' a quality or an action to one Person of the Trinity is to attribute to that Person something which is in fact common to all there but which has a special affinity with one Person because of his place in the Trinity. Thus, although Creation is the work of all three Persons, it is naturally associated with the Father, because he is the begetter, source, and origin within the Trinity. Similarly, beauty is the possession of the whole Godhead, but is particularly associated with the Son, for the reasons mentioned. So Aquinas is not ruling out a connection between beauty and the Holy Spirit. But, as it happens, he does not discuss this question. The same is true of St Bonaventure, the medieval thinker who gives the widest role to the concept of beauty in his theology. He too associates beauty with the Word, as the likeness and splendour of the Eternal Light, and describes him as the 'Eternal Art, by which, through which and according to which all beautiful things are formed'.[26]

---

[25] *On Christian Doctrine*, i. 5.
[26] *Itinerarium* (*The Soul's Journey to God*), ch. 2, §§7–9. See the discussion by Hans Urs von Balthasar in his *Glory of the Lord: A Theological Aesthetics*, ii, trans. Andrew Louth *et al.* (1984), 260–362; also Edgar de Bruyne, *Études d'esthétique médiévale*, iii (Bruges, 1946), 214–16 and 298–9, for the differences between Aquinas and Bonaventure on this point.

There were, however, some minor figures in the medieval period who mentioned the connection made by the early Fathers between the Holy Spirit and beauty, even if they did not develop it much further. Rupert of Deutz mentions the craftsmen Bezalel and Oholiab in his discussion of Exod. 35 and asks 'who can doubt that these or all arts of this type are gifts of God?'; he concludes that the arts are to be used for the service of God.[27] The example of Bezalel was discussed in a more interesting way by Theophilus, the twelfth-century writer of one of the earliest treatises on church decoration, who explores it in terms of the seven gifts of the Holy Spirit. He refers to Exod. 31: 1–11 and draws the moral that the artist who embellishes God's house will firmly believe that his heart has been filled with the Spirit of God. He then explains this in terms of the seven gifts of the Holy Spirit (derived from Isa. 11: 1–2): through the spirit of wisdom the artist knows that all created things come from God; through that of understanding he has received the capacity for skill; through that of counsel he displays his gift by working and teaching; through that of fortitude he works vigorously; through that of knowledge he is master of his skill; through that of godliness he regulates his work and its rewards; and through that of fear of the Lord he remembers that he can do nothing of himself.[28]

The connection between the Holy Spirit and beauty is also found occasionally in the liturgy, for example in the twelfth-century hymn 'Amor Patris et Filii' (no. 438 in *The English Hymnal*), which begins:

> Love of the Father, love of God the Son,
> From whom all came, in whom was all begun;
> Who formest heavenly beauty out of strife,
> Creation's whole desire and breath of life.

A different line of thought is glimpsed in the *Summa* attributed to the thirteenth-century English theologian, Alexander of Hales, which suggests that 'beauty in the divine [is] from the order of the divine persons', that is, the relation of the Son to the Father, from whom he is generated, and their

[27] *De Trinitate et Operibus Eius. In Exod.* bk. 4 (*PL* 167: 744b).
[28] Theophilus, *The Various Arts*, trans. C. R. Dodwell (London, 1961), 62–3.

relation to the Holy Spirit, who proceeds from both of them.[29] This remark, however, is made in reply to an objection, and is not explored any further.

The simple connection between the Holy Spirit and beauty made by some early Christian Fathers recurs at the Reformation in the work of Calvin. Although he did not favour the use of painting and sculpture in churches, Calvin followed many others in appealing to the example of Bezalel as showing that all the arts come from God and are to be respected as 'divine inventions'.[30] He also described music as one of the 'excellent gifts of the Spirit', when discussing Jubal, the inventor of the harp and the organ, in his commentary on Genesis.[31] As regards natural beauty, Calvin quotes Gen. 1: 2, which describes the Spirit of God as moving over the waters at Creation, and says that it shows: 'not only that the beauty of the universe (which we now perceive) owes its strength and preservation to the power of the Spirit but that before this adornment was added, even then the Spirit was occupied with tending that confused mass'.[32]

We find, however, a much fuller and deeper development of these ideas in the work of the eighteenth-century New England theologian Jonathan Edwards. He keys his discussion of aesthetics into a fully developed Trinitarian theology, according to which the Spirit's mission of beautifying is grounded in his role within the Trinity. This theology, moreover, explores Augustine's idea that the Holy Spirit is the harmony of the Trinity.

For Edwards, God's beauty or 'lovely majesty'[33] is pre-

[29] Alexander of Hales, *Summa Theologica*, pt. i. inq. 1, tract. 3, q. 3, art. 2, ad 2 (Quaracchi edn., i, n. 103, p. 163).

[30] See vol. iii of Calvin's Commentaries, trans. Charles W. Bingham (Grand Rapids, 1950), 291, 297; also his *Institutes*, i. 11. §12; ii. 2 §16.

[31] John Calvin, *Commentaries on Genesis*, ed. John King (Grand Rapids, 1948), 218.

[32] *Institutes*, i. 13. §14, trans. Ford Lewis Battles. See Abraham Kuyper, 'Calvinism and Art', ch. 5 of his *Lectures on Calvinism* (Grand Rapids, 1953), for a good discussion of Calvin and Calvinism in relation to aesthetics; also his *Work of the Holy Spirit*, trans. H. de Vries (Grand Rapids, 1975), 19, 27–31; and Léon Wencelius, *L'Esthétique de Calvin* (Paris, 1937; reprinted Geneva, 1979).

[33] Jonathan Edwards, *A Treatise concerning Religious Affections*, ed. John E. Smith (New Haven, 1959), 265, 298 f. Roland Delattre's *Beauty and Sensibility in the Thought of Jonathan Edwards* (New Haven, Conn., 1968) is a very comprehensive and helpful treatment of Edwards's thought here.

eminent among his attributes: God is beautiful, indeed beauty itself, and the source and foundation of all beauty in the world. He says that the Father created the world with his Son (he cites John 1: 3, Col. 1: 16, and Heb. 1: 10 on this point[34]), and that the Holy Spirit, being the harmony, excellence, and beauty of the deity, has the particular function of communicating beauty and harmony in the world.[35] This function follows from the Spirit's role within the Trinity: in his *Essay on the Trinity* Edwards says that the Father and Son delight in each other, and breathe forth the Holy Spirit in love and joy, thus 'the Holy Ghost, Being the Love and Joy of God, is his beauty and happiness, and it is in our partaking of the same holy Spirit that our Communion with God consists'.[36] Here, of course, he is taking for granted the Augustinian view of the Trinity, which regards the Holy Spirit as proceeding from the Father and the Son, and as the bond of love between them. But he gives the tradition a novel twist in construing this love as the source of beauty, and indeed as beauty itself.

Edwards says that the Holy Spirit has three functions with regard to creatures: to quicken, enliven, and beautify all things; to sanctify intelligent beings by communicating God's love (which he *is*) to them; and as the Comforter to comfort and delight the souls of God's people (*Essay*, pp. 97–102). He introduces the first of these functions by appealing, like Calvin, to Gen. 1: 2, which he glosses to read 'the Spirit of God moved upon the face of the waters or of the Chaos to bring it out of its Confusion into harmony and beauty', and by quoting Job 26: 13, which he translates as 'God by his Spirit garnished the heavens' (p. 90; again, there is a play on words between 'wind' and 'spirit'); and he concludes 'whose office can it be so Properly to give all things their sweetness and beauty as he who is himself the beauty and Joy of the

---

[34] Jonathan Edwards, *Miscellaneous Observations on Important Theological Subjects*, ed. John Erskine (Edinburgh, 1793), 434.

[35] Jonathan Edwards, *Miscellanies*, §293, in Harvey G. Townsend (ed.), *The Philosophy of Jonathan Edwards, from his Private Notebooks* (Westport, Conn., 1972), 260.

[36] Jonathan Edwards, *Essay on the Trinity*, ed. George P. Fisher (New York, 1903), 108.

Creator' (p. 98). Thus the Holy Spirit plays a particular role within creation, of communicating God's love and beauty to the world.

The two functions of beautifying and sanctifying are closely related, for Edwards; indeed they are identical, for God's beauty *is* His holiness, and our sanctification is the most significant manifestation of our participation in His beauty. Edwards describes God's holiness as 'The infinite beauty and excellence of his nature' in his *Essay* (p. 97); and in his *Dissertation concerning the End for which God created the World* he says that when God communicates virtue and holiness to creatures, the latter share in His 'moral excellency, which is properly the beauty of the divine nature',[37] a sharing which he compares to the brightness of a jewel reflecting the sun. Again, the Holy Spirit plays the particular role of making the soul partake of God's beauty, because 'Holiness, which is as it were the beauty and sweetness of the divine nature, is as much the proper nature of the Holy Spirit, as heat is the nature of fire'.[38]

Edwards does not associate beauty with the Holy Spirit alone, for he sees the Son, too, as the image of God's glory, and therefore as manifesting His beauty. In a *Miscellany* on the 'Excellency of Christ' he says that when we are delighted with flowery meadows, green trees and fields, rivers and murmuring streams, singing birds, and all the other glories of nature, we should see them as 'the emanations of the sweet benevolence of Jesus Christ', which have the 'footsteps of his sweet grace and beauty'; but he is more interested in moral and spiritual beauty, hence he ends, characteristically, by saying that we find the most proper image of Christ's beauty in the human soul.[39] He says, too, in one of his sermons that 'it is this sight of the divine beauty of Christ, that bows the wills, and draws the hearts of men'.[40] Edwards does not see any inconsistency here, for he thinks that we should not

---

[37] Ch. 1, §3; in *The Works of Jonathan Edwards*, viii, *Ethical Writings*, ed. Paul Ramsey (New Haven, 1989), 442.

[38] Edwards, *Religious Affections*, 201; cf. 257.

[39] *Miscellany* 108, quoted by Delattre, *Beauty and Sensibility*, 181.

[40] 'True Grace Distinguished from the Experience of Devils', in *Works*, Bohn edn., ii (London, 1865), 49.

separate the Word from the Spirit within the Godhead, nor
ignore the influence of the Spirit in the life and work of
Christ. In the same sermon he says that it is the saving grace
of God's Spirit that enables us to apprehend divine beauty;[41]
and in another sermon he says that the light of the Holy
Spirit, which is 'a kind of emanation of God's beauty', gives a
'sense of the heart' whereby the saints discover 'the divine
superlative glory and excellency of God and Christ'.[42] It
would seem, then, that Edwards regards the being and the
works of the two Persons as complementary, an idea which
Roland Delattre expresses neatly: 'The divine beauty that *is*
the Holy Spirit *appears* especially in the Son'.[43] This comple-
mentarity applies both to their relation within the Godhead
and to their missions in the world. Edwards uses an analogy,
found in some of the early Christian Fathers, that of the sun,
to summarize his position at the end of his *Essay*: the Father
is represented by its substance or inner constitution, the Son
by its brightness and glory, and the Spirit by its beams—the
rays of the sun and their beautiful colours, he says in
conclusion, well represent the Spirit.

Edwards's treatment raises many difficult questions about
the relationship between the Son and the Spirit, and about
his use of the Western, Augustinian model of the Trinity. I
shall return to those issues in Chapter 4, where I shall
contrast his approach with that of a contemporary Russian
theologian, Paul Evdokimov. As an Eastern Orthodox,
Evdokimov does not share Edwards's Augustinian view of the
Trinity. For him the Person of the Holy Spirit is hidden and
the procession a mystery. Nevertheless he concludes his
book, *L'Art de l'icône: Théologie de la beauté*, by quoting St
John of Damascus, 'The Son is the image of the Father and
the Holy Spirit is the image of the Son' (*On the Orthodox
Faith*, i. 13), a principle which he has earlier spelt out in
terms of the beauty of the Son being the image of the Father,
who is the source of Beauty, and revealed by the Spirit of

---

[41] Ibid. 48.

[42] 'A Divine and Supernatural Light, Immediately imparted to the Soul by the
Spirit of God, shown to be both a Scriptural and Rational Doctrine', ibid. 15–16.

[43] Roland Delattre, *Beauty and Sensibility in the Thought of Jonathan Edwards*,
156.

beauty.[44] Like his compatriots Bulgakov and Florensky, he echoes Irenaeus when he maintains that no one can represent the image of the Lord except by the Holy Spirit, for the latter manifests and makes audible the Word (pp. 12 *f.*); a view which he encapsulates when he says 'The Father pronounces his word and the Spirit manifests it, he is the *Light of the Word*' (p. 15). Despite their different views of the procession of the Holy Spirit, he and Edwards have a very similar account of the Spirit's revelatory role and mission in the world. Evdokimov's remark 'The figure of Christ is the human visage of God, the Holy Spirit reposes on him and reveals to us the absolute Beauty, divine—human . . .' (p. 20) expresses Edwards's thought perfectly.

Edwards's approach can also be compared to that of perhaps the greatest modern writer on theological aesthetics, Hans Urs von Balthasar, who allots the Holy Spirit a subsidiary role in his *Herrlichkeit*[45] (curiously, Edwards is nowhere mentioned in its three thousand or so pages!). The subtitle of this work is *A Theological Aesthetics*, but its author understands the term far more widely than most writers on the topic; for he is returning to the original Greek sense of aesthetics as 'perception'. John Riches rightly says that von Balthasar's theology 'is *aesthetic* because it consists in reflection on what it is that enables us to *perceive* the drama of the Cross and the *descensus* and the Resurrection as the revelation of the divine glory'.[46] But since, as this remark also indicates, von Balthasar's concern is with the manifestation of God's *glory*, and hence His beauty, his work is also an aesthetics in the more limited and conventional sense. Moreover, he draws an analogy between carefully attending to a work of art and contemplating the Christian mystery: in both cases we behold what is presented to us.[47]

---

[44] Paul Evdokimov, *L'Art de l'icône: Théologie de la beauté* (Paris, 1970), 298, 29. Evdokimov's book, as the title suggests, is largely devoted to the theology of icons, which allots a particular role to the Holy Spirit in giving icons a sacramental character: see especially pt. 2, ch. 5 and pt. 3, ch. 8.

[45] Now being translated as *The Glory of the Lord: A Theological Aesthetics* (Edinburgh, 1982–).

[46] John Riches (ed.), *The Analogy of Beauty* (Edinburgh, 1986), 181.

[47] Von Balthasar, *The Glory of the Lord*, i, trans. Erasmo Leiva-Merikakis (Edinburgh, 1982), 465; cf. 140–1.

Like most Western writers, von Balthasar associates divine beauty especially with the Son; and indeed the whole of *Herrlichkeit* can be regarded as an extended meditation on the idea that God's glory is manifested in the self-emptying of Christ. He describes Christ as the form (*Gestalt*) of God, and therefore as the aesthetic model of all beauty;[48] and, with reference to John 15: 26 and 16: 14, he ascribes to the Holy Spirit the role of witnessing to the Son (as the Son witnesses to the Father), by creating within us the ability to perceive God by apprehending the form of the Son.[49]

Like Edwards, von Balthasar also accepts the Augustinian position that the Holy Spirit proceeds from both Father and Son, and he draws his aesthetics into this Trinitarian pattern. Since for him the Spirit is the bond of love between Father and Son, the Spirit in some sense gives form to the Trinity. He says that since the Holy Spirit is the unity of both Father and Son, he transfigures both of them in their unity, and is therefore the Spirit of form and giving form, as well as a Spirit of love and enthusiasm; hence 'In this incomprehensible unity he is the locus of the beauty of God.'[50] Although he does not mention Edwards, von Balthasar is here approaching very closely the latter's development of the idea that the Holy Spirit is the harmony of the Trinity.

We shall return to von Balthasar's work in Chapter 4. My purpose at the moment is only to mention briefly *some* of the writers who have considered our topic over the last two millennia, and to see what questions their discussions pose. Of course, the writers I have mentioned are diverse: for some of them aesthetics is of peripheral concern, for others, e.g. von Balthasar, it is a leading theme in their theology. They are, moreover, writing in very different contexts, with varying purposes. Irenaeus is the early Father who does most to

---

[48] Ibid. 609. He goes on to remark on the next page that the manifestation of God in Christ cannot be reduced to any worldly categories of beauty: there is an *Aufhebung*, in that 'the categories of aesthetics are not simply annihilated, but rather raised above themselves in an incomprehensibly positive way . . . in order to contain something which is infinitely greater than themselves' (610); cf. 477 and vol. vii, trans. B. McNeil (Edinburgh, 1989), 316.

[49] Ibid. i. 602, 247; cf. 605–6, 249.

[50] Ibid. 494. I shall analyse this passage in ch. 4.

celebrate the goodness of the created world, for the reasons given; and his remarks on the adornment of the world by the Holy Spirit are a by-product of his treatment of the role of Wisdom in Creation. This concern with Wisdom recurs, in a very different way, in Bulgakov's work. Jonathan Edwards, on the other hand, is concerned (among other things) to stress the importance of beauty as a divine attribute, relating it to the biblical concept of divine glory, and to bring out the role of the Holy Spirit both within the Trinity and in the world. Likewise, von Balthasar gives the divine glory and its reflections in this world a central place in his *Glory of the Lord*. I shall say more about the theological preoccupations of some of these writers as we encounter them in due course. But it will be seen already that we have uncovered a grand theme, on which some of the greatest minds in Christendom have touched, and which raises many fascinating and important theological questions. The theme also emerges sometimes in non-theological contexts, as in Peter Shaffer's play *Amadeus* or in some popular views of artistic inspiration. There are also some parallels in non-Christian religions, for instance the Hindu idea that there is an interplay between the physical beauty of the world and the presence of the beauty of the Lord Krishna.[51]

THE DOG THAT DIDN'T BARK

Before going on to look at those questions, let us, however, raise a further query: why is it that although many theologians of widely different times and places (and there are some others not so far mentioned, e.g. Simone Weil) have raised our topic, few have developed it to any extent? We have seen how in the medieval period it was some minor writers, rather than Aquinas and Bonaventure, who discussed it. And in more recent times most theological aesthetics, at least in Western Christianity (and there has been little enough of it there) has continued the Augustinian tradition of emphasizing the Son's

---

[51] See, for example, Rāmānuja's *Vedārthasamgraha*, trans. S. S. Raghavachar (Mysore, 1978), para. 220, pp. 172–3; and Ananda Coomeraswami, 'Asiatic Art', in his *The Traditional Doctrine of Art* (Ipswich, 1977) for some other parallels.

role. Barth, for example, like von Balthasar, describes the Son as the radiant light and archetype of God's glory, and sees the Incarnation as the supreme revelation of God's beauty; although he says that 'the triunity of God is the secret of His beauty', he fails to bring out the role of the Holy Spirit in this connection, apart from saying that the creature is glorified through his work.[52] There has, of course, been a great outpouring of books on the Holy Spirit since around 1970. But again the link between the Holy Spirit and aesthetics is almost wholly ignored, both in books and articles of learned theology and in the more popular works associated with the Charismatic Movement.[53] Why this silence? If Sherlock Holmes found it significant that the dog did *not* bark during the night, then the silence of theologians too on certain topics may be revealing!

The theological reasons for this silence are, I believe, summed up simply in the two terms, 'the Holy Spirit' and 'beauty': they both represent underdeveloped areas of theology taken in themselves, let alone in terms of the connection between them. There are relatively few official Church teachings and classical theological treatises on the Holy Spirit; and in them little is said about the Spirit's role in nature or in history and culture, for traditionally they have concentrated on Christology, Trinitarian theology and ecclesiology, and, more recently, on the subjective experience of the individual believer. The Spirit's role in Creation is of course acknowledged with reference to Gen. 1:2 and 2:7, but it is seldom discussed much further, at least by Western theologians, both Catholic and Protestant.[54] The omission of a consideration of the Holy Spirit's connection with aesthetics follows from this wider omission.

[52] Barth, *Church Dogmatics*, iii, pt. 1, trans. T. H. L. Parker *et al.* (Edinburgh, 1957), 661, 670.

[53] I have come across a few short articles which represent the inspiration of artists as a gift of the Holy Spirit: see Robert Faricy, 'Art as a Charism in the Church', *Thought*, 57 (1982), 94–9; id., 'Art and the Holy Spirit', *Theological Renewal*, 16 (Oct. 1980), 27–32; and Peter D. Ashton, 'The Holy Spirit and the Gifts of Art', *Theological Renewal*, 21 (July 1982), 12–23.

[54] This tendency is noted by Wolfhart Pannenberg, for instance, in 'The Doctrine of the Spirit and the Task of a Theology of Nature', *Theology*, 75 (1972), 8–21; and by Kilian McDonnell, 'The Determinative Doctrine of the Holy Spirit', *Theology Today*, 39 (1982), 142–61.

The lack of a theology of beauty, both of beauty in general and of divine beauty in particular, follows in part from fear and suspicion of the question, expressed in pejorative terms like 'aestheticism' and 'élitism'. At best, beauty has often been treated as a Cinderella, compared with the attention paid by theologians to her two sisters, truth and goodness, an attention manifested in theology's predominant concern with doctrine and ethics, and resulting in the intellectualization of religion in recent centuries. Some theologians, indeed, do not even recognize her sisterhood: von Balthasar draws attention to Kierkegaard's disjunction of aesthetics and religion, and blames it for the banishment of the aesthetic from the realm of theology both by Kierkegaard himself and by his more recent Catholic and Protestant followers.[55] At worst, beauty has been treated as a meretricious Hellenistic import, who will distract and indeed corrupt good Christians. Barth describes the treatment of divine beauty by Pseudo-Diony-sius—which was so influential on many medieval thinkers, for example Aquinas—as 'hardly veiled Platonism', which was ignored by the Reformers and by later Protestant orthodoxy. He warns his readers that beauty is a risky concept in relation to God's perfections, because of its connection with the ideas of pleasure, desire, and enjoyment, and its secular and Greek associations (*CD* ii, pt. 1, p. 651; Barth does acknowledge beauty as a divine perfection, but treats it only as auxiliary to God's glory). But, as we shall see in Chapter 3, the attribution of beauty to God is not just Platonism but is rooted in the old Testament, especially in the Psalms, composed over a thousand years before Pseudo-Dionysius wrote, and there is no particular reason to think that it had only an auxiliary role there. One feels that there is perhaps what some people would call a 'Puritan hang-up' at the back of Barth's remarks, despite his later tributes to Mozart: a tendency to regard beauty as a matter of sensual pleasure, something not important, which should not, therefore, be associated with the serious business of religion. Even those who have widened their concept of

---

[55] Von Balthasar, *The Glory of the Lord*, i, 50. Compare his discussion of St Augustine in ii, esp. 123–9, where he draws attention to his mistrust of the senses and of the imagination.

beauty to include moral and spiritual beauty have often failed
to relate these to natural and artistic beauty, and so have
tended to depreciate the latter as being transitory or as
restricted to what is bodily.

Often, too, there is a suspicion that the worship of beauty
may indeed be just that; and hence a substitute for religion.
Shelley's *Hymn to Intellectual Beauty* uses the language of
religion; and indeed Romanticism has been described as 'spilt
religion'. Hence, in one of his letters to André Gide, Paul
Claudel exclaimed: 'As for what people call "Art" and
"Beauty", I had rather they perished a thousand times over
than that we should prefer such creatures to their Creator and
the futile constructions of our imagination to the reality in
which alone we may find delight.'[56] There is the fear, which
we have already encountered in Clement and Augustine, that
the pursuit of sensuous beauty may become a trap which
keeps people away from searching for nobler forms of beauty.
But beyond that there is the suggestion found in some modern
writers that the cult of art may actually become a surrogate
religion. The American essayist Tom Wolfe makes the sweep-
ing judgement in a lecture that 'today, art . . . is the religion
of the educated classes'.[57] Nicholas Wolterstorff warns of the
dangers of a 'religion of aestheticism', which becomes a
substitute for the Christian gospel of redemption and liberation.[58] He finds such a religion in the cults of beauty and
aestheticism of Flaubert and Pater in the last century, and
more recently in some of Herbert Marcuse's work. Such cults
tend to have their élites, both of purveyors and consumers.
Wolterstorff draws attention to the priestly, indeed godlike,
role given to artists in recent centuries, and remarks that since
the fifteenth century it has been commonplace to compare
them with God the Creator, yet this would once have been
regarded as an impious comparison. He points also to the role
of what he calls 'our institution of high art' today, which uses

[56] *The Correspondence between Paul Claudel and André Gide*, trans. John Russell
(London, 1952), 42.
[57] 'The Social Psychology of the Arts', quoted in Hilary Fraser, *Beauty and Belief:
Aesthetics and Religion in Victorian Literature* (Cambridge, 1986), 233.
[58] Nicholas Wolterstorff, *Art in Action: Toward a Christian Aesthetic* (Grand
Rapids, 1980), 50.

special buildings like theatres, museums, and concert-halls, and regards works of art as mostly intended for contemplation, away from the rest of our lives. He agrees with André Malraux's comment that the art museum is by way of becoming a sort of shrine today.[59] (I sometimes wonder whether gourmet-restaurants also fulfil a similar function for some people!)

Wolterstorff's attack is mainly on the cultural élitism of the contemporary art-world. Others have sharpened the attack by pointing to the obsessive and sometimes demonic aspects of art. Gilson comments that since the artist, unlike the saint, finds his perfection in his creations, which demand everything of him, his vocation may become an all-demanding obsession, with which even God must not interfere, for 'God is a temptation against art as art is one against God.'[60] Jaroslav Pelikan points out how Nietzsche turned away from his earlier aestheticism and from his enthusiasm for Wagner, realizing the addictive quality of art: to confuse the holy with the beautiful can be demonic, for it may mask the will-to-power and rob the holy of its questioning and challenging power; or it may be a narcotic self-deception, whereby people vainly try to dull the horrible sense of loneliness and defeat that dogs every step.[61]

The considerations which I have mentioned so far do something to explain why many theologians have not been much concerned with aesthetics. But they do not, I think, justify such a stance. Some of them are exaggerated and can easily be countered by pointing out that aestheticism is a disruption of the correct order of things or a corruption, and not an essential aspect of interest in the arts as such: Wolterstorff points out rightly that when sensory delight becomes a surrogate God, this is a case of treating a limited good as an ultimate good, rather than of treating something evil as good.[62] There are, however, some further considerations that

---

[59] Ibid., esp. pt. 2, §§ 1–2 and 12–14.

[60] Étienne Gilson, *L'École des Muses* (Paris, 1951), 263. Ch. 9 of this book has an interesting discussion on the differences between an artist and a saint.

[61] Jaroslav Pelikan, *Fools for Christ: Essays on the True, the Good and the Beautiful* (Philadelphia, 1955), ch. 5.

[62] Wolterstorff, *Art in Action*, pt. 3, ch. 1, §4.

I must mention which are relevant to any attempts to construct a theology of beauty. Many of them are concerned specifically with the concept of beauty, whilst others range more widely, for instance with regard to the scope of a theological aesthetics and the difficulties involved in developing one today.

SOME MODERN PROBLEMS

It is commonly said nowadays that beauty is simply a matter of what pleases us, that what pleases people differs from individual to individual and from culture to culture, and in any case that the concept is an outmoded one. Thus Wladislaw Tatarkiewicz says in an article with the significant title 'The Great Theory of Beauty and its Decline' that 'in our own century we have been witnesses to a crisis not merely in the theory of beauty but in the very concept itself'.[63] Later on I shall dispute these contentions and argue that the concept is not obsolete. It is certainly true, however, that most of the theologians mentioned by me so far were writing against the background of a very different view of aesthetics from that prevalent today, and that beauty is no longer quite as central a concept in aesthetics as it was once. Recent philosophical aesthetics has been preoccupied with a wide range of questions, such as the ontological status of a work of art, the phenomenology of aesthetic experience, the nature of representation and expression, and the criteria of aesthetic judgement; whilst other writings on art tend to stress creativity, imagination, and the evocation of emotions, and to dwell on the uniqueness of a work of art, its novelty and mystery. The nature and grounds of aesthetic judgement is regarded as only one topic among many, and even here the consideration of beauty often plays a minor role and is regarded as unhelpful by many people: J. L. Austin once made the famous comment 'if only we could forget for a while about the beautiful and get down instead to the dainty and the dumpy'.[64] This displace-

---

[63] *Journal of Aesthetics and Art Criticism*, 31 (1972–3), 165–80. I quote from 169.
[64] J. L. Austin, 'A Plea for Excuses', in *Philosophical Papers* (3rd edn., Oxford, 1961), 183.

ment of the concept seems to have started in the eighteenth
century, when other concepts like 'sublime', 'picturesque',
and 'taste' were introduced into critical discussion.[65] Of
course, beauty continued to be a central concept in the
aesthetics of both Kant and Hegel, and the latter gave a very
metaphysically ambitious role to it in his philosophy in
general; and later nineteenth-century writers, for instance
Ruskin, had a very 'high' and often indeed religious view of
it. But by now people's ideas of beauty had been much
affected by Romantic art (which Hegel regarded as the highest
form of art), and they had come to place a lot of stress on the
content, rather than the form, of a work of art, and on its
ability to move us emotionally through its meaning. Many
writers, too, had come to see music as offering the more
fundamental aesthetic experience, an important development
in itself but also for us, given that much traditional theology
meditated on the *vision* of God and tended to take the visual
arts as its paradigms.

The twentieth-century depreciation of beauty is partly a
reaction against such high-minded views of art and beauty,
and partly a result of philosophical scepticism. The word
seems to create so many problems: what is beauty, why do we
find it so difficult to define and to judge, why do people disagree so much about it, is it in things themselves or rather, as
people say, 'in the eye of the beholder'? Ludwig Wittgenstein
remarked that the concept has done a lot of mischief,[66] whilst
Mikel Dufrenne says that it seems useless or dangerous for his
purposes and so he prefers to use other, more precise terms,
like 'pretty', 'sublime', and 'graceful'. Dufrenne also claims
that at times the term has been used to promote the ideals of
classical art, that is harmony, purity, nobility, and serenity,
and has thus led to an arbitrary and sterilizing dogmatism.[67]

This depreciation is found not only amongst critics and

[65] See Jerome Stolnitz, '"Beauty": Some Stages in the History of an Idea', *Journal
of the History of Ideas*, 22 (1961), 185–204.
[66] See his *Culture and Value*, trans. Peter Winch (2nd edn., Oxford 1980), 55;
also his *Lectures and Conversations on Aesthetics, Psychology and Religious Belief*,
ed. Cyril Barrett (Oxford, 1966), i, §§7–9, p. 3.
[67] Mikel Dufrenne, *The Phenomenology of Aesthetic Experience*, trans. Edward
Casey *et al.* (Evanston, Ill., 1973), pp. lviii–lx.

philosophers but also among many artists, who reject or
disregard the traditional view that their role is to celebrate the
beauty of creation. An extreme form of such a reaction is
found in the 'anti-art' of Marcel Duchamp, exemplified in his
famous *Fountain*—which is a urinal. This perhaps is just a
case of shocking the bourgeoisie. But Wolterstorff (who
himself regards beauty as a usable concept, though not a
sufficient nor a necessary condition of aesthetic excellence)
mentions a few more serious examples, e.g. Robert Morris's
metal construction *Litanies*, for which the maker disclaims *all*
aesthetic quality and content, and quotes a remark made by
the American painter Barnett Newman, 'here in America,
some of us, free from the weight of European culture, are
finding the answer, by completely denying that art has any
concern with the problem of beauty and where to find it.'[68]

It may turn out that European (and other) culture will have
the last word. But the questions I have raised do create
difficulties for anyone concerned with theological aesthetics.
One simple way out of such difficulties is simply to omit the
concept of beauty from our discussion. After all, the texts
about Bezalel and Oholiab in Exod. 31 and 35 do not mention
beauty when they mention artistic skill as a gift of the Spirit,
so there is nothing to stop us regarding the arts as gifts of the
Holy Spirit without our bothering to develop a theology of
beauty; and even if we regard natural and artistic beauty as
gifts of God, does not the tendency to regard them as
sacraments or likenesses of divine beauty threaten God's
transcendence? In other words, there may be room for a
theological aesthetics which allows a place for the Holy Spirit
but is much less ambitious than that of Jonathan Edwards and
others, one which either side-steps the concept of beauty
altogether or at least limits itself to the claim that the Holy
Spirit is the beauti*fier* and so declines to speculate about
God's beauty and its relation to earthly beauty.[69]

---

[68] Wolterstorff, *Art in Action*, 54.

[69] Calvin Seerveld's *Rainbows for the Fallen World* (Toronto, 1980) is one such
example of a 'chastened' aesthetic; see pp. 181 and 196 for the role of the Holy
Spirit. As also is Wolterstorff's work. I should be inclined here to name such a
chastened aesthetic 'The Calvinist Thesis', were it not that Jonathan Edwards
constitutes such an outstanding exception.

I think that these more limited views are plausible, but that they fail to do justice to the fullness of the biblical witness and of Christian tradition. The proposal to write off the concept of beauty is a drastic one; and it is, I think, also premature. For it is noticeable that since Tatarkiewicz wrote the article from which I have quoted, there have been two important books by writers in the Anglo-American analytical tradition of philosophy, Mary Mothersill and Guy Sircello, devoted to a consideration of the concept, both of them defending the view that beauty is a real property of things;[70] not to mention works by writers from the Thomist and other intellectual traditions.[71] It has also been remarked (by Tatarkiewicz himself, among others[72]) that some of the concepts which have replaced beauty, especially that of the 'aesthetic', run into similar difficulties of definition and analysis.

The solution which I shall adopt is to continue to employ the concept of beauty, but to draw on other concepts as well, for both aesthetic and religious reasons. It has often been pointed out that the term 'beautiful' seems inappropriate to many great works of art: are *King Lear*, Beethoven's *Grosse Fuge*, Grünewald's *Crucifixion* at Colmar, *The Magic Mountain*, and Sophocles' *Oedipus Tyrannus* exactly 'beautiful'?[73] In some of the cases we may perhaps borrow Yeats's phrase 'terrible beauty'.[74] But even this seems inappropriate to, say, George Grosz's drawings. We prefer to describe *King Lear* and such works as powerful, moving, magnificent, sublime, and so on. Thus even if we decide that we can surmount or at least live with the problems associated with the concept of beauty, there is no reason why we should restrict ourselves to it, for there seem to be other kinds of aesthetic value—and even the phrase 'aesthetic value' is an inappropriate description of Shakespeare's insight into human psychology or our

---

[70] Mary Mothersill, *Beauty Restored* (Oxford, 1984); Guy Sircello, *A New Theory of Beauty* (Princeton, NJ, 1975).

[71] For examples, Armand Maurer, *About Beauty* (Houston, Tex., 1983), and some of the essays in H. G. Gadamer, *The Relevance of the Beautiful and other Essays*, trans. Nicholas Walker (Cambridge, 1986).

[72] 'The Great Theory of Beauty', 178.

[73] See Wolterstorff, *Art in Action*, 163, and Monroe C. Beardsley, *Aesthetics: Problems in the Philosophy of Criticism* (2nd edn., Indianapolis, 1981), 509.

[74] The line 'a terrible beauty is born' forms the refrain to the poem *Easter 1916*.

appreciation of a powerful imagination.[75] The same is true from a religious point of view: why should we suppose that the presence of the Holy Spirit in works of art should be confined to their beauty? The Spirit is commonly associated with truth, and the truth which is the fruit of insight and experience is sought in literature and in some other arts. Likewise, the Spirit is associated traditionally with warming the heart, so again there may be a connection to be made with the 'affective' and moving qualities of art, with its ability to stir our feelings and imagination and to enlarge our emotional range (and also, perhaps, with its didactic and moral aspects, even if this is an unfashionable standpoint today). The Spirit's modes of action are manifold, and need not relate only to beauty or even 'aesthetic value'. We may distinguish different media, too, looking perhaps for imagination and moral insight in literature, emotion in music, and so on. Some arts reflect the world of nature whilst others look more to the inner world, corresponding perhaps to the different realms of the Spirit's presence and action, in creation and in the human heart. Thus many aspects of works of art may have a theological significance, and specifically a connection with the Holy Spirit. Moreover, modern aesthetics, because it has enlarged the field of discussion, may give *more* scope to such a theological approach to art, rather than threaten it.

I am suggesting, then, that we should 'loosen up' our approach in various ways, and that we may well profit from doing so: we should consider other characteristics besides beauty, and also bear in mind that the early Christian Fathers had a wider conception of it than our current one (in any case, the Greek *kalos* has wider connotations than the English 'beautiful'); and we should look at other functions of art besides its ability to please us, for example its symbolic, representative, expressive, and emotionally moving capacities.

There remains, however, a further question raised by my proposal to open up the discussion: how wide should our exploration be in terms of the territory covered—should we look, say, at architecture and cookery as well as music and

---

[75] See David Pole, *Aesthetics, Form and Emotion*, ed. G. Roberts (London, 1983), chs. 1 and 2(ii) for this point.

natural beauty? Typically, theological aesthetics tends to draw its examples from the fine arts,[76] especially music, painting, sculpture, and literature, and from natural beauty; and one can see how certain works and media seem particularly appropriate: many people besides Barth have drawn attention to the 'unearthly' beauty of much of Mozart's music, and in general, music seems most germane to an approach centring on the Holy Spirit. Both Aquinas and Hegel give preference to arts connected with sight and hearing, e.g. painting and poetry, though for different reasons.[77] One notices that some arts get short shrift from writers on theological aesthetics, for example architecture (apart from discussion of specifically religious buildings). And indeed this seems a difficult medium to relate to our theme: how might an architect inspired or guided by the Holy Spirit approach his or her task? How would one tell whether a building was the result of divine inspiration? (I once heard the American writer Norman Mailer, in an expansive mood, declare in a televised discussion that modern architecture is inspired by the Devil!) The cinema, too, is relatively neglected, and cookery almost wholly so (though Calvin Seerveld's *Rainbows for the Fallen World* has a section with the engaging title 'Glory to God in the Kitchen'), perhaps because of the view exemplified in Aquinas' work, that of all the senses taste and smell are the least cognitive, hence they are unconnected with beauty (Simon Tugwell notes, however, that fragrance was widely mentioned in the early Church as a mark of the Holy Spirit's presence[78]). Even if we take one of the arts most cherished by theologians, music, how far do we extend our investigations—to minor

---

[76] Both Maritain and Wolterstorff note that the modern classification of the 'fine arts' emerged only in the eighteenth century: earlier generations distinguished rather between the 'servile' and the 'liberal' arts, and included architecture and the pictorial arts under the former. See Jacques Maritain, *Art and Scholasticism*, trans. J. W. Evans (New York, 1962), ch. 4, and Wolterstorff, *Art in Action*, pt. 1, §4.

[77] See Aquinas, *Summa Theologiae* (henceforth abbreviated as *ST*), 1a2ae. xxvii. 1 ad 3, who argues that beauty has reference to the cognitive powers, and therefore excludes tastes and smells; and Hegel, *Aesthetics: Lectures on Fine Art*, trans. T. M. Knox (Oxford, 1975), i. 38–9, who says that the spirit is made sensuous in art through the senses of sight and hearing.

[78] Simon Tugwell, 'Faith and Experience V: Religious "Natural History"', *New Blackfriars*, 60 (1979), 74. Again, cf. Aquinas, *ST* 1a2ae. xxvii. 1 ad 3.

classical masters like Hummel, to 'light classical' composers like Eric Coates, to jazz, and to pop music?

My approach to these interesting and insufficiently discussed questions will be a practical one: the appeal to the Holy Spirit seems most appropriate in the case of works of art and examples of natural beauty which we find profound and moving, so I shall start from such cases without committing myself to drawing any limits. Likewise in my discussions of beauty and aesthetic value I shall work outwards: in the next two chapters I shall start with an examination of the concepts of beauty in general and divine beauty, and then go on to look at other relevant aesthetic concepts. Then in the following two chapters I shall focus on the role of the Holy Spirit and the nature of inspiration. Finally in Chapters 6 and 7 I shall discuss the relationship between aesthetic qualities and the divine perfections, and explore the view that beauty and related qualities anticipate the restoration of all things in the life to come. In the case of all these topics we shall have three main tasks: to draw together what has been said by theologians and other writers of widely scattered times and places, to show how it can be fitted into a coherent and developed theology of the Holy Spirit, and to explore its plausibility in the light of our contemporary experience and understanding of aesthetics.

2

Types of Beauty

DESPITE the difficulties of analysis and the availability of a wide range of other aesthetic terms, the word 'beautiful' is still in common use. It is certainly not an abstruse or technical term. It is used mainly to give a verdict on something or someone, which can then be justified in terms of more detailed aesthetic judgements, or else it is used of particular aspects or properties. In the latter case, as Guy Sircello points out, the adverb 'beautifully' is often used to qualify another term: thus an autumn sky can be beautifully limpid, or a play beautifully constructed.[1]

Statements about beauty and other aesthetic qualities are often lumped together with moral judgements, and categorized as 'value judgements'. There are, however, some important differences between them. Moral judgements are commonly made about whole classes of actions, like abortion or lying, whereas aesthetic ones usually start from the individual and are rarely made about a whole class. So people may praise the beauty of a particular painting by, say, Turner, but do not usually have occasion to say that all his paintings are beautiful (though this may be true; I am not ruling out *all* generalizations in aesthetics). Hence Mary Mothersill argues that it is futile to force aesthetics into the mould of ethics: the basic judgements of ethics are themselves lawlike, but those of aesthetics are about why a particular object is pleasing, affecting, exhilarating, and so on.[2] Moreover, she argues, the canon of classics has an important exemplary role in aesthetics: thus the judgement that 'The *Iliad* is a great poem' has something like the same status as 'One ought to tell the truth' (though I think that it is worth pointing out that

---

[1] Guy Sircello, *A New Theory of Beauty* (Princeton, NJ, 1975), §5.
[2] Mary Mothersill, *Beauty Restored* (Oxford, 1984), 170–5.

saints and heroes, like St Francis of Assisi or Captain Oates,
sometimes play an analogous role in ethics).

Since our basic aesthetic judgements are made in response
to particular objects, we do not *reason* our way to them,
although we may try to justify them retrospectively. Nor do
such judgements involve the will, except perhaps for when we
try to appreciate something which does not attract us immediately but which has been commended by someone we respect.
But even then we cannot *make* ourselves discern beauty or
some other aesthetic quality. Hence John McDowell points
out correctly that we regard aesthetic valuing as more like
seeing than deciding or choosing[3] —which is what one would
expect, given the etymological origin of the term 'aesthetics'.

But on what occasions do we make such judgements? The
main point to be made in this chapter is that there is a *vast*
range of occasions, embracing the moral and the spiritual as
well as the artistic. I shall also argue that there are analogical
likenesses between them; and I shall end by discussing the
religious significance of beauty and other aesthetic concepts.

THE VARIETY OF BEAUTY

Most contemporary aesthetics is concerned with works of art;
indeed, as Ronald Hepburn points out, many twentieth-
century writers define aesthetics as the philosophy of art.[4]
This tendency was already anticipated by Hegel, who preferred the phrase 'philosophy of fine art' to 'aesthetics' and
claimed that the beauty of art is higher than that of nature,
for it is *'born of the spirit and born again*, and the higher the
spirit and its productions stand above nature and its phenomena, the higher too is the beauty of art above that of nature'.[5]
There are many good reasons for criticizing the neglect of
natural beauty: it ignores an important source of aesthetic
pleasure, one which is appreciated by many ordinary people,

---

[3] John McDowell, 'Aesthetic Value, Objectivity, and the Fabric of the World', in
Eva Schaper (ed.), *Pleasure, Preference and Value* (Cambridge, 1983), 1–16, esp. 5.

[4] Ronald Hepburn, 'Contemporary Aesthetics and the Neglect of Natural Beauty',
in his *'Wonder' and Other Essays* (Edinburgh, 1984), ch. 1.

[5] Hegel, *Aesthetics*, i, trans. T. M. Knox (Oxford, 1975), 2. Cf. 118–52 for
Hegel's discussion of natural beauty.

and thereby limits the scope of aesthetics. But there is an additional consideration relevant to our enquiry: for many religious believers nature has a sacramental aspect, in that its beauty is a sign of God's inventiveness and generosity, and perhaps also of His own beauty.

Let us, therefore, start with both natural and artistic beauty, and move outwards from there. At first sight it seems that Aquinas' trio of wholeness, harmony, and radiance provides a good summary of the conditions for beauty, applicable to a beautiful landscape, a symphony, or a picture. But Aquinas apparently thinks that all the three conditions are required:[6] now there seem to be many cases where only one or two are applicable, for instance the blue sky of an autumn day has radiance and perhaps in some sense wholeness, but 'harmony' seems less appropriate because of the lack of differentiated parts. Hegel draws attention to the beauty of sensuous material, like polished surfaces or a mirror-like lake, and compares them with the purity of the sky, of musical notes, and of colours (*Aesthetics*, 141–2). Likewise, Plotinus writes of the beauty of colours, the light of the sun, gold, and the stars (not to mention noble conduct, excellent laws, and virtues), in questioning the equation of beauty with symmetry (*Enneads*, i. 6.1). Guy Sircello goes a step further, and claims that tastes, smells, and touches can be beautiful, too, though he acknowledges that we lack an adequate vocabulary to describe them.[7] It seems, then, that Aquinas' analysis is too wide to cover what might be called 'beautiful simplicity'.[8]

We can easily modify Aquinas' analysis in the way suggested, by saying that only one or two of his three conditions are required (indeed Aquinas himself does not always insist on all three conditions, e.g. in *ST* 2a2ae. 145. 2). But there are many forms of beauty which his analysis, whether modified or not, fails to capture. I am thinking primarily of things which strike us as beautiful because they are profound and moving; but there is also the kind of beauty which Yeats's

[6] *Summa Theologiae*, 1a. xxxix. 8.
[7] Sircello, *A New Theory of Beauty*, §20.
[8] A phrase used by Marsilio Ficino in his *De Amore* (a commentary on Plato's *Symposium*), Speech 5, ch. 3, when making the same point as Plotinus.

phrase 'terrible beauty' seems to fit. Aquinas' analysis, like
much ancient and medieval aesthetics, seems more appropriate to the visual arts and, more generally, to things which are
appreciated for their form. But in many arts, e.g. literature
and music (especially Romantic works) beauty is often to a
larger extent a matter of meaning and feeling. The aria 'I
know that my Redeemer liveth' in Handel's *Messiah* no doubt
has, in some sense, wholeness, harmony, and radiance, but it
also seems profound, noble, and moving to many people, and
thereby to have great beauty. Or think of Rembrandt, who,
Baudelaire said (contrasting him with Raphael), 'shakes his
rags before our eyes and tells us of human sufferings'.[9] In
such cases Aquinas' trio of conditions seems weak and limited,
as it does too in the case of later, Romantic art. Moreover, in
some cases, for example Grünewald's *Crucifixion* at Colmar,
his analysis seems almost wholly inappropriate, perhaps,
again, because this exemplifies a 'terrible beauty'.

One may of course argue that Rembrandt's and Grünewald's works are not beautiful, though they may perhaps have
some other aesthetic merit. A few years after Baudelaire was
writing, Ruskin criticized Rembrandt for being careless of all
living form and accused him of aiming 'to paint the foulest
things he could see—by rushlight', such as 'the lamplight
upon the hair of a costermonger's ass'.[10] Such examples are
legion in the history of criticism. But usually later generations
have sought to enlarge their standards of what is beautiful to
cover what may have seemed strange or novel at first. Thus
John Drury points out how Rembrandt's nudes are questioning
Renaissance concepts of beauty (he also suggests, with reference to Isa. 53 and Phil. 2, which speak of the lack of
comeliness of the Suffering Servant and the self-emptying of
Christ, that Christianity may be recommending a new kind of
beauty[11]); or rather, I would prefer to say, they are questioning

---

[9] Charles Baudelaire, *Art in Paris, 1845–1862*, ed. and trans. Jonathan Mayne
(London, 1965), 47.
[10] John Ruskin, *The Cestus of Aglaia*, ch. 5; Library edn. of Ruskin's Works, xix
(London, 1905), 109.
[11] John Drury, 'God, Ugliness and Beauty', *Theology*, 76 (1973), 531–5. Jürgen
Moltmann points to the way in which the Fourth Gospel speaks of the *doxa* of Jesus
in his suffering and death, and says this leads to a transformation of values (*Theology
of Play*, trans. R. Ulrich, New York, 1972, 41–2).

the *limits* of traditional notions of beauty, for there is nothing to stop one appreciating *both* Botticelli's *Birth of Venus* and Rembrandt's nudes.

One of the earliest and most ambitious attempts to widen our concept of beauty was made by Plato. In the *Symposium* he recommends lovers of beauty to ascend from beautiful bodies to beautiful souls, observances, laws, and fields of knowledge and learning, until they come to Beauty itself (210–11); and in the *Laws* he praises the beauty of justice (ix. 859d; such an enlargement of the scope of beauty is easier to recommend in Greek than in English, for even in ordinary usage *kalos* covers a much wider range of things than 'beautiful'; like the French *beau* and *belle*, it is often better translated as 'fine'). His work was known by many of the early Christian Fathers mentioned in the previous chapter, and it made it easier for them to argue that spiritual and divine beauty are more valuable than physical and artistic beauty.

Talk of the beauty of good deeds and of virtue was, however, a commonplace in the ancient world, so that we need not look exclusively at the influence of Plato. Aristotle, for example, says that virtue is beautiful (*Rhetoric*, 1366ª 35), and Cicero speaks of the splendour and beauty of virtue (*De Officiis*, ii. 10. 37). Such talk is not limited to the ancient world or to Christian theologians: Hume, for instance, wrote 'There is no spectacle so fair and beautiful as a noble and generous action' (*Treatise*, iii. 1. 2). This way of speaking has not entirely disappeared today: we talk of sweetness of character or moral deformity, and admire especially those who not only lead good lives, but seem to do so without strain or struggle, and with sweetness and joy (as opposed to 'muscular Christians' and others, who have to grit their teeth and make an obvious effort). This idea of moral beauty is captured when people say that someone is a 'lovely person'; the phrase is a bit stale now, but it does convey the idea of a beautiful personality, which need not go with a beautiful appearance.

Another form of beauty to which Greek philosophers drew attention was that of intellectual beauty: Aristotle, for instance, associated beauty with mathematics.[12] Again, this

---

[12] *Metaphysics*, xiii. 3. 1078ª33–ᵇ2; cf. Plato *Timaeus*, 53–4 on the beauty of geometrical figures.

notion has survived: we commonly speak of the beauty of
scientific theories and of the elegance of mathematical proofs.
Nicholas Wolterstorff points out that other aesthetic qualities
besides beauty can be ascribed to non-perceptible entities like
stories or proofs, e.g. 'dramatic', 'awkward', 'coherent', and
'convoluted'.[13]

The ascription of beauty to virtues and to intellectual
entities is of great theological importance, because it shows
that beauty is not restricted to material things and may
therefore, perhaps, be ascribed to God. There is a common
tendency to think of beauty in terms of colours, shapes,
sounds, bodies, and so on—things which we experience
through our senses. Hence we find difficulty with the notion
that God, who has no body or matter, is described as
beautiful. But the recognition of intellectual beauty, at least,
may prove to be liberating when we come to consider the
divine beauty, in Chapter 3, for it shows that even in non-
theological contexts there is still some room for the idea of an
immaterial beauty.

In practice, Christian theologians have paid more attention
to moral beauty than to intellectual, and have seen the former
as one kind of likeness to God. Thus St Cyril of Alexandria
says that the power of the Holy Spirit perfects us in the image
of the Creator in every form of virtue, and that those who are
saved return to the original beauty of their nature.[14] Sometimes theologians have widened the idea by speaking of the
beauty of wisdom[15] (following the Book of Wisdom 8: 2), and
of the beauty of holiness—a phrase which has become familiar
in English because it is used in some of the Psalms in the
Authorized Version, e.g. Ps. 29: 2 (though some recent
translations prefer the more accurate 'holy array'). Jonathan

[13] Nicholas Wolterstorff, *Art in Action: Toward a Christian Aesthetic* (Grand
Rapids, 1980), pt. 2, §9.
[14] *In Jn. Ev.*, bk. 9 (*PG* 74: 277 b–d); *Dialogue 5 on the Holy Trinity* (*PG* 75:
988d).
[15] Thus St Bonaventure includes wisdom (which for him has moral connotations)
under spiritual beauty, which, he says, surpasses bodily beauty (*Commentary on
Wisdom*, vii. 29, *Works*, Quaracchi edn., vi. 159). He also says that true beauty
dwells in the beauty of wisdom, and the external is merely its copy (*Hexaem*, xx. 24;
Works v. 429b). Ficino includes both moral and intellectual virtue in beauty of soul
(*De Amore*, Speech 6, ch. 18.)

Edwards, for example, says that 'holiness is in a peculiar manner the beauty of the divine nature'.[16] He does not limit holiness to God, for he goes on immediately to say that the moral image of God in the saints, i.e. their holiness, is their beauty; and indeed that the beauty and brightness of the angels in heaven consists in their holiness. From a very different perspective, Gerardus van der Leeuw regards the concept of the holy as including beauty (though in general the thrust of his *Sacred and Profane Beauty: The Holy in Art* proceeds in the opposite direction, stressing that the beautiful is holy).[17] A related conception is the beauty of divine grace— a conception which would be natural in some languages, for example Greek, in which *charis* (grace) is commonly used of gracefulness and charm. Thus in one of his poems Gerard Manley Hopkins refers to 'God's *better* beauty, grace'[18] (he often mentions kinds of beauty transcending the physical which may yet be acknowledged in aesthetic terms, e.g. of mind, character, and soul. Also, he regards Christ as the divine archetype of created beauty and as having made the principles of perfect physical and moral beauty manifest in the created world through the Incarnation[19]).

Some writers have drawn parallels between aesthetic and spiritual beauty. Thus the medieval writer Thomas of Cîteaux, in his commentary on the Song of Songs (a text which, not surprisingly, gave rise to many patristic and medieval discussions of beauty, though most of them ignored its straightforward erotic significance) correlated different kinds of external beauty with kinds of beauty of soul, comparing, for example, the beauty of things without blemish to the beauty arising from purification from sin.[20] Aquinas describes

[16] Jonathan Edwards, *A Treatise concerning Religious Affections*, ed. John E. Smith (New Haven, 1959), 257.

[17] Trans. D. E. Green (London, 1963), 333.

[18] 'To what serves Mortal Beauty?', *Poems* (4th edn.; Oxford, 1970), no. 62, p. 98. Aquinas too writes of the beauty (*decor*) of grace, which, he says, comes from the shining of divine light (*ST* 1a2ae. cix. 7).

[19] See Hilary Fraser, *Beauty and Belief: Aesthetics and Religion in Victorian Literature* (Cambridge, 1986), 68 *ff*.; also 28 *ff*. for John Henry Newman's appreciation of the beauty of grace; and 221 for Walter Pater's curious phrase 'the elegance of sanctity'.

[20] *PL* 206: 309.

the saints as the beauty of the house of God, for divine grace, which beautifies like light, shines in them (*In Ps*. xxv. 5). He applies his general analysis of beauty to the virtues, remarking that just as beauty or charm arise from good proportion and radiance, 'so also beauty of spirit consists in conversation and actions that are well-formed and suffused with intelligence' (*ST* 2a2ae. 145. 2); although beauty goes with every virtue, it goes especially with temperance because of its measured and fitting proportion, and because it holds down the forces of debasement (*ST* 2a2ae. 141. 2 ad 3). Likewise, Alexander of Hales followed Augustine in defining beauty in terms of measure, form, and order, and said that these are found in spiritual as well as physical matters: 'just as beauty of body consists in the congruence of the arrangement of parts, so, too, beauty of soul derives from the harmony of energies and the ordering of powers'.[21]

Not surprisingly, many Christian writers have ranked moral and spiritual beauty above aesthetic, as we have already seen in the last chapter. St Bernard, for example, sees beauty of soul as consisting in humility and sanctity, and as manifesting itself in speech, appearance, movement, and even laughter; he contrasts it with physical beauty, which is transitory and corruptible.[22] An interesting variation on this theme is the depreciation of physical beauty in this life, but going with an extolling of the glory of the resurrected body. Thus the *Spiritual Homilies* ascribed to St Macarius say that spiritual persons spurn earthly splendour because they have invariably 'tasted another ineffable beauty and have participated in other riches'.[23] A few pages later, however, Macarius says that at the day of resurrection 'the glory of the Holy Spirit rises up from within, covering and warming the bodies of the Saints. This is the glory they interiorly had before, hidden in their souls, for what they now have, that same then pours out externally into their body.'[24]

Talk of inward beauty and spiritual beauty seems suspect

---

[21] *Summa Theologica*, i (Quaracchi edn.), n. 103.

[22] *On Song of Songs*, xxv. 6, xlv. 3, lxxxv. 11 (*PL* 183: 901d, 1000c, 1193b–d).

[23] Homily 5, §5, in *Intoxicated with God*, trans. George A. Maloney (Denville NJ, 1978), 53.

[24] Homily 5, §9 (Maloney, 60); cf. 32, §3 and 34, §2 (Maloney, 179, 184).

to many people today. The latter phrase is perhaps redolent of Hegel nowadays.[25] But more generally there is the suspicion that these phrases imply that such kinds of beauty are indeed purely inward; or that they are regarded in a Dualistic sense, that is, as denoting the characteristics of an immaterial and indivisible substance, the soul, which is separated from the body at death. Now some of the early Christian Fathers, for instance Cyril of Alexandria, were indeed Dualists, and were unconcerned with physical beauty. One can, however, speak of spiritual beauty without committing oneself to this view: Mozart's music seems to many people to merit such a description, but clearly this has nothing to do with metaphysical Dualism. Likewise, people may regard moral beauty as more valuable than physical without being committed to Dualism, for they may have in mind the transitory nature of physical beauty and its tendency to beguile us and distract us from more important things. This would seem to be St Bernard's position: Tatarkiewicz argues that Bernard is not a Dualist, but is rather discussing beauty as part of ethics.[26] Likewise the Buddha pointed to the transitoriness of physical beauty when he said 'If only this beauty of women were imperishable then my mind would certainly indulge in the passions.'[27] Yet such reservations need not prevent people from acknowledging *both* physical and other kinds of beauty (as Roger Fry, for example, found an interweaving of spiritual and sensuous beauty in the works of Giotto[28]). But Dualists are reluctant to do so because they depreciate physical beauty, whilst others may, by contrast, recognize only this kind of beauty, or at least regard moral, spiritual, and intellectual beauty as such merely in a remote and derivative sense.

We have seen, then, that both Plato and Christian tradition have sought to enlarge the concept of beauty in two ways: by including moral, spiritual, and intellectual beauty; and by appealing to some form of supramundane beauty. But which is primary? Clearly the writers whom I have mentioned

---

[25] e.g. his *Aesthetics*, i. 518.
[26] *History of Aesthetics*, ii. 185. Bernard's asceticism should also be considered.
[27] Quoted by John Passmore, in *The Perfectibility of Man* (London, 1970), 125.
[28] Roger Fry, *Vision and Design* (Penguin edn., Harmondsworth, 1937), 112–49.

thought that physical and aesthetic beauty were the least important.[29] Clearly, too, Plato thought that the Form of beauty was the source of all kinds of beauty; and, as we shall see in the next chapter, many Christian writers have treated God as the source and exemplar of beauty. But such a ranking of types of beauty is compatible with regarding aesthetic beauty as primary in the order of knowledge. It is, after all, in encountering natural beauty and works of art (not to mention seeing a beautiful catch in cricket) that most of us first learn the concept of beauty and other aesthetic concepts, even if later we range more widely and perhaps conclude that other forms of beauty are more valuable.

BEAUTY AND ANALOGY

But why should we go along with such an enlargement of the concept of beauty? What is there in common to all the varieties of beauty, or to the things described as beautiful? One very unitary answer has been mentioned, that of Plato, who regards all beautiful things as participating in the Form of beauty. We may see subsequent writers who have looked for a single definition of beauty as standing in this tradition, even if they have very different metaphysical views from those of Plato. There is, however, an alternative approach which must be mentioned, which sees the different forms of beauty as analogically related.

Aquinas regards the class of analogical predicates as a third class besides those of 'univocal' and 'equivocal' (*ST* 1a. xiii. 10). Univocal terms are those which have the same sense and, according to him, denote things in the same metaphysical category; equivocal ones have a number of different senses, e.g. 'pen', which denotes both a writing implement and an enclosure for animals. Analogical terms are a middle category; they have a number of different senses, but those senses are related. The example which Aquinas constantly uses, bor-

---

[29] Tatarkiewicz points out that although most medieval writers regarded spiritual beauty alone as really important, William of Auvergne regarded physical beauty as the primary form of beauty, and moral beauty only as beauty in comparison with outward, visible beauty, in his *De bono et malo*, 207 (*History of Aesthetics*, ii. 216).

rowed from Aristotle, is that of 'healthy': a person, a seaside resort, and a complexion can all be described as 'healthy'. But these senses are not all quite the same, for it would be strange to ask if I am healthier than Blackpool or than your complexion. On the other hand, these uses are not equivocal, for 'healthy' is not ambiguous in the way that 'pen' is. Aquinas' answer is that 'healthy' is properly predicated of people and animals, but also of other things in so far as they are causes or signs of health. Thus climates, diets, and medicines are healthy if they contribute to good health, and complexions and specimens of blood or urine are healthy if they are signs of good health. Aquinas regards perfection-terms like 'good' and 'wise' as analogical, and thereby as applicable to God.[30]

Now Aquinas himself does not include 'beautiful' in his lists of analogical terms. But his discussions of beauty suggest that it has some similarities with such terms, hence many neo-Thomists have concluded that it too should be regarded as analogical. In his commentary on Pseudo-Dionysius' treatise *The Divine Names* Aquinas argues that 'beautiful' and 'beauty' are attributed to God and to creatures in different ways, and that God gives beauty to all creatures according to their proper nature: thus the beauty of a spirit differs from that of a body, as does the beauty of this and that body (he then goes on to say that beauty consists in harmony and radiance).[31] Likewise, in his commentary on Ps. 45: 2 (Vulgate Ps. 44: 2), when discussing the beauty of Christ, he says that beauty, like health, is predicated in different ways. Hence Jacques Maritain, citing these texts, concludes that beauty is relative to the proper nature and end of things and is, therefore, analogical: 'Like being and the other transcendentals, it is essentially *analogous*, that is to say, it is predicated for diverse reasons . . . of the diverse subjects of which it is predicated:

---

[30] *ST* 1a. xiii. 2, 5, 6; see my 'Analogy Today' (*Philosophy*, 51, 1976, 431–46), for further details of Aquinas' views and the problems they raise.

[31] *In Librum Beati Dionysii De Divinis Nominibus Expositio* (Turin, 1950) ch. 4, lectio 5, §§335, 339. The treatise on which Aquinas was commenting, *The Divine Names* (henceforth abbreviated as *Div. Nom.*), was originally attributed to the Dionysius the Areopagite mentioned in Acts 17: 34, though it is now ascribed to a Syrian monk of the late 5th and early 6th centuries. See Hans Urs von Balthasar, *The Glory of the Lord: A Theological Aesthetics*, ii (Edinburgh, 1984), 144–210 for a discussion of Dionysius.

each kind of thing *is* in its own way, is *good* in its own way, is *beautiful* in its own way.'[32]

Similar claims have been made by non-Thomists. R. W. Church, for example, points to the difficulty of finding any empirical common characteristic for all cases of beauty and, echoing Aristotle's criticisms of Plato's notion of the Form of the Good, rejects the view that 'beauty' is the name of a trans-empirical nature or form assumed to be common to different single beauties; he denies that 'Beauty as such' could be the beauty of anything at all. Instead, he argues for what he calls 'analogous resemblances': instead of looking for a nature or form common to diverse beings, we should look at the context, at the type of thing being described. Beauty, he concludes, 'has no single and unique referent, and it derives its meaning in every case of its use from the connotation of its context'.[33] More recently, some writers have applied Wittgenstein's notion of 'family resemblance' to aesthetics. Wittgenstein argued that we use the word 'game' of many different things, not because we have discovered a common definition or essence of all games, but because there is a network of similarities between them.[34]

This line of thought seems to explain a number of features of beauty and to cover some difficulties. If we were told that *Nightingale Glade* is beautiful we would be unclear what is meant unless we knew whether it was a place, a painting, a piece of music, or a perfume. Even if we were told that it has harmony and radiance, we would be little enlightened, for these characteristics too vary according to the category of things being described. Similarly, although it makes sense to say that Titian's *Bacchus and Ariadne* is more beautiful than Watteau's *Departure for Cythera* (we would, however, want to know why), it is unclear what would be meant if we said

---

[32] Jacques Maritain, *Art and Scholasticism*, trans. J. W. Evans (New York, 1962), 30. See also n. 66 on 172–4.

[33] R. W. Church, *An Essay on Critical Appreciation* (London, 1938), ch. 1, esp. 53–6. I quote from 53.

[34] Ludwig Wittgenstein, *Philosophical Investigations*, trans. G. E. M. Anscombe (Oxford, 1963), §§65–6. The notion has been applied to aesthetics by, amongst others, W. E. Kennick in 'Does Traditional Aesthetics Rest on a Mistake?', *Mind*, 67 (1958), 317–34.

that either of them was more beautiful than the Taj Mahal or Beethoven's 'Eroica' symphony. It is, however, sometimes possible to compare things of different categories, not by saying that one is more x than the other, but by using word frames of the form $a : b :: c : d$. Thus Simone Weil says that 'Beauty is to things what sanctity is to the soul'[35]; and Jonathan Edwards's remark in his essay 'The Beauty of the World' that 'How great a resemblance of a holy and virtuous soul is a calm, serene day'[36] could be drawn out in the form

holiness and virtue : a human soul :: calmness and serenity : the weather

Some of the examples of analogy which Aquinas gives can be drawn out in this way, for example, our knowledge : created beings :: God's knowledge : His essence (iv *Sent.* 49. 2. 1 ad 2). Later Thomists coined the phrase 'Analogy of Proper Proportionality' to describe such cases.

A further consideration, which I have already touched on, is that we sometimes enlarge our conceptions of beauty to accommodate a new example or type. If the change is a radical one, then we have, as Moltmann argues, a transformation of values. Usually, however, we enlarge our conceptions only when we note some resemblance between the new examples or types and our accepted canon of beauty. Again, there is an analogical relationship, perhaps a 'family resemblance', between the new and the old.

The claim that beauty is an analogical concept has often gone together with the claim that it is a transcendental one, that is, a concept, like 'one' or 'good', which may be applied to things in different categories and indeed, some say, to all being. Again, this claim was not made explicitly by Aquinas himself, for he does not include beauty in his lists of transcendentals (e.g. in *On Truth*, i. 1 and xxi. 3), but some of the things which he says have led his followers to make the claim

[35] Simone Weil, *First and Last Notebooks*, trans. R. Rees (Oxford, 1970), 139.
[36] In *Images or Shadows of Divine Things*, ed. Perry Miller (reprint, Westport, Conn., 1977), 136. Edwards regards the secondary beauty of the natural world as a 'type' or image of love or charity in the spiritual world. See also his *The Nature of True Virtue*, ch. 3, in *The Works of Jonathan Edwards*, viii, *Ethical Writings*, ed. Paul Ramsey (New Haven, Conn., 1989), 562–4.

on his behalf (also some other medieval thinkers regarded beauty as a transcendental, because all things have form[37]). Aquinas does say that goodness and beauty are the same in being (though we distinguish them logically); hence Armand Maurer concludes that he too regarded beauty as a transcendental.[38] Likewise Maritain says, just before the passage which I have already quoted, that

Like the one, the true and the good, the beautiful is *being* itself considered from a certain aspect; it is a property of being . . . Thus everything is beautiful, just as everything is good, at least in a certain relation. And as being is everywhere present and everywhere varied the beautiful likewise is diffused everywhere and is everywhere varied. (*Art and Scholasticism*, 30)

We can agree with these authors that beauty is transcendental, in the sense that it can be ascribed to many categories of things; for we have already seen that actions, virtues, theories, and proofs can be beautiful, as well as landscapes and works of art. I am less happy, however, about talking of being itself as beautiful, since there is a risk that such a generalized claim makes the notion vacuous. At this point, many neo-Thomists distinguish between transcendental and aesthetic beauty, though, again, Aquinas himself does not explicitly make this distinction. Thus Gary Greif treats the latter as a subclass of the former: 'when the beautiful is realized in that grade of being which is clearly perceived by the human intellect as perfective of itself, the beautiful is contracted to the grade of aesthetical beauty', and says that aesthetic beauty is denominated from its having a special degree of being, which is clearly experienced by us as having wholeness, consonance or

---

[37] St Bonaventure says that everything that exists has form, and what has form has beauty (ii *Sent*. 34. 2. 3; Quaracchi edn., ii. 814); cf. Tatarkiewicz, *History of Aesthetics*, ii. 237, 288, and E. J. M. Spargo, *The Category of the Aesthetic in the Philosophy of St. Bonaventure* (New York, 1953), 34 *f*., 37 *f*., for further references. St Albert the Great says that all beings share in beauty and goodness, and he sees 'resplendence of form' as essential to the former. Cf. his *De Pulchro et Bono*, cited in Tatarkiewicz, *op. cit.*, 243; and Umberto Eco, *Art and Beauty in the Middle Ages*, trans. H. Bredin (New Haven, Conn., 1986), 25.

[38] Armand Maurer, *About Beauty* (Houston, Tex., 1983), ch. 1; he cites *De Div. Nom.*, §§340, 355 and *ST*, 1a. v. 4 ad 1. See Umberto Eco, *The Aesthetics of St. Thomas Aquinas*, trans. H. Bredin (London, 1988), ch. 2, for a helpful discussion.

proportion, and radiance.[39] In terms of this distinction, our concern in this chapter is with aesthetic beauty.

SOME OTHER AESTHETIC CONCEPTS

We noted in the last chapter that beauty is not as central a concept in much modern aesthetics as it was in ancient and medieval aesthetics, and that the modern critical vocabulary extends very widely and includes concepts like 'graceful' 'elegant', 'profound', 'moving', 'joyous', 'lively', 'imaginative', 'life-enhancing', 'illuminating', and 'sublime'. Of course, some of these terms were found in earlier times, too; and 'beautiful' is still a very common term of appreciation and judgement. The more striking characteristic of modern aesthetics, however, is that it recognizes certain aesthetic qualities which were not previously acknowledged, at least not explicitly. R. A. Sharpe remarks that 'a great deal of art is uncomfortable, upsetting and even horrifying, and is not valued any the less on that account'.[40] One can think of many works of art which exemplify Sharpe's judgement: just to take painters, there are Grünewald and George Grosz already mentioned, and Goya and Francis Bacon. Such cases create difficulties not merely for the concept of beauty, but for some more modern concepts, for example aesthetic pleasure, which seems too weak a term for some cases and wholly inappropriate in others. Hence Hugo Meynell prefers the term 'satisfaction' to 'pleasure', and asks 'can one really be said to derive pleasure from *King Lear* or Kafka's *Metamorphosis?*'[41] A good question, but I am not sure that 'satisfaction' is much better for the examples he gives, and I find it wholly inappropriate to, say, Goya's 'black' paintings. In the case of art which disturbs us, 'dissatisfying' might be a more appropriate term! Meynell rightly points out

---

[39] 'The Relation between Transcendental and Aesthetical Beauty according to St Thomas', *The Modern Schoolman*, 40 (1963), 163–82; I quote from 179. See Roland A. Delattre, *Beauty and Sensibility in the Thought of Jonathan Edwards* (New Haven, Conn., 1968), 53–4 for a critique of the notion of transcendental beauty in the wide sense of the term.

[40] In Eva Schaper (ed.), *Pleasure, Preference and Value* (Cambridge, 1983), 86–7, Sharpe follows T. S. Eliot in suggesting that the minimum claim we make of art is that it should not bore us.

[41] Hugo Meynell, *The Nature of Aesthetic Value* (Albany NY, 1986), 25.

a few pages later that 'Good art expands consciousness in a way and to a degree that good entertainment does not' (p. 38), but he needs to reckon with a wider range of qualities. Even the term 'aesthetic value' seems too vague, or inappropriate, for grotesque, disturbing, and horrifying art.[42]

Such types of art may have a theological significance, for they remind us that there may be arts of the Fall and redemption, as well as those which hymn the beauty of creation. John W. Dixon argues indeed that the different types of Christian art correspond to the principal events in the Christian drama: there are the arts of creation, in which people record the facts of creation or rejoice in the process; the arts of image, in which they probe into the structure of creation, explore its relations, and seek to understand its parts and order; the arts of the Fall, in which they penetrate into the tragedy of existence and investigate the nature or consequences of the Fall, fallen existence itself, or the kind of world resulting from the Fall; and the arts of redemption, where the artist is occupied with the redemptive act itself or the kind of world that results from the transfiguration of creation in redemption.[43] Later on, Dixon remarks that much art of the late nineteenth and early twentieth centuries will not fit into this framework, for it is the most important body of Western art created outside the influence of the Church, and often indeed is in open rebellion against all the Church stands for; he warns us against trying to 'baptize' such work prematurely.[44] He might have pressed those remarks further and discussed what could be called diabolical art, i.e. that art which celebrates ugliness and evil. Some critics of Francis Bacon's painting might say that it fits into this category. Such art raises difficult questions both about the nature of evil and about its own artistic merits.

All this, however, has taken us far afield from our original consideration of beauty. The variety of categorizations discussed helps explain why not all aesthetic qualities fall under

---

[42] See Mikel Dufrenne, *The Phenomenology of Aesthetic Experience*, trans. Edward Carey *et al.* (Evanston, 1973) 465–6.

[43] John W. Dixon, *Nature and Grace in Art* (Chapel Hill, 1964), 72.

[44] Ibid., 186.

the concept of beauty. On the other hand, this concept is still a central one, perhaps *the* central one, in aesthetics, for it is widely used both in ordinary language and in critical discussion. Often, indeed, it is still used as a catch-all for all forms of aesthetic excellence. We can accept such usage, provided that we keep in mind not only the analogical character of the term 'beautiful' but also the vast range of other aesthetic terms. Roger Scruton has suggested the following helpful general classification:

(i) terms used primarily in judgements of aesthetic value, e.g. beautiful, graceful, and elegant;

(ii) descriptions of formal or technical accomplishment, e.g. balanced, well-made, rough;

(iii) predicates normally used of our mental and emotional life, e.g. sad, joyful, agitated, sincere, vulgar, and mature;

(iv) those referring to the expressive features of works of art, e.g. expressing the transiency of human life. Closely related to these are:

(v) 'affective' terms, used to express or project particular human responses, e.g. moving, exciting, evocative, tedious, enjoyable:

(vi) 'comparison' terms, e.g. masculine, bloated, warm or cold (of colours).

He also includes descriptions of works of art in terms of what they represent, their truthfulness and their genre.[45]

OBJECTIVITY AND STANDARDS

Scruton's classification is helpful, because it indicates that questions about the objectivity of aesthetic evaluations and about criteria for the application of aesthetic terms must have regard to the type of concept being considered. Judgements about the fifth group, 'affective' terms, involve consideration of the feelings of those who are apprehending a work of art: a work which sets out to be exciting and exhilarating must be deemed to have failed in this purpose if few people are in fact

---

[45] Roger Scruton, *Art and Imagination* (London, 1974), 30-1.

excited or exhilarated by it. On the other hand, estimates of
whether a work is rough or well-made involve looking at the
materials used, judging what is appropriate both to the nature
of the materials and to the artist's intentions, and assessing
how much effort has been put into the work. Many of
Scruton's other categories require similar exercises of judgement: we decide whether something is balanced or graceful,
for example, by looking at a number of its features and by
comparing it with other things which are regarded as having
these qualities to a greater or lesser degree. Such judgement
is required in the ascription of many other terms besides
aesthetic ones: was John Henry Newman a saint? is someone's
driving negligent? There may be a scale of comparison in
such cases: thus being delicate may be the mean between
insipidity and crudity or garishness. People may disagree
about the location of particular examples on such a scale. But
some judgements seem to be ruled out: it would be difficult
for a pale colour to be labelled as gaudy or garish, and for a
fast-moving piece of music to be solemn.[46]

In the case of beauty, two seemingly contradictory tendencies often jostle with each other: people want to explicate the
criteria which govern their use of the concept, yet they also
want to leave the nature of beauty something of a mystery.
The former tendency is motivated by the desire to delineate
the sorts of reasons which warrant an ascription of beauty,
and to explain the logical relationship between such ascriptions and the reasons on which they are based. Yet in fact it
has proved difficult to provide an agreed list of sufficient and
necessary conditions for the ascription of beauty to things in
general. Many of the candidates, e.g. Aquinas' wholeness,
harmony, and radiance, are vague, or else they already
covertly embody an appeal to beauty. We seem to have here a
problem analogous to that raised in ethics with regard to the
relationship between 'is' and 'ought', or between descriptive
and evaluative terms. But in aesthetics we are, as I pointed
out at the beginning of this chapter, usually dealing with the
particular; hence there is also a suspicion of those who would

---

[46] See Frank Sibley, 'Aesthetic and Nonaesthetic', *Philosophical Review*, 74
(1965), 135–59.

seek to capture beauty in their theories and rational schemes. This suspicion was expressed classically by Schiller at the beginning of his *On the Aesthetic Education of Man*, when he said of beauty 'its whole magic resides in its mystery, and in dissolving the essential amalgam of its elements we find we have dissolved its very being'.[47] Other writers have made the same point in terms of the indescribability of beauty: we may apprehend it, and yet be unable to describe it, for we are struck speechless with admiration;[48] or in terms of the strangeness of beauty. Thus Baudelaire says: *'The Beautiful is always strange*. I do not mean that it is coldly, deliberately strange, for in that case it would be a monstrosity that had jumped the rails of life. I mean that it always contains a touch of strangeness, of simple, unpremeditated and unconscious strangeness . . . try to imagine a *commonplace Beauty*!'[49] Now if we could invent a theory to explain beauty, it would spoil the whole thing: it would be like constructing a cage for a butterfly. Hence Dufrenne calls for an aesthetics 'which recognizes beauty without creating a theory of beauty, because basically there is no theory to create'.[50]

The ancestor of some of the more philosophical presentations of this view is Kant, who thought that judgements of taste are universal, because the beautiful pleases universally, but that there can be no objective rule of taste whereby the beautiful can be defined by means of concepts.[51] But a more practical consideration is often operative: if we could set out a theory of beauty giving the necessary and sufficient conditions for its ascriptions, we would have a recipe for producing beauty. Yet it seems that no such recipe exists. In his *L'Éducation sentimentale* Flaubert says of one of his characters, a painter, 'Pellerin used to read every book on aesthetics, in the hope of discovering the true theory of the beautiful; for

---

[47] Schiller, *On the Aesthetic Education of Man*, trans. Elizabeth M. Wilkinson and L. A. Willoughby (Oxford, 1967), Letter i, §5. Similarly, Simone Weil says 'There are three mysteries, three incomprehensible things, in this world. Beauty, justice, and truth' (*First and Last Notebooks*, 292).

[48] See Étienne Gilson, *Painting and Reality* (London, 1957), 209.

[49] Charles Baudelaire, *Art in Paris*, 124.

[50] Dufrenne, *The Phenomenology of Aesthetic Experience*, p. lxiii.

[51] Kant, *Critique of Judgement*, §§6, 9, 16–17.

he was certain that he had only to find it to be able to paint masterpieces.'[52] Flaubert is poking fun at such an idea; yet in past centuries people have sought for such theories, and have indeed concocted mathematical formulae—I am thinking of the famous Golden Section, which finds a recipe for beauty in the formula $A : B :: B : C$ (where $C = A + B$).

Yet, mysterious though beauty may be, it is usually a function of other properties of things, even if we cannot provide an exact formula. What then is its relation to these other properties, of colour, line, shape, melody, style, and so on? Many contemporary writers on aesthetics wish to modify Kant's dictum that the beautiful cannot be defined by means of concepts, and see it as an emergent property which is supervenient on other characteristics. Frank Sibley argues that concepts like 'delicate', 'graceful', and 'elegant' are emergent, in that we justify their use by appealing not only to other terms but to non-aesthetic ones, for example when we judge that something is delicate because of its pastel shades and curving lines. There is a relation of dependence, signified by terms like 'makes', 'due to', 'results from', and 'is responsible for'; but Sibley sees this relation as a looser one than entailment, for he denies that non-aesthetic features are logically sufficient conditions for applying aesthetic terms.[53] Similarly, Guy Sircello analyses beauty (which Sibley does not discuss) in terms of what he calls 'properties of qualitative degree', which differ according to the kind of thing in question but include the delicacy, depth, richness, and vividness of colours, the clarity and brilliance of sounds, and serenity, calmness, and joy in people. He argues that if something is beautiful, it is always so in terms of certain other characteristics: thus beauty is not a property, but a way in which things have other properties, e.g. being beautifully vivid, rich, calm, and so on.[54] Mary Mothersill disagrees with Sircello in that

---

[52] Pt. 1, ch. 4 (Everyman edn., London, 1956, p. 36).
[53] Frank Sibley, 'Aesthetic Concepts', *Philosophical Review*, 68 (1959), 421–50; and 'Aesthetic and Nonaesthetic'. For attempts to analyse further the relations of supervenience and emergence, see Jerrold Levinson, 'Aesthetic Supervenience', *Southern Journal of Philosophy*, 22 suppl. (1983), 93–110; and John Bender, 'Supervenience and the Justification of Aesthetic Judgments', *The Journal of Aesthetics and Art Criticism*, 46 (1987–88), 31–40.
[54] Sircello, *A New Theory of Beauty*, esp. §5.

she thinks that beauty *is* a property of things; but she too thinks that things are beautiful if they please us in virtue of their aesthetic properties, e.g. the 'bluish grey' and 'wavelike contour' of a particular picture.[55]

Such views are recent developments of what has traditionally been called an objective view of aesthetic value, i.e. one which regards beauty and other such qualities as inherent in the nature of things and not just, as is said, in the eye of the beholder. They face, therefore, certain common objections: that people disagree both about ascriptions of beauty to particular things and about the criteria for such ascriptions, that there is no way of resolving such disagreements, that we cannot appreciate what other cultures find beautiful, and so on. There are equally common replies to such objections: that we should not expect the kind of exactness in aesthetics that we find in some sciences, that aesthetic qualities are subtle and elusive so it is hardly surprising that people disagree about them, that there are disagreements and undecidable areas in other supposedly more 'objective' fields, that aesthetic disputes can sometimes be resolved (perhaps more easily than many moral disputes can be) by getting someone to see a feature of a work of art or a landscape that he or she has missed, that we find a lot of agreement too in aesthetics and could look for other explanations of disagreements besides 'tastes differ', e.g. prejudice, self-deception, and lack of effort or of perception, and so on. In the case of beauty, Sircello points out that disagreements are not surprising, given the indefinitely large number of 'properties of qualitative degree' and the way in which they apply in various ways to different sorts of object, the difficulty of describing them, and people's limited experience of them. He classifies types of disagreement, distinguishing, for example, disagreements about particular properties like vividness of colour from ones where an object may seem to be beautiful with respect to one set of properties but not with regard to another set. He argues that most disagreements stem from the failure of the disputants to reveal the grounds of their judgements, a lack of perception or sensitivity in one of

---

[55] Mary Mothersill, *Beauty Restored* (Oxford, 1984), 153, 347–53.

them, or a disparity in their experience of the relevant qualities.[56] Sircello does not discuss the problems raised by art of alien cultures, such as Indian or Chinese music. But here it can be argued that a failure to like or appreciate such works often stems from a lack of understanding. In so far as sets of artistic symbols are analogous to languages and other communication systems, then a failure to appreciate may be assimilated to a lack of understanding of a language or of an idiom. Certainly, being attracted by the beauty of a language or a piece of music presupposes some such understanding, which may require a long period of learning; and indeed any aesthetic appreciation requires training in attention and observation.

The issues which I have just summarized are part of a debate which has been going on for centuries and will, I suspect, continue long into the future. I have no desire to go over familiar ground by recapitulating ideas and theories which can be found in many books on aesthetics. But it has to be said that the theological consideration of these issues introduces certain new factors. If indeed God created the world with all its beauty, and such beauties are reflections of His beauty, then it seems that there are theological grounds as well as philosophical for a broadly 'realist' or 'objectivist' position. Thus theology rules out certain views a priori and favours others; and this is not surprising, for we find a similar situation in ethics, where, for instance, wholesale ethical relativism is precluded for a Christian, whilst certain values and principles are normative, even if there may be some flexibility in their application. In the case of aesthetics, Christian theologians, and indeed all theists, start from the assumption that the beautiful aspects of nature are properties put there by God as creator of all things (which is not to deny that beauty may be supervenient on other qualities[57]); they may be led from there to explore the footsteps of the Creator and to rejoice in His creation; many have gone further and

---

[56] Sircello, *A New Theory of Beauty*, §31.

[57] *Contra* Plato, *Phaedo*, 100d, where the question of whether colour and shape contribute to beauty is brushed aside in favour of the explanation of things' beauty in terms of their participation in Beauty itself.

seen the beauty of works of art too as created by God, though in this case indirectly, through His inspiration of artists as 'secondary causes'; and many see both natural and artistic beauty as a reflection of, or likeness to, God's own beauty. Now we have already seen that the objectivity of beauty and other aesthetic properties is defensible on purely philosophical grounds, and I have mentioned some recent defences of such a view. But the point now is that theologians are arguing for the case on other, theological, grounds; and that their arguments are a priori based on the doctrine of Creation. This consideration faces us with an important issue about method in theological aesthetics.

Such a theological approach need not prevent us also looking at the 'subjective' side of the matter, that is, the response and feeling of the beholders, their pleasure, satisfaction, excitement, and so on, even though we regard them as caused by the actual qualities of things (in labelling them as 'subjective' we are not implying that they are unreal or illusory). Aquinas appeals to such responses when he says that 'things are called beautiful which give delight when they are apprehended' (*ST* 1a. v. 4 ad 1); and McDowell notes more generally that a definition of 'objective' need not exclude reference to how things affect sentient subjects.[58] Even though aesthetic qualities are regarded as inherent in things, we must also consider peoples' individual likes and dislikes, fashion, and all the factors which, both in an individual and in a particular historical era, may lead people to perceive and appreciate those qualities, or prevent them from doing so. It is often remarked that a liking for the scenery of the Alps and the English Lake District developed only in the late eighteenth and early nineteenth centuries, encouraged by Rousseau's and Wordsworth's works. But this does not mean that their beauty and grandeur were not *there* previously: perhaps they were waiting, as it were, to be revealed by artists and poets. Conversely, eighteenth-century Classicism was blind to the value of Gothic architecture, and the Romantics were blind to much Renaissance art and to the Baroque. There are in the world different kinds of beauty, which different generations

---

[58] In Schaper, *Pleasure, Preference and Value*, 2–5.

may recognize. Hence variations in taste do not necessarily show that beauty is not in things themselves, for there is no reason why all the properties of things should be discerned by everybody all at once. In any case, a theological aesthetic, like any aesthetic, should allow some latitude for individual preference. We can agree that God created the beautiful range of colours and that a coloured world is more beautiful than a world of black, white, and grey would have been, without insisting that one particular colour is *the* most beautiful one.

The role of 'subjective' factors in aesthetics like perception and appreciation may also be interpreted in theological terms: for as we shall see later, the Holy Spirit may be regarded not only as inspiring artists or writers, but also as inspiring those who understand and appreciate their work. An interesting variation on this line of thought is the idea that nature is a kind of language in which God speaks to us, an idea found in Berkeley[59] and hinted at by Augustine when he says 'God works the sensible and visible things which He wills, in order to signify and manifest Himself in them' (*De Trin.* iii. 4. 10). Such an idea seems to allow for some latitude, in that God may speak through nature to different people in different ways—though not, I think, *wholly* different, for then we would be faced with a set of private languages. If beauty is one idiom of this divine language, then the Holy Spirit may be needed to give an understanding of that idiom. If so, then it would seem that there are theological reasons too for resisting the attempt to work out an exact theory of beauty, setting out a cut-and-dried account of the relevant principles of taste and criteria of application.

THE MORAL AND RELIGIOUS SIGNIFICANCE OF BEAUTY

A theological aesthetic will not only insist on the objectivity of beauty and other aesthetic qualities in the ways mentioned, but is also likely to claim that they have a moral and religious significance. Here we find a gradation in the claims put forward.

Although Kant distinguished the feeling for beauty from

---

[59] The analogy with a language is made explicitly in *Alciphron*, iv, §§7–15.

moral feeling (remarking, *en passant*, that connoisseurs are generally vain, capricious, and addicted to injurious passions!), he maintained that an interest in the beauty of nature is always a sign of refinement and a mark of a good soul, and that the beautiful is the symbol of the morally good.[60] Likewise, he relates his other main aesthetic concept, that of the sublime in nature, to our moral feelings, remarking that without the development of moral ideas the sublime is merely terrifying.[61] He did not, however, make any theological connections, unlike his successor Hegel, who, although he was little interested in natural beauty, saw art as expressing the Divine, and, along with philosophy and religion, as one of the realms of the absolute spirit.[62] We find other very 'high' views of beauty later in the nineteenth century among writers who saw the poverty and squalor of early industrial capitalism as the destruction of God's beauty in nature, a sin against charity, and the source of corruption in art. Thus Ruskin says in his essay 'Giotto and his Works in Padua' that 'As long as England can bear to see misery and squalor in its streets, it can neither invent nor accept human beauty in its pictures.' [63] Such views are less common in the twentieth century, which has on the whole tended to divorce aesthetic and moral considerations, partly because it has often regarded aesthetics as an autonomous discipline (a conception much influenced by Kant, and earlier by Baumgarten), partly because of its suspicion of didactic art. But even nowadays it is often said that the imaginative insights conveyed by art and literature may enlarge a person's vision; and many writers would still want to go beyond this and say that aesthetic experience can issue a moral and spiritual challenge and perhaps serve as a judgement on a shabby sort of life. Von Balthasar, for example, claims that beauty may be a divine summons to change one's life.[64]

The simplest form of a religious interpretation is to see

---

[60] Kant, *Critique of Judgement*, §§42, 59.
[61] Ibid. §29.
[62] Hegel, *Aesthetics*, 7, 94.
[63] In Joan Evans (ed.), *The Lamp of Beauty: Writings on Art by John Ruskin* (London, 1959), 73.
[64] See Hans Urs von Balthasar, *Word and Revelation* (New York, 1964), 138.

things of aesthetic value, whether in nature or art, as gifts of God, which do not by themselves tell us anything about Him other than that He is creative and generous. But people have often gone much further than this. The enjoyment of natural beauty is for many a religious and mystical experience, in which they feel the presence of God in a specially vivid way. It is unlikely, I think, that such an experience would, just by itself, convert someone to a religious belief. But it is often interpreted in terms of an already existing belief, and may help to confirm it. Similarly, certain works of art seem to many people to point beyond themselves, as we saw in the case of Barth's love of Mozart, of whom Martin Cooper also wrote 'Yet even his most sustained frivolities, such as *Così fan tutte*, contain moments of tenderness and glimpses of unearthly beauty to be found in no other composer'[65], a feeling which many people construe in religious terms. Of course, such works of art are appreciated by believer and unbeliever alike, for in a sense beauty stands on its own feet. But the believer may see things in them which the unbeliever does not (and vice versa); and on occasion the former's conception of beauty may be changed or extended by his or her religious beliefs, as Drury and Moltmann suggest. It is such considerations that sometimes lead people to speak of the holiness of beauty (rather than the beauty of holiness): I have mentioned van der Leeuw in this connection, but over a century earlier the Romantic critic Friedrich von Schlegel punctuated an eloquent paean to beauty with the question 'is not the beautiful also holy?' He went on to relate the sense of beauty to humanity's 'fearful unsatisfied desire to soar into infinity' and to its attraction towards God.[66] Many other later writers have drawn attention to the discontent which an intense experience of beauty can leave behind. Such experiences are elusive, do not last indefinitely, and often leave a feeling of longing or dissatisfaction behind. Thus John F.

---

[65] Martin Cooper, 'Mozart and His Age', in *Ideas and Music* (London, 1965), 40.
[66] Schlegel, 'On the Limits of the Beautiful' (1794), in E. J. Millington (ed.), *The Aesthetic and Miscellaneous Works of Frederick von Schlegel* (London, 1860), 417, 419. See his contemporary Schelling's *System of Transcendental Idealism*, ch. 6 (Cotta edn., iii. 620), for the similar claim that 'the infinite represented as finite is beauty', and that works of art are such representations.

Haught says 'Aesthetic frustration stems from the inadequacy of our perceptual faculties to the deep need we have for limitless beauty.'[67] Like Schlegel, he interprets such experiences theistically, in terms of a yearning for God and a sense of His absence, even if people do not explicitly so construe them.

Many of these discussions can be regarded as adaptations of Plato's 'ladder of beauty' in the *Symposium*. The most striking modern example of such an adaptation is to be found in the work of Simone Weil, who explicitly states that the ascent described in *Symposium* 210d–212a is to God's beauty, which is, she says, 'the attribute of God under which we see him'.[68] Weil is perhaps the leading exponent of a 'revelatory' view of beauty in the twentieth century, a century which, just as it has avoided moral interpretations of beauty, similarly has on the whole fought shy of making ambitious metaphysical claims for the concept. Weil thinks that the experience of beauty is an experience of the transcendent, more specifically an experience of God, and that for unbelievers it is a form of what she calls the implicit love of God. She describes the world's beauty as 'the sign of an exchange of love between the Creator and creation',[69] and as 'the co-operation of divine wisdom in creation . . . God created the universe and his Son . . . created the beauty of it for us'. It is Christ's 'tender smile for us coming through matter'; and the love for it 'proceeds from God dwelling in our souls and goes out to God present in the universe'.[70] Again appealing to Plato, she describes beauty as an incarnation of God, come down to earth to save us.[71] Hence she concludes that all art of the highest order is religious in essence, inspired by God.[72] There is also, of course, diabolical art and 'perverted aesthetics',[73] for aesthetic

---

[67] John F. Haught, *What is God?* (New York, 1986), ch. 4. I quote from p. 85.

[68] Simone Weil, *On Science, Necessity and the Love of God*, trans. R. Rees (Oxford, 1968), 129.

[69] Id., *First and Last Notebooks*, 139.

[70] Id., *Waiting on God*, trans. Emma Craufurd (Fontana edn.; London, 1959), 120. Note the seeds of a Trinitarian analysis of beauty in this passage.

[71] Id., *First and Last Notebooks*, 341, 286; cf. id. *Gravity and Grace*, trans. Emma Craufurd (London, 1963), 137.

[72] Id., *Gravity and Grace*, 137; *Waiting on God*, 124.

[73] Id., *Gravity and Grace*, 138; *Waiting on God*, 124.

merit can go with moral harmfulness, and 'The devil also manufactures an imitation of beauty', which can be discerned only by close attention; though, she tells us, the devil cannot inspire an artist to paint a picture which would comfort someone in solitary confinement for twenty years.[74]

We are confronted here with the most ambitious metaphysic of beauty, which sees it as a revelation of God, and indeed as a divine attribute. Weil regards herself as giving a Christian interpretation of Plato; but a similar view is found in Aquinas, especially in his commentary on Pseudo-Dionysius' *Divine Names*, and in some neo-Thomists, like Weil's contemporary Maritain (she missed these parallels because of her dislike of Aquinas and mistrust of Maritain[75]). Such views obviously run counter to the modern tendency we have noted of conceiving of aesthetics as autonomous, and to the common inclination to regard the appreciation of beauty as merely our taking pleasure in the perceived qualities of things.[76] But at the other end, the plausibility of such a metaphysic as Weil's will depend also on whether we can make sense of the idea of beauty as an attribute of God. We shall investigate that idea in the next chapter.

[74] Id., *First and Last Notebooks*, 341. In saying this, Weil is, it seems, ruling out the possibility of there being a diabolical beauty which is still beauty even though morally corrupted (somewhat as an intelligence devoted to evil is still an intelligence).

[75] Her attitude to them stems from her hatred of their ancestor, Aristotle, whom she described as 'the corrupt tree which bears only rotten fruit' (*First and Last Notebooks*, 355). Like a lot of people, she fails to do justice to the Platonic strand in Thomism.

[76] For an early example of an attack on Platonic and theistic interpretations of beauty, see George Santayana, *The Sense of Beauty* (repr. Cambridge, Mass., 1988, with a valuable critical introduction by Arthur C. Danto).

3
God's Beauty

DURING the last few years there has been a renewed interest
in the traditional theological problems associated with God's
existence and nature. Many books and articles have discussed
the coherence of the notion of God in general, and the
problems raised by particular attributes, especially omnisci-
ence and omnipotence. There is, however, one attribute
which is conspicuous by its absence in these discussions,
namely God's beauty. It is, as von Balthasar says, His most
neglected attribute.[1] This neglect does not just extend to
philosophical and theological works: I do not recall ever
hearing a sermon on the question, and it is little discussed in
popular religious books.

There are many reasons for this neglect. We have already
seen, in Chapter 1, how Barth was uneasy with the idea of
divine beauty, because of the connection of beauty with ideas
of pleasure, desire, and enjoyment, and its secular and Greek
associations. If we think of beauty in terms of colours, forms,
harmonies, and so on in things which we sense, it is difficult
to see how it can apply to One who lacks matter, body, and
parts. The question becomes even more difficult when it is
said not only that God is beautiful but that He *is* beauty itself,
the source of beauty in all other things. Of course, similar
problems arise with other divine attributes, like wisdom,
power, and love. But the ordinary believer gets some handle
on these other attributes by trying to discern the relevant
divine actions, for instance God's wise governance of the
universe, His power manifested in natural phenomena or in
holiness, and His love shown in providence and especially,
Christians say, in the life and work of Christ. In the case of
beauty, however, it is difficult to find any corresponding
actions other than God's creation of beauty in the world.

[1] Hans Urs von Balthasar, *Word and Revelation* (New York, 1964), 162.

Those who attempt to fill in the picture here tend to say that the divine beauty is inexpressible, or else to produce something rather formal, for instance by applying Aquinas' trio of wholeness, harmony, and radiance to the divine Being.

At the root of many of these problems, I think, is the fact that we lack a proper vocabulary to support our ascriptions of beauty to God. We have found that generally we use the term 'beautiful' in two ways: as an overall verdict on a work of art or a natural phenomenon, or to qualify another term. Either way, the term is supported by a whole barrage of concepts: by other aesthetic ones like 'elegant' and 'graceful', or by particular words describing the qualities of colours, sounds, and so on. But much of this vocabulary is not available in describing God—what would a pretty, handsome, or elegant God be like? In the case of divine beauty the neighbouring or supporting concepts are drawn from elsewhere: from the language of power (the biblical term 'glory' suggests power as well as beauty, and goes along with terms like 'majesty', 'splendour', and 'strength'), from that of ethics (most people think of Christ's beauty in terms of his moral and spiritual qualities), or from the more general divine attributes of holiness, perfection, goodness, and excellence. God's beauty is also often related to light, in the sense of intellectual or spiritual illumination, and hence to wisdom, knowledge, and truth; and if we use the eighteenth-century term 'sublime' of Him, then again this suggests His grandeur. These considerations do not invalidate our ascription of beauty to God, but they leave us with the tasks of further clarifying the nature of that beauty and of relating it to earthly beauty (of course, the problem differs from language to language, as the terms used to describe beauty may have varying connotations).

We can, of course, evade these difficulties by opting for the less ambitious view of Christian writers on aesthetics like Wolterstorff or Seerveld, who decline to speculate about God's beauty or about its relation to earthly beauty and other aesthetic properties. It might be said that God can create stones without being a stone Himself, so He can create natural beauty and inspire beautiful works of art without being beautiful (or beauty) Himself: and that speculations about His beauty are relics of the Neoplatonism which crept into early Christianity. Thus it is possible to put forward a less ambitious thesis. Such a view, however, does lose a lot of the richness of Christian tradition, which has seen Creation not just in terms of God's giving being to things but also in terms of His imparting His own qualities to them so that they bear some likeness to Him, and, in the present case, of His communicating His glory so that, as von Balthasar says, 'the cosmos is experienced as the representation and manifestation of the hidden transcendent beauty of God'.[2] More seriously for its proponents, this view ignores much of the biblical witness, which not only attributes beauty to God but also has the closely related notion of divine glory as one of its central concepts.

In this chapter I shall look more closely at the biblical and theological sources, and then consider whether we can indeed justify the ascription of beauty to God. Finally, I shall consider some of the wider implications of such an ascription for theology.

GOD'S BEAUTY: THE SOURCES

I have already given a few examples of early Christian Fathers who describe God as beautiful, most beautiful, or indeed as beauty itself in Chapter 1, and there are many other similar examples available. St Hilary after quoting Wisd. 13: 5, says that we know God's supreme beauty from creation and that because the universe is beautiful it is called *cosmos* (there is a play on words here, for the Greek word *cosmos* means both world and ornament or decoration); he asks 'Should not the Lord of this very beauty be conceived of as the most beautiful of all beauty . . .?[3] St Gregory of Nazianzus refers to Plato's analogy between the sun and the Form of the Good, in *Republic*, vi. 508a–509a, and instead draws an analogy with God: just as the sun is the most beautiful of the beings we see, so God is the most beautiful of the beings we know, and the angels are so well modelled on beauty that they commu-

---

[2] Id., *The Glory of the Lord: A Theological Aesthetics*, ii, trans. Andrew Louth *et al.* (1984), 154 (writing of Greek thought from Plato to Plotinus).
[3] *On the Trinity*, i. 7 (*PL* 10: 30bc).

nicate divine light.[4] St Gregory of Nyssa likewise describes God alone as really beautiful, and indeed not just beautiful but existing always by the very essence of beauty,[5] the archetype of all beauty.[6] Thus the idea was familiar enough by the time Pseudo-Dionysius wrote what was probably the fullest and most influential early treatment of it, in his *Divine Names*, round about AD 500. According to him, the Good (which is one of his names for God) is called beauty because it imparts beauty to all things according to their natures: 'And they name it beautiful since it is the all-beautiful and the beautiful beyond all. It is forever so, unvaryingly, unchangeably so . . .' It is not beautiful in only one part or aspect; rather, Dionysius continues, 'In itself and by itself it is the uniquely and the eternally beautiful. It is the superabundant source in itself of the beauty of every beautiful thing.'[7]

Both Pseudo-Dionysius and many of the Fathers whom I have mentioned were influenced by Plato and Neoplatonism. This influence is seen in their liking for Platonic analogies like the sun, their use of language which is reminiscent of the Theory of Forms (things 'partake of' Beauty), and their adopting or adapting the schema of the 'ladder of beauty' from the *Symposium*. There is a striking occurrence of the last of these in Gregory of Nyssa's *Life of Moses*. This work exemplifies the concept of *epektasis*, i.e. the soul's constant stretching-out towards perfection (the word is cognate with that used by St Paul in Phil. 3: 13, where he writes of 'straining forward to what lies ahead'). Gregory says analogously of those who love what is beautiful:

Hope always draws the soul from the beauty which is seen to what is beyond, always kindles the desire for the hidden through what is constantly perceived. Therefore the ardent lover of beauty, although

---

[4] *Second Theological Oration* (*Or.* xxviii), §§30, 31 (*PG* 36: 69a, 72b).

[5] *On the Song of Songs*, 4 (*PG* 44: 836ab).

[6] *On Virginity*, xi (*PG* 46: 368c); cf. his *Catechetical Oration* vi (*PG* 45: 29b). See Heinrich Krug, *De Pulchritudine Divina* (Freiburg im Breisgau, 1902) for further patristic references: bk. 2 of this work is a veritable *catena* of quotations from the early Fathers (it is noticeable, again, how many of them are interested only in *spiritual* beauty).

[7] iv. 7 (*PG* 3: 701cd), trans. Colm Luibheid, in *Pseudo-Dionysius: The Complete Works* (Classics of Western Spirituality, London, 1987), 76–7.

receiving what is always visible as an image of what he desires, yet longs to be filled with the very stamp of the archetype.

And the bold request which goes up the mountains of desire asks this: to enjoy the Beauty not in mirrors and reflections, but face to face.[8]

It is important to realize, however, that although God's beauty and its relationship to earthly beauty were often described in Platonic terminology, the idea does not derive merely from Plato and Neoplatonism but is also found in the Bible. There are a few texts in the Old Testament which ascribe beauty to God Himself (though they do not say that He *is* beauty); most of them, significantly, come from the Psalms. The first one is Ps. 27: 4, 'One thing I have asked . . . that I may dwell in the house of the Lord all the days of my life, to behold the beauty of the Lord'.[9] The Hebrew term *nō'am*, translated here as 'beauty', also denotes 'favour' or 'sweetness', as in Ps. 90: 17, 'Let the favour of the Lord our God be upon us' (it is also used of the sweetness or pleasing nature of wisdom in Prov. 3: 17; cf. 15: 26, and 16: 24). Other such terms ascribed to God are *hāh-dāhr* ('splendour' or 'majesty'), e.g. in Ps. 145: 5, 'On the glorious splendour of thy majesty, and on thy wondrous works I will meditate', and *tiphāhrāh* (translated as 'splendour', 'pride', 'glory', and 'honour' as well as 'beauty'), e.g. in Ps. 71: 8. The term *yŏphee*, which in later Hebrew is probably the nearest term to 'beauty' in the aesthetic sense, is ascribed to God in Zech. 9: 17.[10] Sometimes these terms are used of places associated with God, e.g. in Ps. 46: 6, 'strength and beauty (*tiphāhrāh*) are in his sanctuary', and in Ps. 50: 2, 'Out of Zion, the perfection of beauty (*yŏphee*), God shines forth.'

Such ascriptions are most common in the Psalms, many of which are songs of praise, even love-poems, to God. The attributions of beauty to God there seem to arise from a

[8] ii, §§231–2 (*PG* 401d–404a), trans. A. Malherbe and E. Ferguson, in *Gregory of Nyssa: The Life of Moses* (Classics of Western Spirituality, New York, 1978), 114 f.
[9] See Gerhard von Rad, *Old Testament Theology*, i, trans. D. M. G. Stalker (London, 1975), 364–8 for some comments on the relationship between Israel's cult and praise of God and its sense of the beautiful.
[10] If, following the Mazoretic text, we read 'his beauty'.

powerful experience of His presence or an intense yearning for Him, and the language used is that of joyful praise, awe, and adoration. We find, however, an entirely different approach in a text from the Apocrypha, Wisd. 13: 3–5, used, as we have seen, by Hilary, and also by many later writers. This text describes God as the first author of beauty and creator, and then says that 'by the greatness and beauty of the creatures proportionably the maker of them is seen'. Here we have an inference made from the beauty of the world to God, an ancestor of much subsequent natural theology (it is to be noted that this text does not actually say that God *is* beautiful, though verses 3 and 4 say that He excels over creation, and earlier on wisdom, an emanation of God's glory (7: 25), is described as bright, radiant, and beautiful (6: 13; 7: 10, 29; 8: 2)). Somewhat between these two approaches is that of some of the 'creation' Psalms, which discern God's majesty and glory in the heavens, the waters of the sea, and the beauties of nature, e.g. Ps. 104. Here it is not so much a matter of making an inference as of responding to God's presence and seeing that 'The heavens are telling the glory of God' (Ps. 19: 1).[11] This takes us, however, to the concept of glory, which is much more central to the Bible than that of divine beauty—though I shall claim that they are closely related, and indeed that beauty is a constituent of glory.

'Glory' is used as a translation of the Hebrew term *kabod*, the root meaning of which is 'heaviness' or 'weight'. The term is not restricted to God, for in Gen. 45: 13 Joseph tells his brothers to go and give a full report to their father of the *kabod* which he enjoys in Egypt (i.e. his wealth and distinction); and Isa. 35: 2 exclaims that the wasteland which will bloom and flourish will have the *kabod* of Lebanon and the splendour of Carmel and Sharon bestowed on it. The earlier texts of the Bible applying it to God associate it with a visible phenomenon, particularly of a cloud (Exod. 16: 10; 24:16) or fire (Deut. 5: 24; 2 Chron. 7: 1–3); hence Moses prays that he may see God's glory (Exod. 33: 18 *f.*, 22). It is used of God's manifestations on Mount Sinai and of the events of the

[11] See J. Kellenberger, *The Cognitivity of Religion: Three Perspectives* (London, 1985), ch. 2.

Exodus (Num. 14: 22), of His filling the Temple in a cloud (1 Kgs. 8: 10 *f.*), and of natural phenomena like thunder (Ps. 29: 3–5). Such manifestations render their *locus*, e.g. the Tent of Meeting (Exod. 29: 43), holy; and they are usually linked with God's word. Later the term is used more generally of God's power and splendour, especially in the Psalms (e.g. 96: 3; the eighteenth-century term 'sublime' might sometimes be the appropriate translation). In Isaiah's vision the seraphs proclaim that Yahweh's glory fills the whole earth, and they link it with His holiness (Isa. 6: 3); later on in that book the restoration of Jerusalem is prophesied, in terms of the rising of God's glory like a light (60: 1–3; Ezek. 1: 28 also associates light with Yahweh's glory, and Exod. 34: 29 *f.* describes Moses' face as shining after the theophany on Mount Sinai). The full manifestation of God's glory is put in the future, in the Messianic age, and it will be seen by all mankind (Isa. 40: 5, 60: 1–3, 66: 18–19).

Later on, in the Targums (Aramaic translations and paraphrases of the Hebrew scriptures) the term 'glory' was often used as a substitute for descriptions of God's presence. Because of a growing sense of divine transcendence, Judaism became reluctant to speak of God's direct intervention in human affairs, and used indirect descriptions, especially the three Aramaic terms *memra* (word), *yekara* (glory), and *shekinah* (dwelling). The last of these was the most common, and was used as a way of speaking of God's omnipresence, accessibility, and special activity in the created world, without infringing the doctrine of divine transcendence. Like 'glory', it was often particularly associated with light. In the Septuagint the Greek word *doxa* was used to translate both *kabod* and *shekinah*, and this affected the use of the term in the New Testament: as A. M. Ramsey puts it, 'conceptions which are distinct in Hebrew and Aramaic literature became, in the Septuagint, fused into a unified imagery of God's glory and God's dwelling or tabernacling with His people. This unified imagery is the background of much of the thought of the writers of the New Testament.'[12] Indeed, as Ramsey points

[12] A. M. Ramsey, *The Glory of God and the Transfiguration of Christ* (London, 1949), 20. The first two chapters of this book are a very helpful treatment of the

out later, *doxa* was used to translate many other Hebrew words of kindred meaning, e.g. 'majesty', 'beauty', and 'excellency', hence *doxa* is far more common in the Septuagint than *kabod* is in the Hebrew Bible.[13]

This wide usage of the term *doxa* was inherited by the New Testament, where it is used, for example, of God's reflection in believers, brought about by the Spirit (2 Cor. 3: 18). But the term is used especially of Christ, on whose face the glory of God shines forth (2 Cor. 4: 6), and here again the term often has an eschatological flavour, like the term 'kingdom'. God's glory is seen in Christ, but not fully manifested until his Second Coming (Matt. 24: 30; Mark 8: 38, 13: 26; Luke 9: 26), or on the Cross (John 7: 39, 12: 16; cf. Luke 24: 26). One very striking reference back to the Old Testament is found in the accounts of the Transfiguration, which echo accounts of Moses on Mount Sinai in Exod. 33–4, for instance in their linking of glory with light. Jesus is described as being transfigured before the disciples, his face shining like the sun and his garments becoming white as light; and the disciples are overshadowed by a bright cloud (Matt. 17: 2, 5). The feast of the Transfiguration is an important one in the Eastern

concept of glory, as also is Israel Abrahams's *Glory of God* (Oxford, 1925; repr. in *The Foundations of Jewish Life: Three Studies*, New York, 1973). Von Balthasar's main treatments of the biblical concept come in *Herrlichkeit: Eine Theologische Ästhetik*, iii. 2: *Theologie*, pt. 1, *Alter Bund* (Einsiedeln, 1967; this vol. will be translated as vol. vi of *The Glory of the Lord*), esp. ch. 1, and in *The Glory of the Lord*, vol. vii, pt. 2. It should be noted that for him glory is a more fundamental concept than beauty, for he thinks that the perception of inner-worldly beauty is to be related to divine glory. Hence he regards modern aesthetics (from Baumgarten and Kant onwards) as but a fragment of a true aesthetics: for this point, see *Herrlichkeit: Eine Theologische Ästhetik*, iii. 1: *Im Raum der Metaphysik*, pt. 2, *Neuzeit* (2nd edn., Einsiedeln, 1975; this vol. will be translated as vol. v of *The Glory of the Lord*), esp. sect. 6. Another factor which distances von Balthasar from much modern aesthetics is that he regards beauty as a transcendental, as the splendour of being.

[13] Ramsey, *The Glory of God*, 24. Likewise the word *kalos* is very common in the Septuagint, used, for instance of the refrain in Gen. 1 'and God saw that it was good'. But, again, it must be noticed that the term has wider connotations than 'beautiful', and that its suggestion of attractiveness and desirability makes it more appropriate to God than is the English term (Pseudo-Dionysius claims that the noun *kallos* is linked with *kalein* (to call), for 'beauty "bids" all things to itself'—*loc. cit.*, a connection which had already been suggested by Plato in *Cratylus*, 416c). Hence modern discussions in terms of aesthetic qualities may be somewhat off the track when considering divine beauty.

Church, for the event honoured is regarded as anticipating not only the glorification of the risen Christ but also the eventual transformation of the whole cosmos.

In his discussion of God's beauty and glory, Moltmann remarks that Western Christianity, unlike Eastern, ascribes little importance to the Transfiguration, and remarks that it has one-sidedly emphasized God's dominion, and not His splendour and loveliness, and thus subjected Christian existence to judicial and moral categories. He remarks, too, that although *kabod* and *doxa* are key words in the Bible, they are not so in modern theological dictionaries, and that Barth is the only theologian in the continental Protestant tradition who dares to call God 'beautiful'.[14] I do not know if all the factors which Moltmann mentions are indeed interconnected, but he is certainly right that Western Christianity has given more attention to God's power than to His beauty. This tendency can be seen in the very passage of Barth which Moltmann commends, his discussion of the divine glory, where Barth gives God's beauty only a subordinate role (*CD* ii, pt. 1, §31). Barth admits that *kabod* (and its Greek, Latin, and German equivalents) includes and expresses what we call beauty. But he says that beauty is not a leading concept in treating of the divine perfections, but an auxiliary one, enabling us to see that God's glory is effective (p. 653). We find a similar ambivalence a few pages later, when Barth says of God 'He is the basis and standard of everything that is beautiful and of all ideas of the beautiful' (p. 656), but warns us that we are not dealing with a creaturely concept of beauty, formed from created things. This warning is justified, but Barth leaves the question of the relationship between divine and creaturely beauty hanging in the air; nor does he justify his relegation of divine beauty to an auxiliary role. The source of this ambivalence lies in something which we have already noticed, Barth's wariness of the concept of beauty. We find a very different approach in, for example, Jonathan Edwards (a writer never mentioned by Barth), who both gives beauty a pre-eminent role amongst God's perfections and regards it as taking priority over power in the divine glory, sometimes indeed

[14] Jürgen Moltmann, *Theology of Play*, trans. R. Ulrich (New York, 1972), 38–9.

treating them as almost identical.[15] Edwards, however, is rare among Christian theologians in giving the concept of divine beauty and glory a leading role in his work.

Later Judaism developed some of the Scriptural themes which we have noted. The Talmud describes a kind of ladder of beauty reaching up to Jacob, whose beauty was a reflection of Adam's; but compared with the *shekinah* even Adam 'was as a monkey to a human being'.[16] The implication seems to be that Adam's beauty was a reflection of the divine glory, which was transmitted in a weaker form to his descendants.[17] One of the highest angels in rabbinical angelology bears the name 'Yafefiah' (beauty of God).[18] We find, however, the greatest interest in divine beauty in later Judaism among mystics. An early example is to be found in the *hekhalot* ('palaces') hymns composed by the *merkava* ('chariot') mystics in Palestine and later in Babylonia around the third and fourth centuries CE. The *hekhalot* are the seven heavenly halls through which the visionary aspires to pass, and the *merkava* is the divine throne, in the inner recesses of the seventh heaven. In one of them, the ministering angels sing a paean to the face of God, as they are stationed at their posts by the throne.

Lovely face, majestic face,
face of beauty, face of flame,
the face of the Lord God of Israel when he sits upon His throne
    of glory,
robed in praise upon His seat of splendour,
His beauty surpasses the beauty of the aged,
His splendour outshines the splendour of newly-weds
in their bridal chamber.

Whoever looks at Him is instantly torn;
whoever glimpses His beauty immediately melts away.

[15] Jonathan Edwards, *A Treatise concerning Religious Affections*, ed. John E. Smith (New Haven, 1959), 264 *f*. and 302 *f*. Edwards's fullest discussion of glory is in his *Dissertation concerning the End for which God created the World*. See also Roland A. Delattre, *Beauty and Sensibility in the Thought of Jonathan Edwards* (New Haven, 1968), ch. 6.

[16] *Baba Bathra* 58a, in *The Babylonian Talmud*, xi, ed. I. Epstein (London, 1935), 233–4.

[17] See Chaim Reines, 'Beauty in the Bible and the Talmud', *Judaism*, 24 (1975), 100–7.

[18] *The Jewish Encyclopedia* (New York and London, 1902), ii, 618.

Those who serve Him . . . their hearts reel
and their eyes grow dim at the splendour
and radiance of their king's beauty.[19]

Later on, in the cabbala, beauty is listed as one of the ten
Sefirot, that is, the emanations or manifested world of the
divine.[20] A passage in the *Zohar* (a central cabbalistic text,
written in Spain in the thirteenth century) lists the *Sefirot* and
says, 'If the radiance of the glory of the Holy One, be blessed,
had not been shed over his entire creation, how could even
the wise have apprehended him? He would have continued to
be unknowable, and the words could not be verily said, "The
whole earth is full of his glory" (Isa. 6: 3).'[21]

REASONS FOR ASCRIBING BEAUTY TO GOD

We have found a large and varied number of sources, both
Jewish and Christian, which ascribe beauty to God.[22] We
have found, too, that such ascriptions occur in different
contexts: in prayers of adoration and of yearning for God,
and in hymns praising the divine glory discerned in the
magnificence of nature; and that we have the beginnings of an
inferential approach to God from the beauty of nature in
Wisd. 13: 3–5, even though that text does not specifically
argue to God's beauty. We now have to go on to ask why
these sources ascribe beauty to God, and what justification
they offer. Roughly speaking, my description of contexts
suggests two main approaches: from experience and worship,
and from argument. Let me begin with the latter.

[19] Part of the tract known as *The Greater Hekhalot*, in T. Karmi (ed.), *The Penguin Book of Hebrew Verse* (Harmondsworth, 1981), 196. An even more anthropomorphic vision of God's beauty is to be found in a mystical text, the *Shi'ur Qomah* (ed. Martin Samuel Cohen, Lanham, Md., 1983), probably composed in Babylon in the sixth century CE. I owe these two references to Dr A. P. Hayman and Dr P. M. Morris.
[20] Gershom Scholem, *Kabbalah* (Jerusalem, 1974), 106.
[21] *Zohar*, selected and edited by Gershom Scholem (New York, 1963), 78. Of course, later rabbis also warned that physical beauty can give rise to pride.
[22] Again, there are many non-Christian parallels. For a very realistic account of the Lord Krishna's beauty, see the Alvar hymns, e.g. in *The Tiruvaimoli of Nammalvar*, trans. S. Bharati and S. Lakshmi (Melkote, 1987). I owe this reference to Dr A. Hunt-Overzee.

In an article on the divine perfections, near the beginning
of his *Summa Theologiae* (1a. iv. 2), Aquinas outlines a two-
pronged argument for ascribing perfections to God: He must
have all perfections because of His very nature, as self-
subsistent being, and He must have them because He is the
cause of perfections in creatures, and any cause must always
have the qualities of its effects. He applies this line of
argument specifically to beauty in his commentary on Pseudo-
Dionysius' *Divine Names*. There he says that God is most
beautiful and super-beautiful, both because of His exceeding
greatness (like the sun in relation to hot things) and because
of His causality, as source of all beauty. Because God has
beauty as His own, He wishes to multiply it by communicating His likeness; hence He is the exemplary cause of all beauty
in things.[23]

Aquinas is not merely saying that God is beautiful, but he
is also claiming that He is beauty itself. He argues that God
contains all perfections in His essence (*ST* 1a. iv. 2; xiv. 6),
and, more specifically, he says in his commentary on Pseudo-
Dionysius that beautiful and beauty are not to be separated in
God, because the First Cause, on account of His simplicity
and perfection, comprehends all in one (§336). We have
already met with the claim that God not only is beautiful but
is beauty itself in some of the early Fathers, and it recurs in
the interim, in St Anselm, for example, who concludes that
God must be the supreme beauty for the same reason that He
must be justice and other such qualities. Anselm's argument
is that whatever is just is so through justice (and likewise for
other such predicates); but if God were just in this way, He
would be just through another and not through Himself; but
whatever God is, He is so wholly through Himself and not
through another; therefore God's nature is itself justice, and
God does not *have* justice but exists as justice; it is as
appropriate to say that He is just as that He is justice, and
vice versa (*Monologion*, 16).

Such language is not restricted to philosophical treatments

---

[23] *In Librum Beati Dionysii De Divinis Nominibus Expositio* (Turin, 1950), ch. 4,
lectio 5 (commenting on ch. 4 §7 of Dionysius' work), esp. §§341, 343, 347, 352,
and 354.

of God's being and nature, but is found in more devotional contexts. The twelfth-century Cistercian writer, William of St Thierry, wrote a long commentary on the Song of Songs (again, it is worth noting how many patristic and medieval discussions of beauty occur in commentaries on this text). Commenting on 1: 14 *ff.* he says that when the bride recipro-cates the groom's praises and calls him 'comely' and so on, 'she understands and is convinced that anything praiseworthy she has, she holds from him, who is the good of all that is good and the Beauty of all that is beautiful . . . And since man is made in the likeness of his Maker, he becomes attracted to God; that is, he becomes one spirit with God, beautiful in his Beauty, good in his Goodness . . .'[24]

Now if God *is* beauty, then in Platonic terms He is the Form of Beauty, in which all beautiful things participate. We have already found this way of speaking also in some of the early Fathers, (others, however, e.g. St Augustine,[25] pre-ferred to see the Platonic Forms as ideas in the mind of God). We also find some early Christian writers using Aristotelian terminology, saying that God is the formal cause of beauty. Thus Pseudo-Dionysius says that the Beautiful and the Good is that from which, and in which, and unto which, and for the sake of which things are: efficient, formal, and final cause (*Div. Nom.* iv. 10; *PG* 3: 705 cd.). But this takes us on to the causal argument for divine beauty.

An early example of such an argument is to be found in one of Gregory of Nyssa's homilies on the Song of Songs. Commenting on the bride's panegyric on her lover's hand-someness in the Song, 5: 10 *ff.*, he says 'He who has looked at the sensible world, and has considered the wisdom shining forth in the beauty of things, reasons from what is seen to that invisible beauty and to the fount of wisdom.'[26] Likewise, Augustine, commenting on Rom. 1: 19 *f.*, says that we know

---

[24] *Exposition on the Song of Songs*, st. 8, in 'Cistercian Fathers' series 6, trans. Mother Columba Hart, OSB (Spencer, Mass., 1970), 75–6. There are also later Jewish interpretations of the Song of Songs: see Steven T. Katz, 'The "Conservative" Character of Mysticism', in his (ed.) *Mysticism and Religious Traditions* (New York, 1983), esp. 6–13, for a comparison of Jewish and Christian interpretations.

[25] *On Eighty-three Questions*, no. 46 (*PL* 40: 30). Cf. Aquinas, *ST* 1a. xv. 2.

[26] *Hom. 13 in Cant.* (*PG* 44: 1049d–1052a).

the unchanging beauty of God from the beauty of things.[27] Such arguments are common in Christian tradition and may be regarded as ancestors of what has come to be called the Argument from Design, though it is to be noted that they do not simply argue to the existence of God or to a First Cause, but to one who is beautiful (or beauty), and who is the archetype or exemplar of all beauty.

These arguments are often attacked on obvious grounds: it is said that we cannot apply modes of inference used of particular things or systems to the whole universe, that the qualities of effects are not necessarily to be found in their causes, that a being could not both be beautiful and beauty, or just and justice, and so on. Theistic philosophers have their replies to such objections, but I do not wish to go over familiar ground in the philosophy of religion. Instead, let me note a limitation in the inferential approach which is more germane to our own inquiry. Even if the arguments which conclude that God is beautiful or beauty are valid, they leave the nature of that beauty unclear. At best, they tell us *that* God is beautiful or beauty, but otherwise they leave us in the dark, especially as proponents of such arguments usually insist that God's beauty differs from any other. The claim that God must have beauty because He has all perfections seems to attract Whitehead's gibe about people's paying metaphysical compliments to God.[28] Those who try to fill in the lacuna here from purely philosophical and theological reasoning seem to provide something that is empty and unsatisfying. Thus Maurer seeks to explain God's beauty by using Aquinas' analysis of beauty in terms of wholeness, harmony, and radiance. He analyses God's wholeness or perfection in terms of His being pure existence or existence itself, His harmony or proportion in terms of the relations between the Persons within the Trinity, and His radiance or clarity in terms of His intelligible or spiritual radiance.[29] Such an analysis is skilfully carried out, yet it seems elusive and

---

[27] *Sermon* 241. 1–2 (*PL* 38: 1134); cf. *City of God*, xi. 4 (*PL* 41: 319).
[28] Alfred North Whitehead, *Science and the Modern World* (Cambridge, 1926), 250.
[29] Armand Maurer, *About Beauty* (Houston, Tex., 1983), 113–14.

leaves the reader wanting a clearer understanding of the divine beauty.

I think there are two reasons for this feeling of dissatisfaction. One, noted at the beginning of this chapter, is that we lack an extensive vocabulary for God's beauty. The other is that talk about divine beauty, like any talk about beauty, is liable to seem only word-spinning unless one has some experience of the beauty in question. Now the biblical references to God's beauty and glory which we have looked at seem to be based on experience rather than argument.

A claim to experience God's beauty might be based either on some experience of God, or else on some experience of great worldly beauty which is taken as a manifestation of divine glory (I have suggested that the 'nature Psalms' should be read in this way). This distinction corresponds to W. T. Stace's distinction between introvertive and extrovertive mystical experience: the former kind of experience is a direct apprehension of God or whatever 'ultimate reality' is taken to be the object of such experience, whilst in the latter this apprehension is mediated through our experience of the natural world, for example, Jakob Böhme's experience of nature, 'in this light my spirit saw through all things and into all creatures and I recognized God in grass and plants'.[30]

We find that actual claims to experience God's beauty fall into both the categories just mentioned. Let us look at a few examples of each. In his *On Virginity* Gregory of Nyssa speaks of the inexpressibility of the divine beauty, and describes David as having been lifted out of himself by the power of the Spirit, so that he saw in a blessed state of ecstasy the boundless and incomprehsible Beauty, a Beauty which is invisible and formless[31] (a few pages later Gregory exhorts his readers to mount a ladder from worldly beauty to the vision of Beauty itself through the help of the Holy Spirit[32]). Such an ecstatic state is described some centuries later by a Byzantine writer, St Symeon, the New Theologian: 'before Your beauty I went

---

[30] W. T. Stace, *Mysticism and Philosophy* (London, 1960), 60–79. The quotation from Böhme is taken from his *Aurora*, ch. 19.
[31] Ch. x (*PG* 46: 361bd).
[32] Ch. xi (*PG* 46: 364c, 365bd).

into ecstasies and I was struck with stupor, O Trinity my God', he exclaims in one of his *Hymns of Divine Love*.[33] He also speaks of having had a vision of God's beauty: 'Lord, my God, Father, Son and Spirit! You who in form have no visible shape, but who are all beautiful to those who see You. You with your inconceivable beauty eclipse all other visions. You surpass in splendour the sight of everything else' (no. xxxi, p. 173). His invocation to the Trinity is worth noting, because in some of his *Hymns* he describes his experiences in explicitly Trinitarian terms. He says that it is in the light of the Spirit that those who contemplate Christ see him, and see the Father in the Son, and so adore the Trinity of Persons, God.[34] A third mystic, St John of the Cross, also gives the Holy Spirit a similar role, though it is not spelt out in fully Trinitarian terms. In his *Living Flame of Love* he speaks of the Holy Spirit as casting the shadows of the grandeurs of God's virtues and attributes on the soul, and 'The shadow that the lamp of God's beauty casts over the soul will be another beauty according to the measure and property of God's beauty.'[35] In this passage John seems to be thinking of God's presence in grace, imparting virtues to the soul. But in another work, *The Spiritual Canticle*, he says that God's presence can be of three kinds: by His essence, in all souls; by grace, which may be unfelt; and by a special spiritual affection and presence in devout souls. The last of these may include an awareness of God's beauty: 'This presence is so sublime that the soul feels an immense hidden being is there from which God communicates to her some semi-clear glimpses of His divine beauty.' These glimpses, says John, have such an effect on the soul that, like David yearning and pining for the courts of the Lord (Ps. 84: 2), 'she ardently longs and faints with desire for what she feels hidden there in that presence'.[36] Such experiences, for him, are anticipations of the fruition to be enjoyed in the Beatific Vision.[37]

---

[33] No. 24; in G. A. Maloney's translation (Denville, NJ, 1976), 131.

[34] *Hymn* 11 p. 37; 21 p. 97.

[35] St. 3, §§14–15, in *The Collected Works of St. John of the Cross*, trans. K. Kavanaugh and O. Rodriguez (Washington, DC, 1979), 616.

[36] St. 11, §4, ibid., 449.

[37] *The Spiritual Canticle*, st. 1, §11, st. 39, §1 (ibid. 420, 557).

It will be noticed that these passages from the writings of mystics say little about the nature of the divine beauty: it is largely described in negative terms, as boundless, inconceivable, and so on, though we are also told that it surpasses other kinds of beauty and that it is the source of delight and ecstatic joy. Hence they convey little to those who have not enjoyed experiences of this kind, and we are again faced by the emptiness of words which we found also in the case of inferences to the divine beauty. Umberto Eco remarks of medieval mystics that 'they were always referring to the beauty which they experienced during their ecstasies. Yet they had nothing positive to say. Since God was ineffable, calling Him beautiful was like saying that He was good or infinite: beauty was just a word used to describe the indescribable.'[38]

Such a judgement, however, does not, I think, apply to the other kind of experiences of divine beauty, corresponding to Stace's 'extrovertive' mysticism, in which this beauty is said to be discerned in some powerful experience of natural or artistic beauty. For many people a sense of divine beauty is conveyed by the aria 'How lovely are thy dwellings, O Lord of Hosts', in Brahms's *A German Requiem*. Admittedly, the words of the aria, from Ps. 84, may have a lot to do with this example. But the sense is also conveyed for many by music which is not specifically 'religious'. In an article published to coincide with the première of the film *Amadeus*, the playwright Peter Shaffer remarked that his own apprehension of the divine was very largely aesthetic. To illustrate what he meant, he quoted a striking line from his play *Amadeus*, on which the film was based, put into the mouth of Mozart's rival, the Viennese court-composer Salieri: 'The God I acknowledge lives, for example, in bars 34 to 44 of Mozart's *Masonic Funeral Music*.'[39]

For others, the experience of divine beauty may be mediated through great natural beauty rather than art. Hopkins writes in his poem 'God's Grandeur', 'The world is

[38] Umberto Eco, *Art and Beauty in the Middle Ages*, tr. H. Bredin (New Haven, Conn., 1986), 90.
[39] *The Times*, 16 Jan. 1985. The line quoted occurs on p. 119 of the play (London, 1980).

charged with the grandeur of God. It will flame out, like shining from shook foil.'[40] His work is full of appeals to the presence of God in natural beauty. Moreover, as in the case of some of the mystics quoted, that presence is described in specifically Trinitarian terms, with a particular emphasis on Christ. For Hopkins, the principles of perfect physical and moral beauty, love, and sacrifice have become manifest in the created world through the Incarnation, and Christ is the divine archetype of created beauty.[41] In poems like 'The Windhover' and 'Hurrahing in the Harvest' the beauty of nature is related to Christ; and in his journals Hopkins expresses his feeling that the beauty of our Lord is manifested in the stars or in a bluebell.[42] In associating beauty particularly (though not exclusively) with Christ, Hopkins is following the main Western tradition, as we have seen. But like Jonathan Edwards he finds the beauty of Christ radiating through natural beauty.

It is tempting for those who are not Christians or theists to label such a way of speaking as a 'religious interpretation' of the world. It seems that Hopkins and others are seeing and hearing what we all do, but seeing and hearing it *as* a manifestation of God's glory. Here again we are veering towards a familiar area of philosophy of religion, the discussion of religious experiences, particularly discussions which make use of Wittgenstein's concept of 'seeing as' or John Hick's extension of it, the concept of 'experiencing as'.[43] There are familiar arguments and counter-arguments in these discussions, concerned with conflicts between different people's experiences, the impossibility of showing which is the

---

[40] *Poems* (4th edn.; Oxford, 1970), no. 31, p. 66. It is worth noting that the poem ends with an appeal to the Holy Spirit who 'over the bent | World broods with warm breast and with ah! bright wings'.

[41] See Hilary Fraser, *Beauty and Belief: Aesthetics and Religion in Victorian Literature* (Cambridge, 1986), ch. 2.

[42] *Poems*, no. 36, p. 69, no. 38, p. 70; *The Journals and Papers of Gerard Manley Hopkins*, ed. Humphrey House (Oxford, 1959), 199, 254.

[43] See Ludwig Wittgenstein, *Philosophical Investigations*, trans. G. E. M. Anscombe (Oxford, 1968) pt. 2, xi; and John Hick, *Faith and Knowledge* (2nd edn.; London, 1967), esp. ch. 5; also his 'Religious Faith as Experiencing—As ', in Godfrey Vesey (ed.), *Talking about God* (Royal Institute of Philosophy Lectures 2, London, 1969), 20–35.

correct interpretation except by using some kind of external check, the way people's beliefs condition what they see, and so on. But, again, I wish to avoid this familiar territory. For I do not think that Hopkins was interpreting his experience of nature in the way in which someone does who sees a fortunate occurrence *as* the working of divine Providence. Rather, quite simply, he saw God's glory shining through nature, just as the Psalmist saw it in the heavenly firmament. Similarly, Peter Shaffer, through the mouth of Salieri, is not *interpreting* Mozart's music; but, staggered by the unearthly beauty of some of it, he is labelling it as divine. The boldest and simplest such account is found in Simone Weil, who states that 'In everything which gives us the pure authentic feeling of beauty there really is the presence of God'[44] and who, as we have found, describes divine beauty as 'the attribute of God under which we see him'.[45] For her, a religious believer is not *interpreting* worldly beauty in religious terms, still less is he or she making an inference from it to divine beauty; similarly, the unbeliever is not failing to make an interpretation or an inference, for he or she sees and loves exactly what the believer does. Quite simply, they are both glimpsing God's beauty. Weil describes the love of beauty as a type of the 'implicit love of God': love for it proceeds from God descended into our souls and goes towards God present in the universe.[46] Presumably she regards the unbeliever who has such a love as failing to realize that its object is indeed an attribute of God.

Weil also remarks that the beauty of the world is the most likely way to God for many people in our time, and criticizes Christianity for having so little to say about it.[47] If indeed she is right in thinking that beauty is the attribute of God under which we see Him, then what she says is of inestimable importance for theology, for it would seem that both natural and artistic beauty might be what was traditionally referred to as a theological 'source' (a term usually restricted to Scripture,

---

[44] Simone Weil, *Gravity and Grace*, trans. Emma Craufurd (London, 1963), 137.
[45] *On Science, Necessity and the Love of God*, trans. R. Rees (Oxford, 1968), 129.
[46] Id., *Waiting on God*, trans Emma Craufurd (Fontana edn.; London, 1959), 120.
[47] Ibid. 118, 116.

Church doctrine, and so on). Such a source has, as she remarks, been relatively little exploited, though many theologians quote Dostoevsky's dramatic saying in *The Idiot*, that 'Beauty will save the world.'[48] More commonly, the appeal has been to the moral and spiritual beauty of Christ, and to the beauty of the Gospel—though for Hopkins and a few others these are related to natural beauty, in that they regard nature as manifesting Christ.

I am sympathetic to the approach of Weil and others who claim to discern God's beauty *in* worldly beauty, for it avoids the seeming emptiness of both philosphical arguments to divine beauty and secondhand reports of mystical visions. If it still leaves divine beauty as something of a mystery, part of the reason may be that any kind of beauty is somewhat mysterious. But the account requires further refinement. It needs to be extended to moral and spiritual beauty, following Weil's own parallel between beauty and sanctity: the discernment of the presence of the Holy Spirit in a saint may be analogous to the perception of divine glory in earthly beauty, indeed it may be another version of the same thing. More generally, we need to explain how such a position preserves God's transcendence and how it differs from pantheism. Likewise, if someone starts by pointing to something of great beauty, as Shaffer does in the case of Mozart's work, and calls it divine or a revelation of God, then we need to ask whether the religious terms are being used in their traditional sense and, if so, why the speaker wishes to use terms carrying so much metaphysical freight, as it were. A theist may well say that beauty is divine, but will usually distinguish his position from pantheism by treating the world's beauty as caused by God and as reflecting His glory, in virtue of the divine actions of creation and inspiration.

My conclusion so far, then, is that ascriptions of beauty to God are more commonly based on powerful experiences of God's presence than on inferences; the term beauty seems appropriate to such experiences because of the overwhelming

[48] For instance, Kallistos Ware in 'The Spirituality of the Icon', 198, in Cheslyn Jones, Edward Yarnold, and Geoffrey Wainwright (eds.), *The Study of Spirituality* (London, 1986).

desirability and attractiveness of God. But more commonly still, the ascription of divine beauty is made as a result of experiences of worldly beauty, which is regarded as reflecting divine beauty. This, in turn, raises a further question of the relationship between the two: accounts couched in Platonic terms face the problems of what a Form or principle of *all* beauty would be like, and why God's beauty is supposed to be the form of all beauty, whilst more Aristotelian accounts which describe the relationship in terms of formal or exemplar causality need to explain how God's beauty can be reflected or refracted in so many different ways. I shall return to these issues in Chapter 6, when we look at the question of the relationship between divine and worldly beauty. In the meantime, there is a more pressing issue which needs to be looked at now, because of our specific concern with the Holy Spirit: are we discussing beauty as a quality of the one divine essence, or is the question of the Trinity also relevant to the topic?

THE ONE GOD AND THE TRINITY

Most modern treatments of the being and attributes of God, as I have mentioned, pay little or no attention to His beauty; and most older ones, in so far as they discuss it, do so only very briefly and under the heading of the attributes of the One God (in this they are following Pseudo-Dionysius, who described beauty as a quality of the whole Godhead: *Div. Nom.* ii. 1, *PG* 3: 637b). Those influenced by Aquinas often, as we have seen, deduce God's beauty from His existence, or treat it as one of the transcendentals, concepts which extend to all being and thus supereminently to God. Maritain, for example, argues that beauty is one of the transcendentals, indeed that it is 'the radiance of all the transcendentals united', and then that it is one of the divine names, for God is 'beautiful through Himself and in Himself, beautiful absolutely' and the source of all beauty in created things.[49] Only

---

[49] Jaques Maritain, *Art and Scholasticism*, trans. J. W. Evans (New York, 1962), 30–1 and n. 66. The standard scholastic textbooks followed a similar line, for instance, F. Diekamp, *Theologiae Dogmaticae Manuale*, i (3rd edn.; Paris, 1949), 189.

when he has presented his account in terms of the being of the one God does he mention briefly that in the Trinity beauty is attributed most fittingly to the Son (following Aquinas, *ST* 1a. xxxix. 8).[50] But apart from the last remark, Maritain's account could be accepted by a Unitarian and indeed by any theist.

We have already found, however, that an alternative tradition manifests itself from time to time, which relates the consideration of divine beauty directly to the doctrine of the Trinity. Alexander of Hales's *Summa* suggests that divine beauty depends on the relations between the divine Persons, whilst Jonathan Edwards explains the particular connections between beauty and the Son and Spirit in terms of their role within the Trinity; his Trinitarian treatment is not an extra bit of theology tacked on at the end, as it were, but is essential to his position. Of course, it might seem that an account of the beauty of intra-Trinitarian relations is, if not unknowable, at least remote from the concerns of the ordinary religious believer, as remote as a deduction of the beauty of the divine essence is which fails to relate that beauty to earthly beauty. But such an impression can be avoided if it is claimed that the Trinity in itself (the immanent Trinity) is revealed in the economic Trinity, i.e. the Trinity as manifested in the economy of salvation. Thus Edwards, as well as presenting the divine beauty in terms of a Trinitarian model, also explains how that beauty extends to the world in terms of the complementary work of the Son and the Spirit. Thereby he anticipates the difficulty which von Balthasar sees in adopting a purely deductive approach here: 'such a doctrine of God and the Trinity really speaks to us only when and as long as the *theologia* does not become detached from the *oikonomia* [i.e. economy of salvation], but rather lets its every formulation and stage of reflection be accompanied and supported by the latters's vivid discernibility'.[51] Hence, in so far as this topic has been treated by theologians, more attention has been devoted to explaining how the beauty of the Trinity

---

[50] Maritain, *Art and Scholasticism*, 31–2.
[51] Von Balthasar, *The Glory of the Lord*, i, *Seeing the Form*, trans. Erasmo Leiva-Merikakis, 125.

is manifested to us than to speculating about its nature in itself.

The manifestation of the beauty of the Trinity is most commonly explained in what might be called a linear pattern: the glory of the Father is manifested through his Word and Image, the Son, and the Holy Spirit leads us to see that manifested glory. St Basil expresses this order neatly in one of his letters, 'our mind being enlightened by the Spirit looks up to the Son, and in Him as in an image beholds the Father',[52] and in another one he makes the particular connection with beauty when, citing John 14: 9, he writes of seeing 'the unbegotten beauty in the Begotten'.[53] Likewise, St Cyril of Alexandria, commenting on John 17: 6, says that the disciples were led from the splendour of the Son to the beauty of the Father, from the perfect and absolute image to the very exemplar or archetype:[54] and as we saw in Chapter 1, he maintained that Christ sent the Holy Spirit to restore mankind to its original beauty in the likeness of God.

Later Christian tradition explored the beauty of the Son in a variety of ways. Sometimes it was presented very abstractly, using the biblical terms of Word and Image (both of which, of course, have artistic connotations) to express the relationship between the Son and the Father. But if the Word truly became incarnate, then should we not look for God's beauty in that very incarnation, in which as Dixon says 'the material substance of the earth was deemed worthy not only to proceed from the creative hand of God but to be radiant with the Godhead himself'?[55] Some have seen that beauty as particularly manifest in the glory of the risen Christ, or in its anticipation, the Transfiguration, when Jesus was physically glorified for a time before the eyes of some of the Disciples. Others have preferred to spell it out in terms of his moral and

---

[52] *Letter* 226. 3 (*PG* 32: 849a).
[53] *Letter* 38. 8 (*PG* 32: 340b); see also *On the Holy Spirit*, ix. 23, already quoted in Ch. 1, which connects all three Persons with beauty.
[54] *Thesaurus*, xxxii (*PG* 75: 560d–561a). Cyril uses two different Greek words for the beauty of the Son and the Father, respectively *hōraiotēs* and *kallos*.
[55] John W. Dixon, *Nature and Grace in Art*, (Chapel Hill, 1964), 196. Dixon goes on immediately to say that for the Christian artist physical material is 'radiant with the glory of creation and the new creation that proceeds from the Incarnation' (p. 197).

spiritual beauty, and that of the Gospel he proclaimed. Thus Jonathan Edwards describes the spiritual beauty of Christ's human nature in terms of his many virtues and his holiness, and says that it is the image and reflection of the beauty of his divine nature.[56] In the sermon 'True Grace Distinguished from the Experience of Devils', in which he says that the sight of Christ's divine beauty bows the wills and draws the hearts of man, he also contrasts the beauty and amiableness of Christ that drew men's hearts to him, and are known only by his followers, with his external glory and majesty, which will be manifest to all, even the wicked, at the Day of Judgement.[57]

A stress on Christ's moral spiritual beauty can coexist easily with an acknowledgement of his earthly obscurity and also his defacement during his Passion. Quite early on, the Church appropriated to him Isaiah's prophecies of the suffering servant. But how could he who was the very image of the Father's glory also be the one in whom there was 'no form or comeliness' (Isa. 53: 2)? Some early Fathers claimed physical handsomeness for Jesus, taking Ps. 45: 2, 'You are the fairest of the sons of men', as applying to him, and so took Isaiah's words as referring only to his Passion. This view recurs in one of Hopkins's sermons, where he claims physical beauty for Christ, on the grounds that his body was framed directly by the power of the Holy Spirit, who would not have botched or failed in his work—though he goes on to say that this beauty, like the beauty of wisdom and genius which Hopkins also claims for Christ, is surpassed by the beauty of his character.[58] The majority of writers, however, have felt it unnecessary to make such claims. Thus Cyril of Alexandria interpreted Isa. 53 in terms of Christ's emptying himself and taking the form of a servant (appealing to Phil 2. 7 *ff.*), and asked what need had God of human splendour.[59] St Bonav-

---

[56] Edwards, *Religious Affections*, 258–9. St Bernard says, likewise, that Christ was beautiful in both his divine and human natures, for he is the form and splendour of the Father, and he had the beauty of grace (*On Song of Songs*, xlv. 9; *PL* 183: 1003).
[57] *Works*, Bohn edn., ii (London, 1865), 48–9.
[58] *The Sermons and Devotional Writings of Gerard Manley Hopkins*, ed. C. Devlin (London, 1959), 34–8.
[59] *Glaphyra in Exod.* bk. 1 (*PG* 69: 396ab); In Is. bk. 5, tom. 1 (*PG* 70: 1171ab). The patristic debate is summarized in Heinrich Krug, *De Pulchritudine Divina*, bk. 3, ch. 4.

enture contrasts Ps. 45: 2 with Isa. 53: 2 and with the indignity of Christ's Passion, and says that even in his suffering Christ kept inner gracefulness (*decus*) and intrinsic beauty. He ends on a moralistic note: 'Let us be deformed in our outer bodies with the deformed Jesus, that we may be inwardly reformed with the beautiful Jesus.'[60]

Many Christian writers have gone a step further and seen the Cross as the summit of Christ's beauty, a step which seems at first sight to be a reversal of normal values. St Augustine says in one of his sermons 'He hung therefore on the cross deformed, but his deformity is our beauty.'[61] This line of thought helps to explain again both the lack of interest in aesthetics shown by many theologians and the anxiety of others to distinguish the beauty of God or Christ from any other kind of beauty. Shortly after the passage in the *Church Dogmatics* which we have already looked at, in which Barth both claims that God is the basis and standard of everything that is beautiful and warns against using the concept of beauty in theology, he goes on to describe the Incarnation as revealing 'the beauty of God in a special way and in some sense to a supreme degree'. But, he says, appealing to Isa. 53: 2–3, 'If the beauty of Christ is sought in a glorious Christ who is not the crucified, the search will always be in vain.'[62] We find that this is one of the leading themes of von Balthasar's *Glory of the Lord*. Shortly before the last passage which I have quoted from this work, he alludes to Barth's discussion, and draws two important conclusions: first, Christian beauty must include even the Cross and everything else which a worldly aesthetics discards as unbearable; and, second, 'we ought never to speak of God's beauty without reference to the form and manner of appearing which he exhibits in salvation-history'.[63] It is worth noting now that the leading Scriptural

---

[60] *Vitis Mystica*, ch. 5. Aquinas is very guarded on the issue: after saying that Christ's beauty was fourfold, consisting in his divine form, justice and truth, honest conversation, and beauty of body, he says that he had the beauty which befitted the status and reverence of his condition (*In Ps*. xliv. 2).

[61] *Sermon* xxvii. 6 (*PL* 38: 181).

[62] Karl Barth, ii. pt. 1, 661, 665; cf. Moltmann, *Theology of Play*, 41 f.

[63] *The Glory of the Lord*, i. 124. The theme that the Cross is the point of greatest beauty is also found in Oliver Davies, *Living Beauty: Ways of Mystical Prayer* (London, 1990), ch. 3.

warrant for von Balthasar's stress on the glory of the Cross is
not so much Isaiah's passage about the Suffering Servant as
the Johannine idea that Christ's true glorification on this earth
is to be seen, not in the Transfiguration (which is not
mentioned in the Fourth Gospel), but in the Crucifixion:
speaking of his own death, Jesus is represented as saying 'I,
when I am lifted up from the earth, will draw all men to
myself' (John 12: 32).

There are some profound thoughts here, and one might
risk being accused of gilding the lily in trying to explain them
any further. But there is one startling omission: the Holy
Spirit seems to have almost dropped out of the picture. Von
Balthasar, at this point, sees the Holy Spirit as the one who
enthuses and inspires us towards God through Christ
(p. 121). Barth follows up his discussion of the beauty of the
Incarnation by considering how the glory of God is manifested
externally in the glorification of the creature. He acknowledges
that God's glory is of the whole Trinity and therefore of the
Holy Spirit, and that the spirit is the divine reality active in
the world. But our glorification is spelt out in purely religious
terms: 'If God is glorified through the creature, this is only
because by the Holy Spirit the creature is baptised, and born
again and called and gathered and enlightened and sanctified
and kept close to Jesus Christ in true and genuine faith'
(p. 670). Now, however, it is beauty that has dropped out of
the picture, and piety has taken over. Something is missing
here. Let us, therefore, go on and try to repair these omissions
by returning to the main theme of this study, the connection
between the Holy Spirit and beauty.

4

The Holy Spirit in the Trinity

WE found in Chapter 1 that a long list of Christian theologians, from Irenaeus and Clement of Alexandria in the early Church to more recent writers like Edwards and Evdokimov, have associated the Holy Spirit with beauty. This association applies both to natural beauty, in virtue of the Spirit's role in Creation, and to artistic beauty, which is regarded as inspired by the Spirit. In the latter case, the artist or writer is seen as an instrument of the Spirit or, better, as a 'co-creator'.

Christian tradition assigns the Holy Spirit a parallel role with regard to some other transcendental concepts besides beauty. The promise that the 'Spirit of truth' would lead the disciples to the fullness of the truth (John 14: 17, 16: 13) naturally led to a particular association between the Holy Spirit and truth—and here I do not mean only religious truth. Aquinas thought that every truth, by whomsoever it is said, is from the Holy Spirit (*ST* 1a2ae. 109. 1 ad 1), whilst Calvin said, with reference to the works of profane writers, 'If we reflect that the Spirit of God is the only fountain of truth, we will be careful, as we would avoid offering insult to him, not to reject or condemn truth wherever it appears. In despising the gifts, we insult the Giver' (*Inst.* ii. 2. 15). Likewise, texts like Rom. 15: 16 and Gal. 5: 22 *f*. suggest a special link between the Holy Spirit and sanctification. We have already seen how some of the early Fathers regarded the latter as a kind of beautifying, and indeed as the only kind that is really important, for it is the re-creation of the divine image in us.

We need to go on now to look at the rationale for these claims. In the present chapter I shall approach the question of the relationship between aesthetics and the Holy Spirit from the standpoint of dogmatic theology, especially the doctrine of the Trinity. I shall consider how the particular association of beauty with the Holy Spirit is to be related to that doctrine, and I shall compare Eastern and Western

Trinitarian theologies. In the next chapter I shall approach the matter from below, as it were, by starting from experience and examining the concept of inspiration.

THE HOLY SPIRIT AND BEAUTY

The question of why we should link beauty with the Holy Spirit is really two questions, depending on where one puts the emphasis: why single out *beauty*, and some other aesthetic qualities, and associate them with the work of the Holy Spirit? And why associate them with the *Holy Spirit*? We have already looked at some answers to the first question, when we considered the view that artistic talents are gifts of the Spirit and when we discussed whether beauty is a divine attribute. As regards the second question, the link between beauty and the Holy Spirit is usually made in discussions of the Spirit's role in Creation, or else with reference to some other notions particularly associated with the Spirit, like inspiration, light, wisdom, and joy (again, the point must be made that in associating beauty with the Holy Spirit we are not ruling out a connection with the other Persons of the Trinity).

We saw in Chapter 1 that the earliest Christian theologian to make the link, Irenaeus, did so in the context of discussions of Creation; and that he and later writers supported their case by citing certain biblical texts, especially Gen. 1: 2 and some of the Psalms which mention God's *ruach* (wind, breath, or spirit) in this connection, e.g. Ps. 33: 6. In general, the ascription to the Holy Spirit of a role in Creation simply follows from the doctrines that Creation is the work of God, that the Holy Spirit is God, and that all three Persons are involved in divine works. The last of these doctrines is summed up in the principle 'the external works of the Trinity are undivided', a principle which derives from several early Fathers, for instance Augustine, who denied that the Father made one part of creation, the Son another, and so on: rather, he said, 'the Father through the Son in the gift of the Holy Spirit together made all things and every particular thing' (*On True Religion*, vii. 13).[1] But, as it happens, later Christian

---

[1] *PL* 34: 129. St Athanasius likewise maintained that 'The Father does all things

tradition has had little to say about the Spirit's role in Creation. Although the Holy Spirit is often referred to as *Spiritus Creator* and indeed is described in the Nicene Creed as 'Lord and giver of life', later theologians, especially in the West, have tended to restrict their treatments of the Spirit's work to ecclesiology, the spiritual life, and, more recently, religious experience. Kilian McDonnell remarks rightly that if one loses sight of the relationship of the Spirit to creation and cosmos, then it is difficult to relate him to nature, and to moral, cultural, and political life; and so 'Spirit becomes too sacralized, too tied to holy objects and events'.[2]

Even if we had a developed Trinitarian theology of Creation, we would still need to make particular connections within it between the Holy Spirit and beauty. Irenaeus did so by introducing the Old Testament concept of Wisdom: he identifies it with the Spirit, as he identifies the Word with the Son, says that both Word and Wisdom were with the Father before Creation, and then says that God made all things by the Word and adorned them by Wisdom.[3] The Old Testament does indeed give Wisdom a creative role: Prov. 8: 27 *ff.* describes Wisdom as present with God at Creation. Moreover, that text, in describing Wisdom as delighting God and at play then, introduces an idea which Irenaeus might have exploited had he chosen to develop his theme further than he did, for several modern writers have made a connection between aesthetics and play. Hans-Georg Gadamer, for instance, remarks that aesthetic pleasure tends to be regarded today as a temporary release from the pressures of everyday existence,

---

through the Word in the Spirit, and thus the unity of the Holy Trinity is kept.' (*Ad Serap.* i. 28, *PG* 26: 596a). For a similar position, see St Basil, *On the Holy Spirit*, xvi. 37 (*PG* 32: 133bc); St Gregory of Nyssa, *On the Holy Trinity* (listed by Migne as St Basil, *Letter* 189. 6–7; *PG* 32: 692c–693b); id., *On Not Three Gods* (*PG* 45: 133a); St Gregory of Nazianzus, *Fifth Theological Oration* (*Or.* xxxi.) 14, 16 (*PG* 36: 148d–149a, 152ab); id., *Or.* xl. 41 (*PG* 36: 417bc); St Augustine, *De Trin.* i. 4. 7; 5. 8; iv. 21. 30; v. 14. 15; and St Thomas Aquinas, *ST* 3a. xxiii. 2. The principle that the works of the Trinity are inseparable was first officially defined in the Creed drawn up by a local council at Toledo in AD 675 (Denzinger 284).

[2] Kilian McDonnell, 'The Determinative Doctrine of the Holy Spirit', *Theological Studies*, 39 (1982), 150. See also Jürgen Moltmann, *God in Creation: An Ecological Doctrine of Creation* (London, 1985), esp. 9–13, 94–103.

[3] *Adv. Haer.* iv. 20. 1–3; *Demonstration*, 5.

and argues that it and aesthetic practice should be related to the more fundamental human experiences of play, symbol, and festival.[4] If we push this idea a little further, we have another link with the Holy Spirit through the related idea of joy, one of the 'fruit of the Spirit' listed by St Paul in Gal. 5: 22 *f.*,[5] which Barth sees as radiating from God's beauty (*CD* ii, 1, p. 654) and which Abrahams, quoting rabbinical tradition, insists should be found in those on whom God's glory rests.[6] Wolterstorff gives this theme an eschatological twist when he argues that 'Aesthetic delight is a component within and a species of that joy which belongs to the shalom God has ordained as the goal of human existence'.[7]

Wisdom is also associated particularly with the Holy Spirit through its inclusion in the traditional list of the gifts of the Spirit, a list which derives from Isa. 11: 1–2, where the prophet lists the qualities with which the Messiah will be endowed by the Spirit of God (of course, this association is found earlier in the Old Testament, notably for us in Exod. 31 and 35, which describes the endowments of the craftsmen Bezalel and Oholiab). Similarly, the Spirit is associated especially with perception and understanding (cf. John 16: 8, 13), and with the illumination of the mind. Such an illumination is not, I think, to be conceived of in narrowly intellectual terms; for, as we shall see in the next chapter, inspiration often brings an enlargement of people's emotional and affective range, so that they can see and respond in new ways and thus 'surpass themselves' in their creations. Nor is it to be confined to creativity or activity, for there is also the standpoint of the spectator, listener, or reader to be considered. If

---

[4] Hans-Georg Gadamer, *The Relevance of the Beautiful and other Essays* (Cambridge, 1986), ch. 1. The theme of play is also discussed in his *Truth and Method*, trans. G. Barden and J. Cumming (London, 1975), 91 ff., where Gadamer is concerned to counter what he regards as the subjectivism of much modern aesthetics. See also J. Moltmann, *Theology of Play*, trans. R. Ulrich (New York, 1972), and C. Seerveld, *Rainbows for the Fallen World* (Toronto, 1980), ch. 2.

[5] Cf. also Rom. 14: 17 and 1 Thess. 1: 6. The link is perhaps more natural in Greek, where the words *chara* (joy) and *charis* (beauty, grace) are connected etymologically.

[6] Israel Abrahams, *The Glory of God* (Oxford, 1925, repr. in his *Foundation of Jewish Life: Three Studies*, New York, 1973), 85.

[7] Nicholas Wolterstorff, *Art in Action: Toward a Christian Aesthetic* (Grand Rapids, 1980), 169.

the Holy Spirit's action is often seen as an illumination, then there is the light of contemplation, insight, and realization, as well as that of creation.[8] Such an illumination may require an inner transformation—something also traditionally associated with the Holy Spirit. A. M. Allchin quotes a remark from the Russian classic *The Way of a Pilgrim*, 'The whole outside world also seemed to me to be full of beauty and delight', and goes on to say 'By the transformation of the heart, through the realisation of God's presence there at the centre of man's being, it becomes possible to see that "heaven and earth are full of God's glory".'[9] This idea may perhaps be regarded as a parallel with the traditional doctrine that the inner witness of the Holy Spirit is required in order to see the revelation of God in Christ or in the word of Scripture. But such an illumination is not confined to religious believers, any more than artistic inspiration is—even Calvin, although he thought that the spirit of holiness is given only to believers, allowed that artistic gifts are given indiscriminately by the Holy Spirit, and indeed he acknowledged that they shine more brilliantly among unbelievers.[10] (Religious believers, however, might claim that, in treating both artistic talents and their appreciation as gifts of the Holy Spirit, they have at least the advantage of giving them their right names.)

So far I have approached our topic both by considering the doctrine of Creation and by looking at particular gifts of the Spirit which may be associated with artistic activity and appreciation. Now it is already apparent that there are two seemingly conflicting tendencies at work here: to treat the Holy Spirit as having a part within the collective work of the Trinity, and to assign him particular roles or tasks. Maurice Wiles remarks that there is an inconsistency in the Cappadocian Fathers between their insistence on complete identity of

---

[8] Dorothy Sayers gave this a central place in her treatment of the role of the Holy Spirit in her book *The Mind of the Maker* (London, 1941), in which she argued that there is a Trinitarian structure in all creative work; see esp. chs. 3 and 8. Unfortunately she did not discuss the Spirit's role with regard to beauty.

[9] A. M. Allchin, *The World is a Wedding: Explorations in Christian Spirituality* (London, 1978), 40.

[10] *Inst.* ii. 2. 15–16; A. Kuyper, *Lectures on Calvinism* (Grand Rapids, 1953), ch. 5.

operations in the Trinity and their ascribing different roles within creation to each Person, e.g. the Father originating, commanding, and conceiving, the Son creating, and the Spirit perfecting.[11] Each tendency seems to create difficulties for our particular concern: for if we adhere to the maxim that the external works of the Trinity are undivided, then how can we continue to associate beauty particularly with the Holy Spirit and to describe him as 'Perfecter' or 'Beautifier'? But if we continue to do so, then we must either abandon the maxim or else explain how the other Persons have a connection with beauty, too. The traditional solution of 'appropriation' does not seem to be available to us here, because those who have appealed to it (notably Aquinas) have appropriated beauty to the Son rather than to the Holy Spirit. In any case, appropriation is no longer a popular manœuvre today: it is criticized as unscriptural, as precluding the possibility that every Christian may have a distinct relationship with each Person, as inapplicable to the Incarnation (since only the Son became incarnate), and, in the case of the Holy Spirit, as failing to preserve the emphasis which the sources place on the Spirit's role in the life of Christ, at Pentecost, and in the Church.

It may be possible, however, to preserve orthodox Trinitarianism by both ascribing a proper mission to the Holy Spirit and at the same time associating the other Persons with that mission through their co-presence, on the analogy of saying both that the Son alone became incarnate and that the Father and the Spirit had roles in the Incarnation.[12] If so, we avoid the inconsistency which Wiles discerns in the Cappadocians— though even in their case I am not sure that it is exactly inconsistent to adhere to the principle that the external works of the Trinity are undivided and at the same time to say, as Gregory of Nyssa did, that 'Every good thing and every good name, depending on that power and purpose which is without beginning, is brought to perfection in the power of the Spirit

[11] Maurice Wiles, *Working Papers on Doctrine* (London, 1976), ch. 1.

[12] See Yves Congar, 'Pneumatologie ou "Christomonisme" dans la tradition latine?', in *Ecclesia a Spiritu Sancto edocta: Mélanges théologiques Hommage à Mgr. Gérard Philips* (Gembloux, 1970), 127–40; id., *I Believe in The Holy Spirit*, trans. David Smith (3 vols; London, 1983), ii, 85 ff.; and D. M. Coffey, 'A Proper Mission of the Holy Spirit', *Theological Studies*, 47 (1986), 227–50.

through the Only-begotten God.'¹³ In the case of beauty, I
shall argue that the principle in question does not preclude
the ascription to the Holy Spirit of a particular connection
with beauty: for if the creation of beauty, like all creation, is
a work of the One God, the Spirit may nevertheless have a
particular role *within* that one work. An analogy may be
drawn here with prayer. Prayer is directed to God, but it can
be explained in Trinitarian terms, as when we are advised to
pray to the Father through the Son in the Holy Spirit—an
understanding of prayer which derives from Rom. 8: 15–17
and Gal. 4: 6.¹⁴

To maintain such a point, however, we need to look at the
alternatives. Let us again, as in Chapter 1, adopt a historical
approach, but this time looking at theological positions rather
than individual writers.

TRINITARIAN APPROACHES

The simplest approach to our topic is to say that God, by the
inner agency of His spirit, 'blows through' or 'breathes' beauty
into the world. When people talk of God's spirit, they often
simply mean that God acts in a certain way, particularly by
affecting the human heart, without thinking out the Trinitarian implications of what they are saying. This wider sense of
'spirit' follows the usage of the Old Testament. There the
term is most commonly used to denote the power of God's
inner working in creation, especially in the human heart. We
find that this power is often described in terms of 'penetrating'
or 'permeating'; and that it is frequently associated with the

¹³ *On Not Three Gods (PG* 45: 129 ab), trans. H. A. Wilson; shortly afterwards
Gregory says that there is no difference of nature or of operation in the Godhead (*PG*
45: 133a). St Augustine says, with reference to the account of Jesus's baptism in
Mark 3: 13–17, that the three Persons may be shown separably, though they work
inseparably (*Sermon*, lii; *PL* 38: 354–64). He gives his favourite analogy, of memory,
understanding, and will in the human soul).
¹⁴ See *We Believe in God: A Report by The Doctrine Commission of the General
Synod of the Church of England* (London, 1987), ch. 7; and, more generally, Gérard
Philips, 'Le Saint Esprit en Nous', *Ephemerides Theologicae Lovaniensis*, 24 (1948),
127–35. The Pauline texts quoted raise the interesting question of whether there may
be a specifically Trinitarian experience of the Holy Spirit, i.e. an experience not
merely of a divine energy, but of being caught up in a divine conversation or
perichoresis.

heart, both in the Old and New Testaments. Again, it is well
to be reminded of the metaphorical nature of the term: in
Hebrew and in Greek the terms translated as 'spirit' (*ruach,
pneuma*) also mean 'wind' and 'breath', and there is sometimes
a play on words in the Bible, e.g. in John 3: 8 ('The wind/
Spirit blows where it wills') or 20: 22. The Spirit of God is
often spoken of as endowing people with various gifts, like
prophecy, strength (in the case of Samson), wisdom, and, in
the case of Bezalel and Oholiab, artistic skill.

It was out of such usage that the Christian doctrines of the
Holy Spirit and the Trinity developed; and recently, in
questioning such doctrines, some theologians have advocated
a return to an older and simpler usage. Thus in his book *God
as Spirit* Geoffrey Lampe questions the utility of the Trinitarian model of God, and recommends that the phrase 'the Spirit
of God' be understood, not as referring to a divine hypostasis
distinct from God the Father and God the Son, 'but as
indicating God himself as active towards and in his human
creation . . . in his personal outreach'.[15] Lampe does not
discuss our own particular topic. But if we applied his view to
it, we would come up with something like the simple position
that by the power of the Spirit, God glorifies creation and
inspires people to create things of beauty.

Let us move on from this simple view to look at some
specifically Trinitarian positions. Christianity developed
Judaism's teaching on the gifts and work of the Spirit of God;
but it went far beyond Judaism in hypostasizing that Spirit
into a Person in the Trinity. Moreover, this hypostasization
only occurred after a similar hypostasization of the Word,
believed to have become incarnate in Jesus Christ, from
whose face the glory of God shone forth; and the mission of
the Holy Spirit was seen as being closely associated with the
Incarnation.

The simplest Trinitarian treatment of our theme is to be
found in the Cappadocian Fathers. As we have seen, they
maintain that beauty or glory is of the One God, as also is
the action of beautifying, but this principle does not prevent

---

[15] Geoffrey Lampe, *God as Spirit* (Oxford, 1977), 11. See Maurice Wiles, *Faith
and the Mystery of God* (London, 1982), ch. 7 for a similar view.

them from saying that each of the three Persons has a particular role or function with regard to beauty and beautifying, though these roles or functions are kept in relation to each other and are within a single work. This understanding of things can be expressed in a linear pattern: the beauty or glory of the Father is expressed in the Son, who is the Word or Image of the Father, and in the Holy Spirit because he is the likeness of the Father (as Irenaeus says[16]), or because he is the image of the Son as the Son is the image of the Father (as Athanasius puts it[17]). Gregory of Nyssa uses here the analogy of a series of lamps, one being lit from another.[18] Such a linear pattern may suggest the idea that the Spirit is both beauti*ful* and, in virtue of his mission, beauti*fier*: beautiful as reflecting the Father's glory, and beautifier because of his role in Creation and because of his gifts to us. This simple pattern can be applied to other divine attributes besides beauty.

The Cappadocian Fathers' treatment is repeated and developed by some modern Orthodox writers. Evdokimov, for instance, describes the Father as the source of beauty, and the Son's beauty as being the image of the Father, which in turn is revealed by the Holy Spirit, who is the 'Spirit of Beauty' and the 'Light of the Word'.[19] Although he cannot accept that in his causal origin the Spirit proceeds from or by the Son, Evdokimov allows that at the level of revelation or manifestation the Spirit is in and by the Son.[20] Even if the origin of the Spirit in the Father is a mystery in relation to the generation of the Son, the two Persons share a likeness to each other in virtue of their common origin from the Father; and their work in the economy of salvation is closely related, in virtue of the interdependence of their respective manifestations and missions.

[16] *Adv. Haer.* iv. 7. 4.

[17] *Ad Serapionem*, i. 20, 24; iv. 3 (*PG* 26: 577b, 588b, 640d–641a); cf. St John of Damascus, *On the Orthodox Faith*, i. 13 (*PG* 94: 856b); *On Sacred Images*, iii. 18 (*PG* 94: 1340ab); and St Cyril of Alexandria, *Thesaurus*, xxxiv (*PG* 75: 572a). Aquinas says that one Person in the Trinity imitates another (*ST* 1a. 93. 5 ad 4).

[18] *De Spiritu Sancto contra Macedonianos*, vi (*PG* 45: 1308b); *Contra Eunomium*, i. 36 (*PG* 45: 416c).

[19] Paul Evdokimov, *L'Art de l'icône: Théologie de la beauté* (Paris, 1970), 29, 15.

[20] *L'Esprit Saint dans la tradition Orthodoxe* (Paris, 1969), pt. 1, ch. 6.

We find a different pattern emerging in the West, where the Spirit came to be seen as the bond of love between Father and Son and defined as proceeding from them both. This position is associated particularly with St Augustine, though it was not officially accepted in Rome until early in the eleventh century; and it was not applied to the question of divine beauty until much later on. It would take us too far afield to summarize the reasons for the emergence of this view and the subsequent controversies between East and West which it occasioned. Suffice it to say, for the moment, that Westerners have recommended their view on the grounds that it does justice to the scriptural witness which describes the Spirit both as the spirit of the Father and as that of the Son (e.g. in Matt. 10: 20, Rom. 8: 9, 11, and Gal. 4: 6), that it succeeds in differentiating the origin of the Spirit, who proceeds from the Father *and* Son, from that of the Son, who is generated from the Father alone (whereas Easterners, it is alleged, can make only a verbal distinction between procession and generation, and cannot relate the two), that it boosts the dignity of the Son in depicting him as sharing the Father's origination of the Spirit, and that it gives a fuller account than the East does of the unity and interrelations of the Persons within the Trinity, in that the West links the relationships between the missions of the Persons with their relationships with each other within the Trinity. Let us, rather, look at the application of this view to the attribute of divine beauty by Jonathan Edwards.

Edwards specifically relates the mission of the Holy Spirit as beautifier to his position within the Trinity, and he describes that position in terms of an Augustinian Trinitarian theology, which regards the Holy Spirit as being the mutual love of the Father and the Son, and as proceeding from them both. We saw in Chapter 1 how in his *Essay on the Trinity* he says that the Father and Son delight in each other, so that the divine essence flows out and is, as it were, breathed forth in love and joy, and thus proceeds the Holy Spirit; and that the Spirit's office of giving all things their sweetness and beauty comes from his being the beauty of joy of the Creator (pp. 93 *f.*, 98). In another work, *The Mind*, he again says that the mutual love of Father and Son 'makes the third, the personal Holy Spirit or the holiness of God, which is his infinite beauty',[21] and that creatures participate in excellence and beauty according as God communicates more or less of his Holy Spirit. Likewise, he says in one of his *Miscellanies*:

It was made especially the Holy Spirit's work to bring the world to its beauty and perfection out of the chaos; for the beauty of the world is a communication of God's beauty. The Holy Spirit is the harmony and excellence and beauty of the deity, as we have shown. Therefore, 'twas His work to communicate beauty and harmony to the world, and so we read that it was He that moved upon the face of the waters. (§293)

The references to 'harmony' in this quotation reveal that Edwards has a concept of beauty typical of his time, to be related to what Takarkiewicz calls 'the Great Theory of Beauty' which sees beauty as consisting especially in the proportion of parts.[22] Edwards also defines beauty in terms of consent and agreement, or 'sweet mutual consents'.[23] This conception of beauty both gives his account its plausibility and reveals its limitations.

In associating beauty with the Holy Spirit, and indeed identifying the latter with the divine beauty, Edwards is not precluding a connection with other Persons in the Trinity, for he also bears witness to the beauty of the Son and to the way in which it is displayed and reflected in the world. Edwards sees Christ as manifesting the divine beauty, because he is the image of God and because he was filled with the Holy Spirit, and thereby attracting people to him; but he thinks that it is the Spirit's function to beautify creation and to work through

---

[21] §45 para. 9, in *The Works of Jonathan Edwards*, vi, *Scientific and Philosophical Writings*, ed. Wallace E. Anderson (New Haven, Conn., 1980), 364.
[22] 'The Great Theory of Beauty and its Decline', *Journal of Aesthetics and Art Criticism*, 31 (1972–3), 167.
[23] *The Nature of True Virtue*, ch. 1, in *The Works of Jonathan Edwards*, viii, *Ethical Writings*, ed. Paul Ramsey (New Haven, Conn., 1989), esp. 540 ff; *Images or Shadows of Divine Things* ed. Perry Anderson (repr. Westport, Conn., 1977), 135. Aquinas finds harmony, connection, and joy appropriate to the Holy Spirit because he proceeds from the other two Persons and is the bond between them, and because they rest joyfully in each other (*ST* 1a. 39. 8). But he fails to draw out the conclusions about beauty which Edwards does.

human hearts. [24] Thus despite the originality of his thought on the Holy Spirit, Edwards is also influenced by the predominant Western tradition, found in Augustine, Aquinas, and Bonaventure, which associates beauty especially with the Son. Most of the Western theologians who have discussed the matter since Edwards have followed this tradition: von Balthasar's *Glory of the Lord* is centred round the idea that God's glory is manifested in the self-emptying of the Son, and discusses the role of the Holy Spirit only as a subsidiary theme. Likewise, van der Leeuw describes the Incarnation as the summit of beauty in his *Sacred and Profane Beauty: The Holy in Art*, and brings in the Holy Spirit only peripherally, for instance when discussing the principle that icon-painters must be illuminated by the Spirit. [25]

In recent decades, with the growth of the ecumenical movement, there has been the beginning of an attempt to effect a *rapprochement* between East and West by desisting from the polemics of past centuries and seeking for a common doctrine of the Holy Spirit. On the Western side there has been the suggestion that the *filioque* clause might be dropped from the Creed and the recognition that Western theology has paid insufficient attention to the possibility that there is a personal mission of the Holy Spirit; on the Eastern side there has been the recognition that the two theologies may be complementary in many respects rather than contrary to each other, and that, if understood in a certain way, the *filioque* clause expresses a possible theological opinion which cannot

[24] See esp. his *Essay on the Trinity*, ed. George P. Fisher (New York, 1903), 89, 98, and 101, and *Miscellanies* §§94 and 293 in *The Philosophy of Jonathan Edwards from his Private Notebooks*, ed. Harvey G. Townsend (Westport, Conn., 1972); also Roland A. Delattre, *Beauty and Sensibility in the Thought of Jonathan Edwards* (New Haven, Conn., 1968), ch. 7. A further distinction with regard to the roles of the Son and the Spirit both within the Trinity and in their missions is made in *Miscellanies* §448. There Edwards explains that God is glorified within Himself in two ways, by being manifested in His own perfect idea, the Son, and by delighting in Himself by flowing forth in his Holy Spirit in infinite love and delight towards Himself; likewise he glorifies Himself towards His creatures in two ways, by being manifested in their understanding, and by communicating Himself to their hearts and wills. Thus, he says, 'God is glorified not only by His glory's being seen, but by its being rejoiced in.'

[25] Gerardus van der Leeuw, *Sacred and Profane Beauty*, trans. D. E. Green (London, 1963), 340, 328–9, 176.

be rejected out of hand. One of the most considerable contributions to this conciliatory discussion is Volume iii of Yves Congar's *I Believe in the Holy Spirit*.[26] There he argues that many of the Greek Fathers of the fourth and fifth centuries allowed for a dependence of the Spirit on the Son in the life of the Trinity, and that it was only in the time leading up to the rupture between East and West in AD 1054 that Eastern theologians attacked the Western position as unacceptable. He recognizes, however, that the Westerners need to do justice to the fact that the Holy Spirit proceeds principally from the Father, as source or origin of divinity. He therefore recommends the use of the phrase 'through the Son' (the formula *per filium* was in fact agreed upon by the Council of Florence in 1439), and suggests that the *filioque* clause be suppressed, provided that its non-heretical character is recognized.[27] On the Eastern side, Evdokimov recognizes that Photius' formula that the Holy Spirit proceeds 'from the Father alone' was a polemical one, no more jusitified by Scripture than the *filioque* clause, and that the controversies about these formulae unfortunately made the subtle question of the relation between the Son and the Holy Spirit into the subject of political dispute. He suggests that the narrow question of the causal origin of the Spirit must give way to the wider question of the relationships between the Persons in revelation: the Father reveals himself through the Son in the Holy Spirit, and there is a dialectic between all three Persons.[28]

---

[26] Congar, *I Believe in the Holy Spirit*, esp. ch. 4. See also Lukas Vischer (ed.), *Spirit of God, Spirit of Christ: Ecumenical Reflections on the Filioque Controversy* (London and Geneva, 1981), and Germain Leblond, 'Point de vue sur la procession du Saint-Esprit', *Revue Thomiste*, 78 (1978), 293–302.

[27] In his later book *Word and Spirit* (trans. D. Smith, London, 1986), ch. 7, Congar favours the continuance of both Eastern and Western traditions, rather than seeking a common formula, provided that both sides recognize the Creed formulated by Constantinople in 381 as fundamental. The 'through the Son' formula is of course found long before Florence, e.g. Gregory of Nyssa writes of the Holy Spirit drawing his being from the Father through the Son in his *Letter* xxiv (*PG* 46: 1089c; cf. his *Contra Eunomium*, i (*PG* 45: 464bc), where he writes of the Son as cause of the Spirit), and John of Damascus, *On the Orthodox Faith*, i. 12 (*PG* 94: 849b). Moltmann (in Vischer, *Spirit of God*, 164–73) discusses yet another formula, 'the Holy Spirit, who proceeds from the Father of the Son'.

[28] *L'Esprit Saint*, pt. 1, ch. 6. See also S. Bulgakov, *Le Paraclet* (French trans., Paris, 1946), 123–4, 182, for a similarly eirenic position, which may be contrasted with the polemical stance of Vladimir Lossky, e.g. in his 'The Procession of the Holy

Eastern theologians have usually opposed the idea of the Holy Spirit as the bond of love between Father and Son,[29] because of its association with the *filioque* position, which they reject. But here again recent theology has opened up the possibility of conciliation. David Coffey suggests that besides the traditional 'procession model' there is also what he calls a 'bestowal model' or 'model of return' for understanding the Trinity. According to the latter model, the Father bestows his love on the Son generated by him, the Son in return bestows his love on the Father, and this mutual love is the Holy Spirit. Now since the Father begets the Son, the Holy Spirit is in the first instance his love for the Son, hence in a sense the Spirit proceeds from the Father alone. But he is also the Son's responding love, and therefore their mutual love. Yet the Son's love of the Father is an answering love, requiring the Father's love for him as its condition of possibility. So this model recognizes both the Father as source of love and the mutual love of Father and Son, and thus it may serve as a way of reconciling East and West. Moreover, it has the advantage of indicating the circular movement in intra-Trinitarian relations.[30]

Coffey also contributes to a possible ecumenical theology of the Holy Spirit by arguing that there may be a personal mission of the Holy Spirit, something suggested by other recent Western theologians. Traditionally, the West has tended to construe the maxim 'The external works of the Trinity are undivided' as meaning that divine actions in the

Spirit in the Orthodox Triadology', *Eastern Churches Quarterly*, 1948, suppl. 2, 31–53, and *The Mystical Theology of the Eastern Church* (London, 1957), ch. 3.

[29] Though the idea is not entirely unknown in the East: Gregory of Palamas writes of the Spirit as the mutual love of Father and Son (*PG* 150: 1144d–1145a). David Coffey thinks that the position that the Holy Spirit is the mutual love of the Father and the Son, which Augustine usually based on the *filioque*, can be supported through Scripture independently of the latter position, although it presupposes and completes it. See his 'The Holy Spirit as the Mutual Love of the Father and the Son', *Theological Studies*, 51 (1990), 193–229.

[30] See id., *Grace: The Gift of the Holy Spirit* (Sydney, 1979), esp. pt. 1, ch. 2 and pt. 4, ch. 10, and the article cited in the previous note. Cf. von Balthasar, *Spiritus Creator: Skizzen zur Theologie*, iii (Einsiedeln, 1967), 114–15, for a similar model. Coffey goes on to develop a theology of grace, according to which those who are filled with grace, which *is* the Holy Spirit, participate in this mutual love.

world are always those of the One God (whereas the East
construes it more in terms of the Father working through the
Son and perfecting through the Holy Spirit). Thus the Spirit's
mission of sanctification has often been taken as referring to
the sanctifying action of the Trinity as such, which is 'appropriated' to the Holy Spirit because of his role as bond of love
within the Trinity.[31] Perhaps also the view that the Spirit is a
bond of love has made it difficult to envisage him as an agent
or as a Person, even in the special sense of the term used of
the Trinity. Yet Scripture does speak of the Spirit as acting
in the life of Christ, as manifesting himself at Pentecost, as
dwelling in the hearts of believers and distributing his gifts,
and as guiding the early Church. Hence some recent Western
theologians have argued that the Holy Spirit does indeed have
a proper mission: to promote the epiphany of the Son, to make
Christ present after his death, and to remind us of all he said
and did, to work in the Church and to move us to prayer.[32]
Acknowledging such a proper mission does not entail violating
the maxim 'The external works of the Trinity are undivided',
for the mission may involve the other two Persons, just as,
again, the fact that the Son alone became incarnate does not
exclude the other two Persons having had a role in the
Incarnation (von Balthasar notes the role of the Holy Spirit at
Christ's conception, according to Luke 1, and says that here
the Father is the sender and giver of a commission, the Son is
sent and undertakes the commission obediently, and the Holy
Spirit lets the Son become man through a creative act[33]). In
any case, it has been argued that the maxim applies only to
God's *efficient* causality, and not, say, to His imparting grace,
which also involves His formal or quasi-formal causality.[34]

[31] See Columba Marmion, *Fire of Love* (London, 1964), ch. 4, and Edward
Kilmartin 'The Active role of Christ and the Holy Spirit in the Sanctification of the
Eucharistic Elements', *Theological Studies*, 45 (1984), 225–53.

[32] In addition to the works by Coffey and Kilmartin already cited, see J. Webster,
'The Identity of the Holy Spirit: A Problem in Trinitarian Theology', *Themelios*,
9(1) (1983), 4–7; J. Milbank, 'The Second Difference: For a Trinitarianism without
Reserve', *Modern Theology*, 2(3) (1986), 213–34; and Heribert Mühlen, *Der Heilige
Geist als Person in der Trinität, bei der Inkarnation und im Gnadenbund: Ich—
du—wir* (Münster, 1969).

[33] Von Balthasar, *Spiritus Creator*, 107–8.

[34] Karl Rahner, 'Nature and Grace', in his *Theological Investigations*, iv, trans.
K. Smyth (London, 1974), ch. 7, 165–88, esp. 177; Coffey, *Grace*, pt. 1, ch. 3.

This acknowledgement of the mission of the Holy Spirit has, not surprisingly, gone hand in hand with a recovery of a sense of the doctrine of the Trinity as being something of importance in the life of ordinary believers and not just a topic of theological speculation, and with a concern for Jesus's relationship with the Father and the Spirit in his life and work.[35] Unfortunately for us, however, none of this writing has been related to our particular concern with divine beauty; similarly, none of the works which I have mentioned as recognizing a proper mission of the Holy Spirit pay any attention to his role in beautifying the world, and indeed, more generally, they have little to say about his presence in nature, culture, and history—note, for instance, how little of Congar's trilogy touches on these questions.[36] So, now that I have set out the main Trinitarian positions, let us return to our main topic and ask whether the differences between these positions which we have explored, particularly the disputes between East and West, are of any practical concern to us.

EAST VERSUS WEST

The question of the practical relevance of different Trinitarian theologies for us now can be approached from two directions: we can ask whether these variations make any difference in practice for our topic; but we can also ask, conversely, whether our consideration of the relation between the Holy Spirit and beauty throws any light on the doctrines of the Trinity and of the Holy Spirit in general. The latter question involves consideration of, first of all, the mission of the Spirit, then of the economic Trinity (i.e. the Trinity as revealed to us in God's salvific work), because the Spirit's mission is related to the work of the Father and the Son, and lastly, if we assume that the economic Trinity is to be related to the Trinity as it is in itself, of the immanent Trinity. At first sight there seem to be advantages on both sides: the East, at least

[35] e.g. in Walter Kasper's *Jesus the Christ*, trans. V. Green (London, 1976) and his *The God of Jesus Christ*, trans. M. J. O'Connell (London, 1984).
[36] The part most relevant is *I Believe in the Holy Spirit*, ii, 218–28. See also his *Word and Spirit*, ch. 8.

until recently, has acknowledged more than the West the personal mission of the Holy Spirit, *perhaps* because its lack of the *filioque* clause (though, logically, there is no incompatibility between the two), and has, maybe because of this acknowledgement, done more to develop a theology of beauty specifically related to the Holy Spirit. On the other hand, the example of Jonathan Edwards's appeal to the idea of the Holy Spirit being the bond of love in the Trinity might be cited as showing that the Western view contributes something distinctive to the theology of beauty.

Despite their rejection of the *filioque* clause, many Eastern theologians connect the Holy Spirit's role as beautifier with his function of manifesting the Word. This, again, is because they associate closely the mission of the Spirit with that of the Son, without wanting to surmise from this anything about the Spirit's origin within the Trinity. We have already seen how Evdokimov assigns the Spirit the role of manifesting the beauty of the Son, who is the Word and Image of the Father, and that he describes the Spirit as 'the Light of the Word'. Evdokimov's position may be compared with that of another Orthodox theologian, Sergius Bulgakov, in his book *Le Paraclet*.[37] Bulgakov goes beyond other Orthodox thinkers in labelling the Son and the Spirit as a 'dyad', and in arguing that the divine wisdom is the double unity of these two Persons. Moreover, in discussing the procession of the Holy Spirit, he allows that the Spirit proceeds *on* the Son, to repose on him, and that the Son's presence is the indispensable condition of the Spirit's procession from the Father (pp. 173 *f*.). But he takes a similar line to Evdokimov in describing the Spirit's revelatory role and mission in the world: he says that each Person in the dyad reveals the Father in his own way, the Son as Word and as content, and the Spirit as the actualized reality of this content, as beauty, for, he says, 'the reality of truth felt is beauty' (p. 176). Thus their functions are complementary, and indeed there is a 'reciprocal transparency' (p. 176); as he puts it: 'The Spirit is the transparency of revelation, the Son is he who *is* in this transparency, its content . ... The Word becomes an abstract

---

[37] See esp. ch. 4 'The Dyad of Word and Spirit'.

idea if he does not receive his concrete reality in the Spirit' (p. 182). Like Evdokimov, he compares the Spirit to light: we do not see light itself, but it is only through it that the sun becomes visible to us. As regards natural beauty, Bulgakov sees Creation in terms of the Father's working through divine Wisdom, and again the Spirit, as he puts it, realizes the 'words' of being, which are of the Logos, as forms, and thus is the 'Artist of the World'; and 'The beauty of the world is the effect of the Holy Spirit, the Spirit of Beauty, and Beauty is Joy, the joy of being' (p. 193). For him, the beauty of nature is evidence of divine wisdom, for it is 'the reflection of the eternal mystical light of divine Wisdom', and '"inanimate" nature reveals itself as "Spirit-bearing", for it witnesses to the Spirit and is His revelation' (p. 194).

It seems, then, that although the Eastern churches reject the *filioque* clause as an account of the eternal origination of the Holy Spirit, they are content to associate the role of the Spirit very closely with that of the Son, both in revealing the Father and in Creation. Indeed, at one point Bulgakov writes of there being an inevitable *practical* 'filioquism' in the theology of the Holy Spirit, as far as his relation with the Son is concerned.[38] Apart from Bulgakov's more speculative thoughts about the 'dyadic' nature of divine wisdom, there is nothing of this Eastern theology which would be unacceptable to a Western theologian, even if some of its ideas are unfamiliar because the West has often tended to start its theology from the common essence of the Godhead and has consequently given insufficient attention to the roles of each Person of the Trinity in Creation and revelation; and when it has considered the roles of the Persons, the West has given more attention to the way in which the Son manifests the Father, than to the Spirit's role in illuminating the Word (and this perhaps, again, does something to explain why Aquinas and some other theologians have 'appropriated' beauty to the Son and have failed to develop an aesthetic of the Holy Spirit,

---

[38] Bulgakov, *Le Paraclet*, 182. Similarly, Dumitru Staniloae is willing to use phrases like 'goes out from', 'shines out from', and 'is manifested by' of the Son–Spirit relationship (in his 'The Procession of the Holy Spirit from the Father and his Relation to the Son, as the Basis of our Deification and Adoption', in Vischer, *Spirit of God*, 174–86).

which they might have done had they followed Evdokimov and others in considering the Spirit's role in the manifestation of the Word). But what of those few Western theologians who have developed such an aesthetic, and who have also accepted the *filioque* clause? Has their acceptance of this clause, and of the accompanying position that the Holy Spirit is the bond of love between Father and Son, made any specific contribution to their aesthetic?

Both the Western writers whom we have considered so far, Edwards and von Balthasar, specifically appeal to the Augustinian positions which I have mentioned, especially the second one, when they discuss the connection between the Holy Spirit and beauty. Edwards derives the Holy Spirit's mission as beautifier from his role within the Trinity (and also the Son's, as image of beauty, likewise), and he explains both the role and the mission in terms of harmony, consent, and agreement, in that the Holy Spirit, being the harmony and beauty of the Godhead, has the particular function of communicating beauty and harmony in the world. Von Balthasar uses the concept of form (*Gestalt*), rather than of harmony, as his key concept here. First of all, he defines beauty in terms of form, specifically a pleasing and radiant form through which we discern a content.[39] Then he describes the Son as the form which manifests the content of the Father; this form is the aesthetic model of all beauty, and it is placed visibly before us in the Incarnation, in which God shows and bestows *himself*, so that the Christ-form, which reveals the beauty of God, is the archetype of all beauty.[40] Thirdly, he relates the concept of form to the Holy Spirit in a very distinctive way: he says that the Spirit proceeds from the Father and the Word, and 'He transfigures both realities in their unity, since he is the unity of both and witnesses to this fact. Thus, he is at once the Spirit of form and formation [*Gestaltung*] and a Spirit of love and enthusiasm. In this incomprehensible unity he is the locus of the beauty of God.'[41] This obscure but

[39] Hans Urs von Balthasar, *The Glory of the Lord: A Theological Aesthetics*, i, 151. In iii, 103 he says, with reference to Dante, that beauty is the expressive form of the good and the true.
[40] Ibid. i, 153–4, 319, 477, 606, 609, 611.
[41] Ibid. 494.

pregnant remark is to be related to von Balthasar's general view that the Holy Spirit is the personal unity of the mutual self-surrender of Father and Son in love, and that in being both the fullness and the fruit of this love he unites them in a vital way and so holds the love in a Trinitarian form.[42] The most daring application of this idea occurs in his theology of Holy Saturday, in which von Balthasar depicts the Spirit as the uniting bond between the Father and the Son when the latter underwent the experience of abandonment in his death and descent to Hell. In their extreme separation then 'the Spirit unites Father and Son while stretching their mutual love to the point of unbearability'.[43] This role may be illustrated by the analogy of a marriage vow, which is both the subjective 'content' and the objective 'form' of the partners' love. Von Balthasar also gives the analogy, drawn from the work of Heribert Mühlen, of the way in which, when a personal relationship develops, the 'We' transcends the 'I-You', and describes the Spirit as the personal 'We' beyond the 'I-You' of the Father and the Son.[44] He goes on to discuss the mission of the Spirit in terms of this love. He sees the overflowing fullness of the mutual love of Father and Son as the source of its eternal fruitfulness in the work of the Spirit: the love, which the Spirit *is*, cannot be separated from the working of this love in us, for in pouring himself out as Spirit God is the love which is given in our hearts.[45]

Von Balthasar's discussions of the revealing function and

---

[42] For von Balthasar's pneumatology in general one should consult, besides the intermittent discussions in *The Glory of the Lord, Prayer*, trans. A. V. Littledale (London, 1961), some of his essays, esp. in *Spiritus Creator*, and *Theologik iii: Der Geist der Wahrheit* (Einsiedeln, 1987). John Randall Sachs's doctoral dissertation, *Spirit and Life: The Pneumatology and Christian Spirituality of Hans Urs von Balthasar* (Tübingen, 1984) is very useful, though it appeared too early to take account of *Theologik*.

[43] 'Mysteries of the Life of Jesus (IV): Jesus' Death on the Cross—Fulfillment of the Eternal Plan of God', in *The von Balthasar Reader*, ed. M. Kehl and W. Löser, trans. R. J. Daly and F. Lawrence (Edinburgh, 1982), 149. See also *The Glory of the Lord*, vii, 214, 389; John J. O'Donnell, SJ, 'The Doctrine of the Trinity in Recent German Theology', *Heythrop Journal*, 23 (1982), 153–67, esp. 156–7; and John Saward, *The Mysteries of March: Hans Urs von Balthasar on the Incarnation and Easter* (London, 1990), ch. 8.

[44] Von Balthasar, *Spiritus Creator*, 115. Cf. *Theodramatik*, ii, pt. 1 (Einsiedeln, 1976), 232.

[45] *Spiritus Creator*, 120.

mission of the Holy Spirit are much less distinctive than his Trinitarian theology: he concentrates on the Spirit's salvific role, and does little to relate what he says to questions about natural beauty, artistic inspiration, and so on. J. R. Sachs says rightly that in terms of von Balthasar's theological aesthetics, the Holy Spirit's role is to enable us to see and understand the *Gestalt* of Jesus Christ and, by drawing us into it, to transform us through its life-giving power.[46] Through the Spirit we see Christ's death and resurrection as the revelation of God's glorious, self-surrendering love, and are led into the reality of this mystery; and we are empowered to 'glorify' the glory that has been given to us through bearing fruit in our own lives. Thus we are told by von Balthasar that the grace of the Holy Spirit creates the faculty which can apprehend and relish the form of revelation, and that his love bestows on us the 'sensorium' with which we perceive God and the taste for Him,[47] and that the Spirit witnesses to the Son, explains the Word, and leads the believer to see and to encounter Christ.[48] The Son takes individual form in the Incarnation, and the Spirit brings the redeemed universe into harmony with that form; so, if the Son is the *expression* of God, the Spirit's role is to make an *impression*.[49] But all this, however eloquently put, takes us along a familiar track: von Balthasar is developing the view that the invisible Spirit leads us to see the visible image of the Father, the Son, and renews us in his likeness, a view which we have seen to be the common teaching of East and West.

Let us now take stock, and ask whether these writers' appeals to the Augustinian positions are essential, or even advantageous, to their aesthetics. Are they simply using the model which they have inherited, or are they developing it to provide something distinctive?

Edwards's case is simpler, and raises questions both about his limited definition of beauty and about why worldly beauty should be taken to derive from the harmony of the Trinity.

[46] Sachs, *Spirit and Life*, 204–5.
[47] Von Balthasar, *The Glory of the Lord*, i, 247, 249.
[48] Ibid. i, 155, 319, 494, 605–6.
[49] Ibid. ii, 116, 348.

As regards the former, we need to reckon with the fact that not all beauty is a matter of harmony, consent, and agreement, as was realized long ago by Plotinus, when he instanced colour, the light of the sun, gold, and so on as militating against the definition of beauty as symmetry (*Enneads*, i. 6. 1). It might also be argued that the concept of harmony already contains the idea of beauty, for we only call a combination of things harmonious if it is found beautiful. Moreover, other accounts of beauty might go naturally with a different Trinitarian theology. I am thinking here particularly of accounts in terms of light (again, note the association between the Holy Spirit and illumination), found in Plotinus and other Neoplatonists, which seem to have influenced Evdokimov and of which an example is given at the end of Edwards's *Essay on the Trinity*, where he includes the sun amongst the images of the Trinity to be found amongst creatures. He sees the substance or internal constitution as corresponding to the Father, its brightness or glory to the Son, and its beams to the Holy Spirit. He does not interpret the analogy in terms of the *filioque*, e.g. by saying that the beams proceed from both the sun's substance and its brightness; and indeed this analogy, versions of which are found in some of the early Fathers,[50] can equally well be construed in terms of an Eastern theology of the Trinity.

Even if beauty could be defined in the way Edwards assumes, we might ask why the harmonies found in the world should be taken to derive from the harmony of the Trinity itself; for a weaker position is available to us here, namely that there is an analogy between the Holy Spirit as the harmony of the Trinity and beauty as the harmony of the world, but that the former plays no special causal role with regard to the latter. But Edwards has a reply here: it is appropriate that the Holy Spirit should play such a role, for 'whose office can it be so Properly to give all things their sweetness and beauty as he who is himself the beauty and joy of the Creator'.[51] It is appropriate because, if the Holy Spirit

---

[50] e.g. in Tertullian, *Against Praxeas*, ch. 8.
[51] Edwards, *Essay on the Trinity*, 98. See again his *Miscellanies* §293 and *The Mind* 45: 9.

is the divine beauty and harmony, and if the world's beauty is a communication of that beauty, then beauty in the world must depend on the presence of the Holy Spirit. But this response still raises the question of whether the Holy Spirit, even if the mutual love and therefore in some sense the harmony of the Trinity, is simply to be identified with the divine beauty, the source of worldly beauty.

Von Balthasar's position is more complex. Much of what he says about the revelatory role and mission of the Holy Spirit would be equally acceptable to the East and to the West; and if part of the Spirit's mission is to be the beautifier, and beautifying involves giving form, then he might be said to be the 'Spirit of formation'. The problem for Easterners is von Balthasar's teaching that the Spirit is the form of the Trinity because he is the mutual love uniting Father and Son, and thus that the Spirit's role in revelation and salvation mirrors his position in the Trinity. But clearly von Balthasar, like many Western theologians, regards this point as an advantage of his position, for it seems to them inconsistent to relate the missions of the Son and the Holy Spirit closely and yet refuse to connect their being within the Trinity. This emerges in his discussion of Bonaventure, whom von Balthasar commends for depicting the external relations of the Persons as reflecting the inner life of the Trinity.[52]

Here we face a fundamental issue in Trinitarian theology which divides East and West. If there is indeed an advantage in the Western position, then it should be extended to theological aesthetics. But is there, again, any reason related specifically to aesthetics which recommends von Balthasar's position? Does it not face a question similar to that raised in the case of Edwards: even if the Holy Spirit is the form of the Trinity, holding together Father and Son, does it follow that the beauty of the world derives from the form or beauty of the Trinity? But this question seems to answer itself, in terms of von Balthasar's theology: for from where else would beauty derive? His position there is more subtle than Edwards's, because the concept of form is more elastic than that of harmony; and his statement that the love between the Father

[52] Von Balthasar, *The Glory of the Lord*, ii, 291.

and the Son, which *is* the Holy Spirit, overflows into our hearts naturally suggests by analogy that the beauty of the Godhead, of which the Holy Spirit is the *locus*, overflows likewise into the pleasing and radiant forms of things.

It seems, then, that von Balthasar and, to a less extent Edwards, have used the Western Trinitarian position in a novel way in their aesthetics. Whilst they are both much influenced by the predominant Western tradition, which associates beauty particularly with the Son, they have not restricted themselves to this but have developed a specifically Trinitarian aesthetic, which allots a vital role to the Holy Spirit, thus avoiding the impoverishment of simply 'appropriating' beauty to the Son.

We are, then, presented with two positions in the authors we have looked at: a Western one, which sees the Holy Spirit as the harmony of the Trinity or the *locus* of divine beauty, which overflows into the world; and a more linear Eastern model, which predicates beauty of all three Persons, but in different ways according to their roles in the Trinity: the Father is the Source of beauty, the Son is the perfect image or replica of the Father and radiates His glory (cf. Col. 1: 15, Heb. 1: 3, 2 Cor. 4: 6), and the Spirit eternally manifests this glory and reflects the image in the world by completing and communicating divine revelation and by creating beauty, and thus is, as it were, the 'point of contact'[53] of the Trinity for us. This model connects closely the roles of the Son and the Spirit, though in a different way from the Augustinian model, and this connection may be seen as a limited case of their reciprocal action in the economy of salvation.

I do not think that a consideration of aesthetic issues will enable us to choose between these two positions, since they both recognize the divine beauty and both acknowledge the mission of the Holy Spirit as beautifier (again, East and West disagree little about the mission of the Holy Spirit or about

---

[53] A phrase used by Kilian McDonnell, though not with reference to a theology of beauty, in his 'The Determinative Doctrine of the Holy Spirit', 149–50; he cites St Basil, *Letter* 38. 4 (*PG* 32: 332c) in which the Trinity is compared to a chain which, once grasped, draws along the other end, 'so he who draws the Spirit. . . . through Him draws along both the Son and the Father'. See also his 'A Trinitarian Theology of the Holy Spirit', *Theological Studies*, 46 (1985), 191–227.

the relationship between the missions of the Son and the Spirit). The differences between East and West depend on the acceptance by the West of Augustine's teaching about the Holy Spirit as the bond of love between Father and Son and about the *filioque*, and on the subsequent development of divergent Trinitarian theologies in the two halves of the Church. It would be beyond the scope of our study to arbitrate on this question, which has been discussed polemically for over a thousand years and which is being treated more constructively now because of the ecumenical approaches of our time.[54] One possible outcome of these approaches is that the two positions may come to be seen not so much as rivals but as alternative theological models which are both permissible. Both models are trying to accommodate various roles of the Holy Spirit, especially as completer or communicator of revelation and as point of contact with the Trinitarian life of God.[55]

So, to end on an eirenic note, both East and West offer us theologies which can accommodate within Trinitarian frameworks our connections between the Holy Spirit and beauty. It has to be said, however, that such theologies are very abstract taken by themselves. Just how does earthly beauty reflect the beauty of Christ? And how does the Holy Spirit work to ensure the reflection of divine beauty in the world? Let us therefore turn from such general theological discussions to look at the place where the idea of the Holy Spirit as beautifier 'touches down' in human experience, in the notion of inspiration, and then consider how earthly beauty may be said to reflect divine beauty. In doing so we move, as it were, from the mountains of dogmatic theology, whose peaks are wreathed in mist, to the sunnier plains of human experience.

[54] See again, for example, Vischer, *Spirit of God*. It is noticeable that most of the contributions concentrate on the *filioque* clause and devote little attention to the associated Augustinian position that the Holy Spirit is the bond of love between Father and Son. It is the latter topic which is far more crucial for Edwards's and von Balthasar's aesthetic.

[55] I have been helped to see this by an unpublished paper written by Dr Sarah Coakley.

5

Inspiration and Imagination

IN inspiration we have a concept which, it seems, will serve as a bridge between the two terms of our enquiry, the Holy Spirit and aesthetics. It is, moreover, a concept which has a use in ordinary life and conversation, unlike some of the complexities of Trinitarian theology discussed in the last chapter. People are familiar with the idea of surpassing themselves by doing something unforeseen or unplanned, or by producing something that means more than they intended or perceived at the time but which nevertheless bears their hallmark. The lives of many artists, writers, and musicians (not to mention scientists and other creative workers) provide plenty of examples. One of the best-known is that of Handel composing *The Messiah*: he wrote the oratorio in three weeks, writing like one possessed, spoke of having been visited by God, and always refused subsequently to accept any money for performances because he felt that it was not really he himself who had composed it.[1]

Many religious believers treat such phenomena as gifts from God, for which thanks are appropriate, because His power has made things possible which would otherwise lie outside human capacities. Some of them have pointed to the parallel between the artist's reliance on inspiration and the saint's need for grace, and the times of dryness which they both often endure.[2] Moreover, in both cases Christians appeal to the work of the Holy Spirit. Some other religions employ similar concepts: perhaps the most familiar one in Western culture is ancient Greek religion, which appealed to the Muses as inspiring the arts, but also to the god Apollo and to

---

[1] See Stefan Zweig, *The Tide of Fortune: Twelve Historical Miniatures*, trans. E. and C. Paul (London, 1940), ch. 4. Rosamond E. M. Harding provides many other such examples in *An Anatomy of Inspiration* (reprint of 2nd edn., London, 1967).

[2] Étienne Gilson, *L'École des muses*, (Paris, 1951), ch. 9.

Athena, the goddess of wisdom. The appeal to the Muses survived the demise of Greek religion, and is sometimes found combined with an appeal to the Holy Spirit. Thus Milton begins his *Paradise Lost* with an invocation to the 'Heav'nly Muse' (line 6), and then switches to 'O Spirit' in line 17; then in Book 7 he makes Wisdom the companion of the Muse Urania; and finally in *Paradise Regained* he simply appeals to the Spirit.[3] Dante seeks the guidance of the Muses, Minerva, and Apollo (e.g. in *Paradiso*, ii. 8*f*.); at the beginning of the *Paradiso* he says that until then one peak of Parnassus (the dwelling-place of the Muses) has sufficed, but now he needs the second peak, that of Apollo (i. 13–18). It would be a heavy-footed approach to ask whether these poets really believed in the existence of the Muses. But it has been argued that we should regard the Muses as the name given by the ancients to what is in fact the Holy Spirit. Thus in one of the rare discussions of the Spirit's role in nature and culture G. Fedotov says 'The muse is the pseudonym under which the ancient poets invoked the inspiring grace of the unknown Holy Spirit (*Ruah*).'[4]

I do not think that we can simply equate inspiration with the work of the Holy Spirit. For the former term has acquired connotations of creativity and originality, whilst the latter includes the presence of grace and a guidance which may sometimes be negative, restraining someone from an unwise or bad action. Moreover, many things regarded as inspirations by the secular world would not be accepted as such by religious people, or might even be regarded as diabolical inspirations. In this chapter I will try to provide a more precise definition of inspiration, and elucidate its connection with the Holy Spirit, and then look at the place of imagination. I shall

---

[3] I have been much helped here by an unpublished paper, 'The Heavenly Muse and the Holy Spirit', by Revd Dr Noel O'Donoghue.

[4] G. Fedotov, 'De L'Esprit Saint dans la nature et dans la culture', *Contacts*, 28 (1976), 212–28; I quote from 218. He goes on to warn that the forces which inspire a poet can tear at him and that the demons can pollute the sacred sources of inspiration. Bulgakov has a more complex position: he treats the Muses and the ancient gods as expressions of a 'natural grace of inspiration', which derives from divine Wisdom and is therefore of the Holy Spirit, but which is not a true divine inspiration but rather the capacity for one. See S. Bulgakov, *Le Paraclet* (Paris, 1946), 203–8.

also consider the question of whether we can explain (or explain away) inspiration.

THE NATURE OF INSPIRATION

Unfortunately consideration of the concept of inspiration has been confined within a limited compass in recent centuries. Christian theologians have been mainly concerned with the question of biblical inspiration; and since the authority of Scripture (especially its truth) has been an important issue for nearly two centuries, they have often had a very intellectualistic view, seeing it as divine instruction or dictation, or as an illumination of the mind. Secular writers have subsumed the question under what has come to be called the 'psychology of creativity', and have sought to investigate the sources of originality among artists, writers, and creative scientists. In so confining the areas of discussion, people have ignored Wittgenstein's advice to feed on a wide diet of examples,[5] and have thus impoverished the concept. A further impoverishment is seen in the way in which people try to fit inspiration into an over-simple explanatory pattern (and here I include both the appeal to the concept of inspiration as an explanation of creativity, and the further question of explaining inspiration itself). There is a widespread tendency, among both religious and secular writers, to see inspiration as a psychological process, the antecedents of which must be traced back either to divine intervention or to unconscious mental processes. Since, however, so many of the relevant factors are, it seems, as yet unkown, inspiration comes to take on the character of an explanatory 'black box' or 'something I know not what'. Thus Rosamond Harding concludes her fascinating study of the operation of inspiration amongst artists and scientists with the following definition: 'Inspiration may thus be defined as the result of some unknown factor accidentally met with operating on the mind of the man of science or artist at that particular moment when it is pent up to a certain tension . . .'[6]

---

[5] 'A main cause of philosophical disease—a one-sided diet: one nourishes one's thinking with only one kind of example.' Ludwig Wittgenstein, *Philosophical Investigations*, trans. G. E. M. Anscombe (Oxford, 1968), pt. 1, §593.

[6] Harding, *Anatomy*, 102.

Such a definition is inadequate for many reasons; but the main weakness to be noted now is that it says nothing of the *quality* of the ideas or products which lead people to describe them as 'inspired'. Rosamond Harding's definition would cover the emergence of the trivial and the mediocre as well as the brilliance of genius.

We need, therefore, a fuller and richer concept of inspiration. I think that the two subjects mentioned earlier, biblical inspiration and artistic or scientific originality, are but fragments broken off from a larger whole. That larger whole is, I believe, the doctrine of Creation (in the next chapter I shall point also to some connections with the idea of revelation). According to this doctrine, men and women are created in God's image and likeness. Some theologians regard human creativity as a likeness of God's creative power, and indeed as a participation in His energies and purposes.[7] The products of this creativity include works of art, but also children, crops, gardens, scientific theories, and many other forms of what patents law calls 'intellectual properties'. In their creation God works through human beings as 'secondary causes', to use the traditional term; we may also use another traditional phrase 'instrumental cause', provided that we avoid any connotations of mechanism or of the supplanting of the human spirit by the divine, and the consequent violation of human freedom. I am suggesting that in many of these cases inspiration is the way in which God through His spirit lets us share in His creativity: for instance, He helps us to imitate His own creation of beauty, and indeed furthers that creation, by acting in and through our creative capacities. As Victor Hugo put it pithily, 'Nature is God's immediate creation, and art is what God creates through the mind of man'[8]—though one

---

[7] See Roger Hazelton, *Ascending Flame, Descending Dove: An Essay on Creative Transcendence* (Philadelphia, 1975), 117 *f.* (drawing on Berdyaev), and Peter D. Ashton, 'The Holy Spirit and the Gifts of Art', *Theological Renewal*, 21 (July 1982), 12–13. The Second Vatican Council mentions the procreation of children in marriage as a way in which we may share in God's creative action: see *Gaudium et Spes* §50, in Walter Abbott (ed.), *The Documents of Vatican II* (London, 1966), 254.

[8] *Philosophie* I. 265, quoted by Monroe C. Beardsley in his *Aesthetics from Classical Greece to the Present: A Short History* (Alabama, 1966) 262. Hegel thinks that God works through artists, as spiritual beings, but as we saw earlier, in Ch. 2, he fails to do justice to God's presence in natural beauty.

might point out that God sometimes uses other parts of nature as secondary causes in creating beauty, as in the creation of coral through coral-insects. Human creative capacities may, of course, be ignored, suppressed, abused, or exercised in a repetitive and humdrum way. It is when they are stretched or raised in a striking way that we are inclined to speak of inspiration.

Before I pursue this matter, however, I need to make two very fundamental points about the nature of inspiration which are often ignored: firstly, the term 'inspiration' means literally 'blowing upon' or 'breathing into', and is not a technical concept either in psychology or in theology; and secondly, as I have suggested in my comment on Harding's definition, it is used to express a judgement about the quality of things, especially with regard to beauty, goodness, and truth, as well as about their provenance. In both these respects the term 'inspiration' is somewhat like that of 'enlightenment'.

My first point can be verified by consulting dictionaries, and by comparing the use of Greek and Latin terms like *epipneō, epipnoia, inspiro, inspiratio*, and *afflatus*. It should also be remembered that inspiration is closely related to another rich and important concept, that of 'spirit'; and, again, that the latter originally meant 'wind' or 'breath' in Greek, Latin, and Hebrew, and that in many biblical passages there is a deliberate play on words. If, as I have argued elsewhere,[9] the Bible often envisages the spirit of God as a power which 'blows through' or permeates people, giving or heightening certain capacities, particularly by producing a change of heart, then it would seem that inspiration was originally seen as an empowering of this kind. Unfortunately 'spirit' has become a dead metaphor for most people by now, so that many contemporary philosophers and theologians are content to define it in terms of immaterial substances or incorporeal persons, without any seeming awareness of its historical background and wealth of connotations. 'Inspiration' too is perhaps going the same way: it is often nowadays used as a synonym for encouragement or incitement. This fact and the dead hand of psychologists may do for it what

[9] See my *Spirit, Saints and Immortality* (London, 1984), ch. 2.

philosophers and theologians have done for the 'spirit'! But
here the living experience of poets and artists may at least
slow down the process of banalization: Shelley, for instance,
was well aware of the metaphorical character of the term when
he mentioned inspiration in his *A Defence of Poetry* and said
'the mind in creation is a fading coal, which some invisible
influence, like an inconstant wind, awakens to transitory
brightness'.[10]

This consideration means that we should not look for an
exact definition of the term; nor should we look for a single
essence of inspiration, either in religious or secular contexts;
nor should we assume that there is a single mode of operation:
sometimes inspired people have felt seized by an external
power, as though someone else acted through them,[11] sometimes it is more like a sudden clarity of perception (perhaps
emerging after a period of tension), and sometimes it comes
as a dark and disturbing force. In any case, as I shall show,
the term has been employed much more widely in the past
than in recent usage. So, again, there are good reasons for
resisting its narrowing.

The second point which needs to be made at the outset is
that to describe someone or something as inspired is usually
to pass a favourable judgement on their quality.[12] This is so
even in the case of trivial or derivative uses of the term, as
when we talk of making inspired choices or guesses. An
'inspired choice' by an employer is the finding of an unexpectedly brilliant performer for a job; and by someone shopping
for presents, it is finding just the right gift. Conversely, to
describe someone or something as 'uninspired' is to criticize
them as boring, mediocre, or unimaginative. To adopt a

---

[10] *Shelley: Selected Poetry, Prose and Letters*, ed. A. S. B. Glover (London,
1957), 1050.

[11] Thus George Eliot told J. W. Cross that 'in her best writing there was a "not
herself" which took possession of her, and that she felt her own personality to be
merely the instrument through which this spirit, as it were, was acting'. (J. W. Cross,
George Eliot's Life, as Related in her Letters and Journals, Leipzig, 1885, iv, 280–1.)

[12] Wittgenstein points to a possible exception to my generalization when he
remarks 'Is this the sense of belief in the Devil: that not everything that comes to us
as an inspiration comes from what is good?' (*Culture and Value*, trans. Peter Winch
(2nd. edn.; Oxford 1980), 87). But I think that we have enough on our plates now
without contending with the Devil too!

strategy of 'Buggins's Turn' is to risk an uninspired choice in promoting employees, as to buy pens, aftershave lotion, and so on may be to betray a lack of inspiration in buying presents. Usually, however, we speak of inspiration when more serious issues are afoot, particularly with regard to outstanding examples of truth (both in the case of scientific discovery and in that of biblical inspiration), beauty, and goodness. Here it is not just a matter of passing a favourable verdict, but of expressing one's wonder. To describe a work of art as inspired is to convey a sense of the mysterious or miraculous, as well as to praise its excellence. Such judgements are often passed by artists on their own work, when they recognize that they have surpassed themselves. In his *Critique of Judgement* Kant remarked that the creator of works of genius cannot describe or indicate scientifically how he brings about his products; he does not know how he has come by his ideas, he has not the power to devise them at his pleasure and according to plan, nor can he give others precepts to enable them to produce similar works. The use of the term 'genius' in such contexts is, Kant surmised, probably derived from *genius*, in the sense of 'that peculiar guiding and guardian spirit given to man at his birth, from whose suggestion these original ideas proceed' (§46, trans. J. H. Bernard).

Sometimes the judgement that someone or something is inspired may be made retrospectively. Again, it is a matter of expressing wonder when discerning extraordinary quality. Thus, in one of the best treatments of the question of biblical inspiration, *Confessions of an Enquiring Spirit*, Coleridge wrote: '. . . in the Bible there is more that *finds* me than I have experienced in all other books put together . . . the words of the Bible find me at greater depths of my being; and . . . whatever finds me brings with it an irresistible evidence of its having proceeded from the Holy Spirit'.[13] Whereas many Christian apologists have inferred that the Bible must be true because God has inspired it, Coleridge seemingly proceeds in the opposite direction and discerns the Bible's inspiration in its quality of spiritual depth. More recently, Karl Rahner has related the question of the inspiration of the Bible to its

---

[13] Ed. H. St J. Hart (London, 1956), 43.

canonicity: he argues that the early Church selected just the canon it did because that canon seemed to crystallize the authentic apostolic faith.[14] Here, too, there is an appeal to the retrospective nature of judgement about the importance of the Bible, though of a different kind from Coleridge's appeal. I would like to extend this point about the retrospective nature of judgement to other oustanding expressions of truth besides the Bible, and to aesthetic qualities also.[15]

WIDENING THE CONCEPT

Later on in the same work, Coleridge calls for a widening of the concept when he distinguishes between the narrow sense of inspiration as 'inspired revelation' and a wider sense of the term where 'the writer speaks or uses and applies his existing gifts of power and knowledge under the predisposing, aiding and directing actuation of God's Holy Spirit' (p. 77). He sees the latter kind of inspiration as something which all Christians might hope and pray for, to be related to the presence of the Holy Spirit in all true believers. A similar distinction was made about the same time by Søren Kierkegaard, in a passage in his *Journals* written in October 1834. There he says that inspiration means either exclusively the activity of the apostles as they were writing the New Testament or something extended over their whole lifetime: 'We find no basis in the New Testament for the former view; on the contrary, what is referred to, the communication of the Holy Spirit, is something which must be regarded as being stretched out over their whole lifetime.'[16] Elsewhere he explained how the communication of the Holy Spirit might transform the lives of contemporary believers. In his discourse 'It is the Spirit that Giveth Life',[17] he describes the Holy Spirit as the 'life-giving

---

[14] Karl Rahner, *Inspiration in the Bible* (New York, 1961).

[15] In the very interesting discussion of imagination in his *A Dish of Orts* (London, 1908) George MacDonald introduces the concept of inspiration by arguing that since there is always more in a work of art than the producer perceived while he produced it, so there is a strong reason for attributing it to a larger origin than man alone (pp. 25 *ff.*; 'Orts', incidentally, is a Scottish term for leftovers).

[16] *Søren Kierkegaard's Journals and Papers*, iii, ed. Howard V. Hong and Edna H. Hong (Bloomington and London, 1975), §2854, p. 265.

[17] This discourse forms pt. 3 of *For Self-Examination*.

spirit', and says that the new life that is given involves a death: death to selfishness, the world, and earthly hope. The Comforter only came after the horrors of Christ's passion and death; but still he came. And he comes now, bringing faith, hope against hope, and real love. But the work of the Spirit, the Comforter, in us is often uncomfortable, Kierkegaard says, for we are treated like horses driven by a skilled coachman who stretches them.

Here, then, we have inspiration subsumed under the communication of the Holy Spirit, the life-giving and transforming spirit. This proposal is, I think, correct. It is in accord with the meaning of the term; and it is not a novel proposal, for if we look back over the centuries, we find that earlier generations of Christians had a far wider understanding of inspiration than our contemporary one. St Thomas Aquinas, for example, used the term *inspiratio* of the Gifts of the Holy Spirit, i.e. wisdom, understanding, knowledge, counsel, piety, fortitude, and fear of the Lord, in *Summa Theologiae*, 1a2ae. 68. 1; he says that they come through divine inspiration and that they dispose people to become readily mobile to this inspiration. Elsewhere, although he employs the terms *inspiratio* and *inspirare* relatively rarely, he uses them of faith, repentance, good intentions, devotion, and holy desires, as well as of prophecy and—very rarely—of Scripture, and also of the Father's inspiring Christ with the desire to suffer for us, by infusing love into him.[18] Similarly, several early Christian Fathers, countering the view that inspiration was limited to the Jewish scriptures, claimed that it was now found in the Church; they spoke of it in connection with, for example, the work of elders, prophets, and preachers, the building of churches and the election of bishops.[19]

[18] For references, see app. 5 of the Blackfriars edn. of the *Summa Theologiae*, xxiv (London, 1974), 131–6. Lancelot Andrewes uses the term 'inspiration' of the descent of the Holy Spirit on the Apostles at Pentecost, and of his continued indwelling in us, and sees this as a 'great mystery of godliness', parallel with the Incarnation. See his sermon on the Holy Ghost of June 1606, in *Ninety-Six Sermons*, iii (Oxford, 1841), 108–9.
[19] For references, see A. C. Sundberg, 'The Bible Canon and the Christian Doctrine of Inspiration', *Interpretation*, 29 (1975), 352–71. There is, of course, pagan usage to be considered, which by this time was variegated. Quintilian, for instance, speaks of an orator inspiring his hearers by his power (*Institutio Oratoria*, ii. 5. 8).

It is hardly surprising that the early Christians used the concept of inspiration so widely, since they would naturally let its use be moulded by the related concept of spirit. Now in the Bible this term, too, is used very widely. When used of the spirit of God, it usually expresses the way in which God works in the world. It is used of Creation (Gen. 1: 2, 2: 7), but usually of more specific, outstanding endowments, for instance, Samson's strength (Judges 14: 6), the skill, perception, and knowledge of the craftsman, Bezalel (Exod. 35: 31), the inspiration of prophets (Num. 11: 25, Ezek. 11: 5), the Gifts already mentioned with reference to Aquinas (Isa. 11: 1 *f.*), the charisms and fruit of the Spirit listed by St Paul (1 Cor. 12: 8–11; Gal. 5: 22), and the guidance of the early Church (Acts 8: 29, 9: 31, 13: 2). It is also often particularly associated with the human heart, e.g. when Ezekiel describes God as promising to send His spirit and create a new heart, removing the heart of stone and giving a heart of flesh instead (Ezek. 36: 26 *f.*). Elsewhere I have argued that we should recognize what might be called 'moral inspiration' or 'inspiration of the heart': for if we already use 'inspiration' of that enhancement of people's capacities whereby they create things of beauty, or perceive and formulate outstandingly striking truths, so, by analogy, we should also use the term of that enhancing of people's capacities in which their emotional and moral range is extended, giving rise to particular creative moral actions or to the perception of new patterns of goodness.[20]

Two other ways in which the concept might be widened are by applying it not just to the initial creative urge but also to the subsequent selection and reworking of material; and by extending it to the reader, hearer, and viewer. The first of these extensions has been made by some biblical scholars, who have pointed out that many books in the Bible were not written by a single author, but were compiled from existing material. There is no reason why we should attribute inspiration only to the person who initiated this process (say a prophet); or for that matter only to the final individual who

---

[20] See my 'Inspiration and the Heart', in Richard Bell (ed.), *The Grammar of the Heart* (San Francisco, 1988), 171–87.

sets down the results of a long process of formulation and reformulation, for the Holy Spirit may be present at each stage of selection and revision.[21] But the point has a much wider application. It is notorious that many artists, writers, and musicians have produced masterpieces only after laborious revision and reworking of their material (Beethoven, for instance, as compared with Mozart). Many, too, have borrowed material from others and improved upon it (Handel is a famous example). There seems no reason why we should not extend the concept of inspiration to the later phases of creation, for God may guide someone in the processes of selecting and revising just as much as in the initial invention. A similar extension of a biblical precedent is proposed in my second suggestion. Traditionally the Holy Spirit has been given the role of assisting the reader or hearer of Scripture to recognize the divine revelation in it. So, by analogy, as I suggested in the last chapter, we need to reckon with the understanding and appreciation of the beholder, listener, and reader in the case of art. It does not seem too far-fetched to use the term 'inspiration' here, for after all it is common to speak of people being inspired by a work of art, and to describe the latter as 'inspiring'.

Any such proposals to widen the concept, however, must bear in mind my initial point that in contemporary usage inspiration connotes excellence, deserving of admiration or wonder. It will not do to claim, for instance, that all Christians are inspired because they have received the Holy Spirit at Baptism. Patently, they are not. And if it is insisted that they are, the term has been widened almost to vacuity.

IMAGINATION AND INSPIRATION

A concept closely related to inspiration, but deserving of a separate treatment, is that of imagination. Their close relationship was acknowledged by the ancients in their assimilation of poetry and prophecy. Plato, for instance, lumps in poets with prophets and holy seers in his *Ion*, 534cd, and

---

[21] This point is made by, for example, Paul Achtemeier, in his *Inspiration of Scripture: Problems and Proposals* (Philadelphia, 1980), chs. 4 and 5.

describes them all as ministers of God; and in his *Phaedrus* he compares the possession and madness inspired by the Muses with the inspired divination of the Sibyl and the priestesses at Delphi and Dodona (244a–245a).[22] I do not think that they should be identified with each other, for imagination is a more specific concept than inspiration, just as inspiration, with its connotations of creativity and originality, is more specific than the working of the Holy Spirit. But inspiration may involve the imagination, as it may involve other mental faculties. Imagination is to be distinguished from inspiration partly because it is usually linked with our perceptions (as the cognate term 'image' suggests; similarly, in German, *Einbildung* is connected with *Bild*, i.e. picture, image, and representation), but mainly because it is an active power of the mind. The latter point is illustrated by the fact that we can ask someone to imagine something, say a scene or what it would be like to live in another century, whereas it makes little sense to tell someone to be inspired. Coleridge described the imagination as the 'esemplastic power', coining a word from the Greek phrase *eis hen plattein* (to shape into one), i.e. an active combining power which brings ideas together.[23] Unlike Plato, he did not regard poetic genius as possession by an alien power, but rather as something which 'sustains and modifies the images, thoughts and emotions of the poet's own mind', so that the poet brings the whole soul into activity, subordinating its faculties to each other, and 'diffuses a tone and spirit of unity that blends and (as it were) fuses, each into each, by that synthetic and magical power to which we have exclusively appropriated the name of imagination'.[24] This is not to deny that imagination is a gift like inspiration; but it is one which we can choose to exercise, and

[22] See A.-H. Chroust, 'Inspiration in Ancient Greece', in Edward O'Connor (ed.) *Charismatic Renewal* (London, 1978), 37–54. G. Fedotov notes that in Latin *vates* signifies both poet and seer ('De L'Esprit Saint'). For a comparison of poetic and religious inspiration, and the role of imagination in both of them, see Austin Farrer, *The Glass of Vision* (Westminster, 1948) and id., 'Inspiration: Poetical and Divine', in F. F. Bruce (ed.), *Promise and Fulfilment: Essays Presented to Professor S. H. Hooke* (Edinburgh, 1963), 91–105.
[23] *Biographia Literaria* (Everyman edn., London, 1956), 91. See Mary Warnock, *Imagination* (London, 1976), 84.
[24] *Biographia Literaria*, 173, 174.

which may be trained to some extent by observation and reflection.

If imagination is an active power, it is one which may, with some qualification, be attributed to God. Coleridge indeed, describes what he calls the primary imagination as 'a repetition in the finite mind of the eternal act of creation in the infinite I AM',[25] whilst others have written of the creation of the world as an exercise of divine imagination. In his book *Faith, Theology and Imagination* John McIntyre quotes Aquinas' remark that God is known 'through the things that are made', and says that we should take it, not as a licence to infer God's existence from the world, following the Five Ways, but rather as an encouragement to look for signs of God's creative hand. We should regard the glories of creation as the expression of God's imagination manifested in His own creation; though, unfortunately, we have lost any perception of God's character as it is revealed in the beauty around us.[26] He then goes on to extend his theme to the work of the Son and the Holy Spirit. In the Incarnation God chose an unexpected and stunningly imaginative way of making his love and forgiveness unmistakably real; and we can conceive of Pentecost as 'the extravagant expression of God's imaginative creative activity in the Spiritual sphere'. This work still continues: 'I would venture to say that the Holy Spirit is God's imagination let loose and working with all the freedom of God in the world, and in the lives, the words and actions, of the men and women of our time.'[27] McIntyre singles out the Charismatic Movement as a contemporary demonstration of the Spirit's working imaginatively: something, he says, which is not dissimilar from the riot of extravagance we see in God's imaginative creativity in a sunset, the magnificence of a rose, or the majestic fury of a storm at sea.

McIntyre is concerned with God's imagination working in Creation, and with the Holy Spirit's imaginative activity in religion. He is not, it seems, concerned here with the human imagination as exercised in the arts, and does not discuss how the Holy Spirit works in this. But we can easily extend his discussion by linking inspiration with imagination, and by

---

[25] Ibid. 167.   [26] (Edinburgh, 1987), 51.   [27] Ibid. 64.

pointing to the liberating and illuminating power of art. The connection here is simply that the Holy Spirit may work through the imagination, as he may work through other mental powers, for instance judgement. In such cases we may speak of an 'inspired imagination'. This link was indeed made by a writer whom McIntyre mentions in an earlier part of his book, George MacDonald. The latter sees the human imagination as a vehicle of divine inspiration, and so he describes a 'wise imagination' as 'the presence of the spirit of God'.[28] This presence enlightens our understanding ('the Maker is our Light',[29]) and accounts for the fact which, as we have seen, MacDonald stresses, that works of art contain more than their producers realized at the time: 'One difference between God's work and man's is, that while God's work cannot mean more than he meant, man's must mean more than he meant . . . A man may well himself discover truth in what he wrote; for he was dealing all the time with things that came from thoughts beyond his own.'[30] MacDonald fails perhaps to do justice to the power of evil imaginings, though he does note that the imagination requires nourishment (especially literature). Like any human power, the imagination can be corrupted, and so its products must be assessed. But then we have seen that it requires discernment to judge whether someone or something is truly inspired, for there may be false claimants to inspiration, if not diabolical inspirations.

Unfortunately the imagination has not received its due from theologians, at least not until recently,[31] perhaps because of its seeming to connote what is unreal, false, or irrational (note how 'imaginary' is often used as a pejorative term, suggesting self-deception. Similarly 'poetry' is sometimes used as an abusive term to describe what is regarded as badly argued or fantastic). The depreciation of the imagination may perhaps be traced back to Plato, who relegates it to the bottom of the Divided Line in *Republic*, vi, below knowledge, reason, and

---

[28] MacDonald, *A Dish of Orts*, 28.   [29] Ibid. 25.   [30] Ibid. 320–1.
[31] In addition to the works by MacDonald and McIntyre already cited, see, for example, James P. Mackey (ed.), *Religious Imagination* (Edinburgh, 1986) and John Coulson, *Religion and Imagination*, (Oxford, 1981).

belief (509d *ff.*; it should be remarked, however, that the term used, *eikasia*, does not have quite the connotations of the English 'imagination', for it can also be translated as 'conjecture'), and who also condemned much poetry for disseminating falsehood about the gods (*Rep.* ii. 377d *ff.*). Those, however, who depreciate imagination and poetry risk suffering what Claudel called the tragedy of a starved imagination.[32] This risk may confront a religion as well as an individual, for if the former lacks imaginative expressions, it may repel people by its banality.

One reason for the suspicion of theologians and others is that imagination is hard to define, for like 'inspiration' the term has a long history, and its modern sense is wider than the ancient and medieval.[33] In any case, as my comment about Plato's Divided Line indicates, the cognate terms in other languages may have varying connotations, leading to misunderstandings. Most modern discussions in English are influenced by Coleridge's treatment, especially his distinction between imagination and fancy. In distinguishing them, Coleridge perceived that much of what people regard as the former is really the latter. For him, fancy consists in rearranging things in new combinations; it 'is indeed no other than a mode of memory emancipated from the order of time and space; and blended with and modified by that empirical phaenomenon of the will which we express by the word *choice*'.[34] If this is correct, then the suggestion of unreality and falsehood really belongs to fancy rather than imagination. One of the functions of the imagination, indeed, is to seek for a deeper truth in our experience, as was realized by George Eliot when she wrote: 'powerful imagination is not false outward vision, but intense inward representation, and a creative energy constantly fed by susceptibility to the veriest minutiae of experience, which it reproduces and constructs in fresh and full wholes'.[35] Like Coleridge, she sees the imagination as a unifying agent. It is not a part of the mind, but

---

[32] Cf. Paul Claudel, *Positions et propositions*, i (Paris, 1926), 175.
[33] Nicholas Wolterstorff prefers to write of 'envisagement' and 'world-projection', in *Art in Action*, pt. 3, ch. 3.
[34] *Biographia Literaria*, 167.
[35] George Eliot, *Impressions of Theophrastus Such*, ch. 13.

rather the whole mind working in a certain way, involving perception, feeling, and reasoning.

If indeed imagination is such a unifying power, then obviously its use is not restricted to the arts, although our present concern is mainly with that use of the creative imagination. The particular exercise I would like to mention briefly now is one brought up earlier when I suggested that there is something that might be called 'inspiration of the heart' or 'moral inspiration', namely in our moral and social life. We speak sometimes of people making imaginative gestures, and we recognize the need for exercising imagination in coming to understand others and cultivating mutual sympathies. Such a sympathetic understanding cannot be reached by those who are concerned only with themselves, for it rests upon the use of the imagination to interpret the outward signs of others' lives and behaviour, and to put ourselves in their place.[36] Imagination, too, may give people a new moral vision, by helping them to see things from an unfamiliar point of view, and thereby perhaps stimulate them to lead deeper and richer lives.[37] The arts, particularly literature, have an important role to play here in extending people's imaginative and moral range. But religious leaders and reformers may play an analogous role, as may saints. We tend to think of the latter as fulfilling the requirements of morality more fully and conscientiously than most of us do. But one of their functions is perhaps to give us a fresh realization of what those requirements are and to suggest new patterns of goodness. Now moral imagination plays an important role here, for it may require imagination to see that we should forgive and love our enemies, help people in the Third World as we do the poor at home, give a low priority to worldly success, and so on. In his *Two Moralities* A. D. Lindsay remarked that saints show imagination, spontaneity, and creativity in their conduct: it is not so much that they do what ordinary people neglect, but they do what has not even occurred to the latter. Thus, he

[36] See Peter Jones, *Philosophy and the Novel* (Oxford, 1975), 48, for this point.
[37] See further Sabina Lovibond, *Realism and Imagination in Ethics* (Oxford, 1983), esp. §45; and Hugo Meynell, *The Nature of Aesthetic Value* (Albany, NY, 1986), ch. 3.

says, '"Gracious" conduct is somehow like the work of an artist'.[38] One might add here that some saints (e.g. St Francis of Assisi) have by the style of their sanctity had an influence akin to that of a pioneering artist on later generations.

INSPIRATION AND EXPLANATION

Although the exercise of the imagination is under our own control, the quality of what is produced is not so. This lack of control is even more pronounced in the case of inspiration, for one of its most commonly noted features is its unpredictability, the way in which it comes suddenly and unexpectedly. Of course, people have recommended various techniques for producing it: Schiller kept rotten apples in his desk; he and Grétry immersed their feet in ice-cold water; Balzac worked wearing a monastic gown, whilst de Musset and Guido Reni preferred magnificent costumes; and the aesthetician Baumgarten advised poets seeking inspiration to ride on horseback, to drink wine in moderation, and, provided that they were chaste, to look at beautiful women.[39] But more often (and more prosaically) artists have been advised to wait, and to prepare for the coming of inspiration by getting on with their work, being open and observant, reading widely, and so on. Thus Rosamond Harding shows that although Tchaikovsky called inspiration a 'supernatural and inexplicable force', he also counselled working regular hours whether or not one feels inspired, saying 'We must be patient, and believe that inspiration will come to those who can master their *disinclination*'.[40] Similarly, in his classic study *The Road to Xanadu: A Study in the Ways of the Imagination*, Livingston Lowes used Coleridge's notebook of 1795–8 to lay bare the ideas and wide programme of reading which formed the soil from which both *The Rime of the Ancient Mariner* and *Kubla Khan* grew. Lowes quotes the mathematician Henri Poincaré as saying 'The unconscious work is not possible, or in any case not

---

[38] A. D. Lindsay, *The Two Moralities: Our Duty to God and to Society* (London, 1940), 50.
[39] See H. B. Levey, 'A Theory Concerning Free Creation in the Inventive Arts', *Psychiatry*, 3 (1940), 229–93.
[40] R. Harding, *The Anatomy of Inspiration*, 12, 35.

fruitful, *unless it is first preceded and then followed by a period of conscious work.*'[41]

The question naturally arises, then, of whether there are states of mind which provide fertile soil for inspiration; and indeed of whether we can cultivate them to prepare ourselves for it. Later on in his *Journals* Kierkegaard wrote 'Just as one does not begin a feast at sunrise but at sundown, just so in the spiritual world one must first work forward for some time before the sun really shines for us and rises in all its glory'.[42] Of course, it might be replied that inspiration is, in theological terms, the communication of the Holy Spirit, which is unpredictable and wholly gratuitous. But at least there seem to be ways of being open to inspiration; and in many cases one might say, putting it sententiously, that inspiration requires aspiration.

This question, in turn, leads on to the more radical questions of explanation which I raised at the beginning, about what sort of explanation an appeal to inspiration provides and whether we can explain inspiration itself.

Recent religious treatments of inspiration largely confine themselves to biblical inspiration, whilst secular ones tend to treat the concept as a psychological or cognitive one, describing the sudden occurrence of good ideas, something which is apparently not under our control. Secular writers recognize that as a matter of history the concept of inspiration is originally a metaphor with religious connotations, but wish to 'demythologize' it by subsuming it under the study of creativity and, in some cases, by replacing the appeal to God or gods with the concept of the unconscious.[43] Many of them realize that it is difficult to explain creativity in terms of any 'covering law' pattern of explanation. As Ian Jarvie puts it, 'Creative achievements are unique events; explanatory progress is made only with repeatable events. Hence there is something

---

[41] Livingston Lowes, *The Road to Xanadu: A Study in the Ways of the Imagination* (London, 1933), 62.

[42] Hong and Hong, *Kierkegaard's Journals and Papers*, v (Bloomington and London, 1978), §5100, p. 39.

[43] See, for example, Arthur Koestler, 'The Three Domains of Creativity', in D. Dutton and M. Krausz (eds.), *The Concept of Creativity in Science and Art* (The Hague, 1981), 17; also his *Act of Creation* (Danube edn., London, 1969).

inexplicable about creativity.'[44] He remarks that purported explanations of creativity are suspect because, if they were successful, they would explain it *away*. Another contributor to the same volume, Larry Briskman, presses the point further when he argues that if we could explain creativity in terms of a covering law, we would be able to deduce its attainment from the presence of certain conditioning factors and also provide a kind of recipe for being creative. He concludes that the most we can explain is the *possibility* of creativity.[45]

At the moment there seem to be two main models of explanation of inspiration or creativity which are prevalent, one secular and one religious, both of which have a psychological slant. The first, associated particularly with Arthur Koestler, sees creativity as the discovery of hidden similarities and the connection of previously unconnected frames of reference. Thus Koestler recommends what he calls 'bisociative' thinking, and says that 'The creative act consists in combining previously unrelated structures in such a way that you get more out of the emergent whole than you have put in.'[46] The second, religious, model sees inspiration in terms of God's working through our psychological processes. William James appealed to such a model when he explained religious experience on the hypothesis that on the 'hither side' the source of saving experiences is the subconscious self, but that on the 'farther side' their source is God.[47] The model has been applied to biblical inspiration by writers who eschew talk of divine dictation or the supernatural communication of divine revelation, preferring instead to construe such inspiration in terms of God's increasing a writer's level of spiritual insight or intellectual vision.[48] Roman Catholic writers often

[44] Ian Jarvie, 'The Rationality of Creativity', in Dutton and Krausz, *The Concept of Creativity*, 109–28. I quote from 112.

[45] Larry Briskman, 'Creative Product and Creative Process in Science and Art', in Dutton and Krausz, *The Concept of Creativity*, 129–55.

[46] Koestler, 'The Three Domains', ibid. 1.

[47] *The Varieties of Religious Experience* (London, 1960), Lecture 20 and Postscript. MacDonald sees God as working through our unconscious in the case of imagination (*A Dish of Orts*, 25).

[48] See M. R. Austin, 'How Biblical is "The Inspiration of Scripture"?', *Expository Times*, 93 (1981–2), 75–9, for examples. Coleridge similarly distinguished 'between the divine Will working with the agency of natural causes, and the same Will supplying their place by a special *fiat*' (*Confessions of an Enquiring Spirit*, 72–3).

appeal here to the notions of 'secondary causes' and 'instrumental causality'; they describe inspiration in terms of the Holy Spirit's working through the ordinary psychological apparatus of the inspired writer (sometimes distinguishing this process from the pagan notion of 'possession', in which the faculties of the writers seemed to be suspended as they went into a trance, and assimilating it rather to the concept of grace).[49]

I think that both these models of explanation are inadequate (though not wholly erroneous). Koestler's model has the general weakness of failing to reckon with a point which I made at the outset, that describing someone or something as inspired is often an expression of wonder, or of admiration for sheer excellence. His recommendation of 'bisociative' thinking gives us a recipe for producing novelties, which may or may not turn out to have the qualities of excellence which are desired (just as taking opium may or may not help to produce poetry of the quality of *Kubla Khan*). There may be an unknown psychological ingredient involved, but it is not the essence of inspiration. But there is also a more specific objection: if I am right in extending the concept of inspiration to the realms of ethics and the emotions, Koestler's approach seems inappropriate in such contexts: are Jesus' words of forgiveness from the Cross indeed an example of bisociative thinking?

The religious model is attractive to many people today because the appeal to the notion of secondary causes conveys some idea of how God may work through the ordinary course of events without intervening miraculously, and so it seems to avoid theological crudity. It is also eirenic, for it sees religious and secular explanations of inspiration or creativity as complementary rather than as rivals: for psychological explanations are seen as attempts to delineate the nature of the mental processes through which the Spirit of God communicates. More generally, the provision of a causal explanation of an occurrence does not preclude our wonder and admiration[50]

---

[49] See Rahner, *Inspiration in the Bible*, esp. 60 *f*.; and James T. Burtchaell, *Catholic Theories of Biblical Inspiration since 1810* (Cambridge, 1969), esp. chs. 1, 4, and 6.
[50] A point made by Ronald Hepburn in *'Wonder' and other Essays* (Edinburgh, 1984), ch. 7.

(again, think of the coral-insects)—a point which is very relevant to Marxist, sociological, and other theories of art which seek to lay bare all the material influences and constraints which may affect creative work: for God may work through many kinds of secondary causes. The trouble is, however, that in practice the model turns out to be either too limited or too general. It is too limited when the concept of inspiration is restricted to biblical inspiration (as it is by, for example, Luis Alonso Schökel, who regards 'inspiration' as a technical term, standing for a charism pertaining to language).[51] Once, however, such a dictatorial limitation of the concept is rejected, because it ignores so much other usage, the model becomes too wide: it does not by itself help us to distinguish inspiration from other ways in which the Spirit works through us, for instance in religious experience, guidance, and assistance. We would need to go on here to convey the notion of creativity, and to make specific connections with the concepts of goodness and truth, and with aesthetic concepts.

The inadequacies of both models stem, I think, from the fragmentation of the concept of inspiration which I noted earlier: both have been developed to cover particular areas, the one scientific creativity, humour, and art, the other the Bible. There is often, too, (particularly in the case of the secular model, perhaps because of its preoccupation with the suddenness and unexpectedness of creative ideas), a tendency to regard inspiration as a psychological process. Wittgenstein's misgivings about labelling understanding, intending, and so on as 'mental processes' (cf. *Zettel* 446, for example) should be borne in mind here. But more specifically, Livingston Lowes made an important point when he concluded his remorseless and wide-ranging study of the sources of Coleridge's inspiration by saying that he could merely lay bare the way in which the poet's creative genius had worked on his material through processes which are common to mankind; but in his case those processes were 'superlatively enhanced'.[52]

---

[51] Luis Alonso Schökel, *The Inspired Word: Scripture in the Light of Language and Literature* (New York, 1965), 45.
[52] Livingston Lowes, *The Road to Xanadu*, 431.

If one were interested merely in psychological processes and their genesis, one could as well do a study of William McGonagall as of Coleridge!

I do not propose now to suggest a further model; indeed, as my citations from Jarvie, Briskman, and Lowes indicate, I am unclear about what an adequate *theory* explaining inspiration would be like—can we explain excellence? We need to ask now whether even the fullest psychological account could ever explain the *quality* of the content of inspiration, and whether religious appeals to inspiration are ever simply attempts to find a causal explanation (for if that is all they are, they face the objection that they may be hypostasizing the putative source of inspiration).

I suggest, in conclusion, that what is characteristic of a religious view of inspiration is that it is put into a wider pattern of explanation, involving an appeal to something like Aristotle's notions of final and formal causes. If we restrict ourselves to the question of whether God intervenes directly in our psychological processes or works through secondary causes (or does both), we are limiting ourselves to the level of efficient causes. But a religious account of inspiration also considers its purpose and context, and the relationship between its content and the nature of God. Even if we *could* explain it in scientific terms (though I do not know what it would be to do so), an explanation in terms of the Holy Spirit would not necessarily be superfluous, for such an explanation is a personal one, which attempts to show the *point* of the process. Religious people regard the purpose of inspiration as being God's communicating to us: for our salvation, in the case of what Coleridge called 'inspired revelation'; and in other cases to enable us to mirror His creativity through moral vision, scientific research, and artistic creation. Similarly, its content may be related to God's nature, for the three activities mentioned may also be seen as ways in which we dimly reflect His perfections. Thus beauty can be regarded as a reflection of God's glory, our goodness as a sharing in His goodness, and our perception of truth as a sharing in His wisdom and knowledge. Inspiration, then, is seen as a mode of God's revelation and also as an expression of His creativity, understanding this not just in terms of His bringing creatures into being and sustaining them, but also in terms of His lovingly communicating His own qualities to them and having a purpose for them; and indeed if we follow some of the writers discussed in the last chapter, it is a taking-up of human beings into the divine life itself.

If this account is correct, then the wonder and admiration which artistic inspiration evokes may be seen as part of our wonder at the manifoldness of creation and at the continued activity of the Holy Spirit in the world. In appealing to the Holy Spirit's working through inspiration we are situating artistic excellence in a theological framework (likewise, in connecting sanctity with the Spirit). Despite the ways in which people have tried to arouse inspiration, some of them bizarre, it seems that they often have to wait for a power beyond themselves, and it is commonly noted that the provision of studios and laboratories and the ready availability of grants and research funds will not necessarily produce creativity in the arts or in science. At the simplest level, the Holy Spirit may be seen as a kind of prompter,[53] energizing us and opening us up to new potentialities within us. Such a role does not exclude the influence of economic and social factors, nor the internal connections with whatever artistic, intellectual, and religious traditions we happen to belong to; nor does it exclude the use of our normal mental processes, e.g. association of ideas, though these may be, as Lowes says, superlatively enhanced. But beyond this, a fuller theological explanation tries to show the point of artistic creativity in terms of its relation to God's perfections and its purpose within His providence. It is within such a picture that the idea of inspiration belongs.

[53] An analogy used by von Balthasar in *Theodramatik*, ii, pt. 2 (Einsiedeln, 1978), 487.

6

Reflections of Divine Beauty

AT the end of the last chapter I suggested that one of God's purposes in inspiration is to diffuse His perfections in the world through the Holy Spirit, as an expression of His creative love, which leads Him not only to make the world but to impart to it something of His own qualities. One exemplification of this suggestion is the widely expressed idea that the beauty of the world is a likeness or a reflection of divine beauty, and that it therefore tells us not only of God's creativity and generosity, but also of His own beauty, which is manifested and shared in the world. Thus beauty can lead us to God. This idea has roots in Christian Platonism, which sees worldly perfections as participating in divine ones, but also in some of the Psalms, which exult in the way in which the earth and the heavens declare God's glory, and (as far as human perfections are concerned) in Gen. 1: 26–7, which states that God created us in His own image and likeness. Of course, this acknowledgement of a likeness to God is balanced by a stress on an unlikeness. In theology we find a range of views, from those who stress the mystery and incomprehensibility of God to those who are struck by His presence in the world (not that the two views are incompatible, for a mystery may be something that is glimpsed rather than wholly unknown); we also find a similar spectrum between those who depreciate earthly beauty because it is, at best, *only* a shadow of something far more splendid, and those who rejoice in it and love to explore its manifoldness, because they see it as a sign of its Creator.

The specific connection with the Holy Spirit here comes through his role in Creation and inspiration, and also through the belief that he helps us to discern reflections of divine glory in the world. In this chapter I shall outline a few accounts of the relationship between divine and created beauty, assess their plausibility, and look at some of the problems they raise, and then outline my own minimal version.

REFLECTIONS, LIKENESSES, AND OTHER RELATIONS

The presence of God's beauty in the world is often expressed metaphorically. Hopkins's line 'The world is charged with the grandeur of God' is one which sticks in the mind; and the next line 'It will flame out, like shining from shook foil' introduces the theme of light, which we find elsewhere in many versions. Ficino, in his commentary on Plato's *Symposium*,[1] describes beauty as 'the radiance of divine goodness', whilst Jonathan Edwards combines the theme of light with the metaphor of a reflection when he says that God is to be loved because He is 'infinitely the most beautiful and excellent: and all the beauty to be found throughout the whole Creation, is but the reflection of the diffused beams of that Being who hath an infinite fulness of brightness and glory'.[2] The cognate analogy of a mirror is also common: in one of his sonnets Michelangelo says that he will only love human beauty because it mirrors God,[3] and Thomas Traherne extends the metaphor more widely in one of his *Centuries*, when he says 'The world is a Mirror of Infinit Beauty, yet no Man sees it' (I. 31). Later on, Traherne describes how he saw the world as a child:

O what Venerable and Reverend Creatures did the Aged seem! Immortal Cherubims! And young Men Glittering and Sparkling Angels and Maids strange Seraphick Pieces of Life and Beauty! Boys and Girls Tumbling in the street, and Playing, were moving Jewels. I knew not that they were Born or should Die. But all things abided Eternaly as they were in their Proper Places. Eternity was

---

[1] *De Amore*, Speech 2, ch. 3.

[2] *The Nature of True Virtue*, ch. 2, in *The Works of Jonathan Edwards*, viii, *Ethical Writings*, ed. Paul Ramsey (New Haven, Conn., 1989), 550–1; see again *A Dissertation concerning the End for which God created the World*, ch. 1, §iii, in *Works of Jonathan Edwards*, viii, 442, for his comparison of the creature's holiness, as conforming to and participating in God's beauty, to the brightness of a jewel reflecting the sun.

[3] *Rime*, ed. Enzo N. Girardi (Bari, 1967), no. 106; *Complete Poems and Selected Letters of Michelangelo*, ed. Robert N. Linscott (New York, 1963), no. 104.

Manifest in the Light of the Day, and som thing infinit Behind
every thing appeared . . . (III. 3)

It is perhaps easier to express the relationship between
God's glory and earthly beauty poetically and metaphorically
than to attain any philosophical or theological exactitude.
Hence prudence might suggest that we stop at this point. But
philosophers and theologians have attempted to go further, so
we must follow them and try to assess their attempts.

The simplest and most common version of the idea which
we are exploring to be found among philosophers and theologians is that worldly beauty is like God's beauty because God
has communicated a likeness of His own beauty; and that
there are degrees of likeness to God according to the extent
that creatures share in the communication, resulting in a
hierarchy of beauty. We find an influential expression of this
position in Pseudo-Dionysius' works, especially *The Divine
Names*. Although he denies that there can be an exact likeness
between creatures and the divine, he describes the Super-
Essential Beautiful (i.e. God) as the source of all created
beauty, its exemplar and the goal of all things. In the passage
from which I quoted in Chapter 3, he says that the Super-
Essential Beautiful is called 'Beauty' because it imparts beauty
to all things according to their nature, and is the cause of their
harmony and splendour 'flashing forth upon them all, like
light, the beautifying communications of Its originating ray'.[4]
Since all the patterns of things pre-exist in the Universal
Cause in a unity,[5] it is the unique pre-existent cause of all that
is beautiful, containing in a transcendent manner the originating beauty of everything beautiful.[6] Thus for him phenomenal
beauties are images of invisible beauty.

Pseudo-Dionysius was much influenced by Plato and Neoplatonism (which saw earthly perfections as emanations of the
Divine), and he in turn influenced many later thinkers,
including Aquinas. The latter's fullest treatment of aesthetics
comes in his commentary on *The Divine Names*, especially
the *lectio* entitled 'On the Beautiful and How it is attributed

---

[4] Ch. iv, §7 (*PG* 3: 701c).   [5] Ch. v, §8 (*PG* 3: 824c).
[6] Ch. iv, §7 (*PG* 3: 701c).

to God'.[7] There, after saying that God is most beautiful and beauty itself, because of His surpassing greatness and because He is the First Cause, Aquinas goes on to say that God has the source of all beauty, for things are beautiful according to their proper form, and every form, whereby things have being, is a participation in divine radiance; similarly, all harmonies, e.g. friendships, proceed from divine beauty (§§347, 349). Thus the beauty of creatures is a participation in the First Cause, which makes all things beautiful, and is a likeness to divine beauty which is shared in things (§337). Elsewhere Aquinas is careful to say that the likeness between creatures and God is not a generic one, for God does not belong to any *genus* (*ST* 1a. iv. 3; xiii. 5 ad 2), and that God is unlike them as well as like them (*Summa contra Gentiles*, i. 29). Likewise, Jonathan Edwards sees God as not only beautiful but as beauty itself and the source of all beauty, yet he also insists that divine beauty differs from all other beauty.[8]

Aquinas' ideas and language in his commentary are, not surprisingly, very reminiscent of Plato, who describes particulars as resembling and participating in their Forms, and in the *Phaedo* says specifically that if there is anything else that is beautiful besides beauty itself, it is only so because it partakes of that beauty (100c). But he also, as we shall see, follows his mentor in borrowing concepts from Aristotle, especially with regard to the different kinds of cause—efficient, final, and so on.

Of course, many early Christian Fathers before Pseudo-Dionysius had expressed these ideas, often in similar language. St Augustine, for instance, writes of imitating God's beauty, and addresses God as He in, by, and through whom all good and beautiful things have these qualities.[9] Likewise, St Gregory of Nyssa uses the Platonic language of 'partaking' and refers to God as the 'Archetype'.[10] In one of his homilies

---

[7] Ch. iv, lectio 5, commenting on ch. iv §7 of Pseudo-Dionysius' work.

[8] Jonathan Edwards, *A Treatise concerning Religious Affections*, ed. John E. Smith (New Haven, Conn., 1959), 298.

[9] I *De ordine*, 8 (*PL* 32: 989); II *De ord.* 19 (*PL* 32: 1019); *Soliloquia*, i. 1. 3 (*PL* 32: 870); cf. *De Fide et Symbolo* 2 (*PL* 40: 182).

[10] *On the Making of Man*, xii. 9 (*PG* 44: 161c).

on the Song of Songs he says that the beloved is beautiful because filled with the image of divine beauty, the archetype of beauty,[11] whilst in his *Catechetical Oration* he describes man as 'beauteous in form, for he had been created as a representation [*apeikonisma*] of the archetypal beauty'.[12] St Cyril of Alexandria also refers to God as the archetypal beauty, to which man is formed by the Holy Spirit (he quotes Gen. 2: 7), which has been impressed on him like a seal, leading to all virtue.[13]

A weaker claim, which might be called an internalization of Plato's Forms, is that creatures are copies of ideas in God's mind. This claim is found in Augustine,[14] and also in Aquinas, who says that every creature is an image of the exemplar type in the divine mind (*ST* 1a. xciii. 2 ad 4). The likeness between creation and God then becomes assimilated to the relationship between a work of art and ideas in the artist's mind.[15]

Terms like 'image' and 'archetype' differ from 'like' in that they convey the notion of the causal priority of an original (the same point applies to mirrors and reflections). Such terms are not symmetrical, whereas the term 'like' is usually so: if *x* is like *y*, then *y* is like *x* (I say 'usually', because there are some exceptions; we say that a son is like his father, but not vice versa, because we regard the latter as the prototype). Aquinas notes that the notion of an 'image' adds something to that of 'likeness', for it suggests the idea of an imprint taken from another, or an imitation; thus one egg is like another, but is not its image (*ST* 1a. xciii. 1, discussing the image of God in man). Likewise, Pseudo-Dionysius argues that although God may bestow a divine similitude upon those who turn to Him and strive to imitate His qualities, He does not

---

[11] *On the Song of Songs*, 5 (*PG* 44: 868 cd).

[12] Ch. vi (*PG* 45: 29b).

[13] In Jn. ix, commenting on John 14: 20 (*PG* 74: 277b–d). For other patristic references, see H. Krug, *De Pulchritudine Divina*, (Freiburg im Breisgau, 1902), bk. 2, pt. 2.

[14] *On Eighty-three Questions*, no. 46 (*PL* 40: 30).

[15] Plato himself has a threefold pattern in his *Timaeus*: the *dēmiourgos* (creator) creates the world with reference to an eternal pattern, so that the natural world is an *eikon* (image) of the unchangeable (28a–30a). He also says that the creator desired that all things should be as like himself as they could be (29e).

resemble them, any more than a man resembles his own portrait.[16]

Of course, not all those who use such terms keep this logical point in mind; and this consideration applies to the great variety of other terms which are commonly used of the relationship between divine and worldly beauty, e.g. vestige or trace,[17] type,[18] sacrament,[19] and revelation.[20] Sometimes they are used indiscriminately, or as so many metaphors; and sometimes they are used carefully and distinguished from each other. Thus St Bonaventure distinguishes between a vestige and an image: every creature has a vestige of God, but only human beings, as rational creatures, have the image of God, in virtue of an 'expressed likeness'.[21] A failure to make such distinctions may lead to theological and philosophical problems. Thus, if art or worldly beauty are described as revelations of God, how is this claim to be taken? Many Christians would accept it in the weak sense that art may convey important truths (including, perhaps, the fruits of mystical states and of spiritual development), and that it and natural beauty may manifest God's power and presence, but would wish to distinguish a stronger and more normative sense of the term 'revelation', reserved for God's manifesting Himself in the salvation-history and prophecies of Israel, for the culmination of this history in the life, death, and resurrection of Christ, and for the records of these in the

---

[16] *Div. Nom.* ix. 6 (*PG* 3: 913c).

[17] Alexander of Hales, *Summa Theologica*, ii (Quaracchi edn.), p. 47, n. 37; p. 49, n. 40.

[18] Jonathan Edwards, *Images or Shadows of Divine Things*, ed. Perry Anderson (repr. Westport, Conn., 1977), 134.

[19] Simone Weil, *Waiting on God*, trans. Emma Craufurd (Fontana edn., London, 1959), 124.

[20] Gerardus van der Leeuw, *Sacred and Profane Beauty*, trans. D. E. Green (London, 1963), 339.

[21] ii *Sent.* xvi. 1. 1 (Quaracchi, edn., ii. 394). He makes a similar distinction in his *Itinerarium*, ch. 1, §2, and then, in a later chapter, describes creatures variously as shadows, echoes, pictures, vestiges, representations, spectacles, exemplars, and exemplifications, whereby we are carried over from the sensible things seen to intelligible things not seen, as through signs to what is signified (ii.11). See the Classics of Western Spirituality edition of his works, ed. Ewert Cousins (London, 1978), 60, 76, 108; also ii *Sent.* i. 1. 1. 2 (Quaracchi edn., ii. 22). Aquinas likewise distinguishes between a vestige and an image: the former is in non-rational creatures and in the non-rational parts of us (*ST* 1a. xciii. 6).

Bible.[22] Similarly, many Christians might acknowledge that art may have a sacramental quality, in that it may be a sign of the divine and therefore in some sense a channel of grace, but would wish to distinguish it from the sacraments of the Church (thus the Eastern Orthodox prefer to describe icons as sacramental rather than as sacraments)—though I think that those sacraments do presuppose what von Balthasar calls the sacramental principle,[23] i.e. the idea that the spiritual can be conveyed through the material, so that their meaningfulness depends on a wider sense of the sacramental quality of things.

The concept of a sacrament, whether widely or narrowly construed, is important in the present context because it presupposes another concept commonly used of the relationship between God and the world, that of a sign. In the Bible, signs of God are extraordinary events regarded as supporting claims that God has spoken or as vouching for someone's authority, such as the sudden consuming of the food Gideon had left on a rock after he had prayed for a sign to confirm the angel's message (Judg. 6: 17) and the miracles of Christ (John 6: 30, Acts 2: 22). But Christian theologians have come to use the term much more widely, partly through the influence of sacramental theology, which sees human gestures and materials like water as vehicles of divine action, and partly through reflection on what is entailed in the doctrine of Creation. Thus the twelfth-century writer, Hugh of St Victor, after saying in his commentary on Pseudo-Dionysius' *Celestial Hierarchy* that visible beauty is the image of invisible beauty, goes on to say more generally that visible things are signs of the invisible.[24] But the use of this term raises some philosophical issues, for a sign may be what C. S. Peirce called an 'iconic' sign, which represents its object because it is similar to it[25] (e.g. an

---

[22] See Harold Osborne, 'Revelatory Theories of Art', *British Journal of Aesthetics*, 4 (1964), 332–47; and Peter D. Ashton, 'The Holy Spirit and the Gifts of Art', *Theological Renewal*, 21 (July 1982), 12–23.

[23] *Prayer*, trans. A. V. Littledale (London, 1961) pt. 3, ch. 2. See also David Jones's important essay 'Art and Sacrament', in Nathan A. Scott (ed.), *The New Orpheus: Essays toward a Christian Poetic* (New York, 1964).

[24] *PL* 175: 949b, 954b.

[25] *The Collected Papers of Charles Sanders Peirce*, ii, ed. Charles Hartshorne and Paul Weiss (Cambridge, Mass. 1960), §276. He construes this category widely: it includes pictures, photographs, and diagrams, but also algebraic formulae (ibid., §279).

inn-sign which is a realistic picture); or it may be one involving language (e.g. some road signs), where the relation between it and its object is one of denotation; or it may be like a medical symptom, where the relationship is causal and inductive (what Peirce calls an 'index'), e.g. boils are signs of impurity in the blood. Only the first type involves a relationship of likeness: the picture of Queen Victoria on an inn-sign may resemble its original, but the words 'Public Footpath' do not *resemble* a footpath, for the relationship between language and reality is not one of resemblance (except in the case of onomatopoeia).[26] Now when theologians say that earthly beauty is a sign of divine or invisible beauty, they mean usually that the former resembles, or is the image of, the latter. But occasionally something more like the linguistic relation of denotation is suggested. In another work Hugh of St Victor writes that 'the whole sensual world is, as it were, a book written by the finger of God'.[27] The idea of nature being a kind of language through which God communicates with us is one explored by other theologians, e.g. by Berkeley in *Alciphron* and captured by John Keble in one of his poems in *The Christian Year*:

> The works of God above, below,
> Within us and around,
> Are pages in that book, to shew
> How God himself is found.[28]

But, again, if the analogy of a book is to be pressed, it suggests a relation of denotation rather than of likeness. Our concern now is with likeness and other such relations, rather than with linguistic representation.[29]

---

[26] See Nelson Goodman, *Languages of Art: An Approach to a Theory of Symbols* (2nd edn., Indianapolis, 1976), esp. ch. 1. I have explored some of the issues raised by Goodman's book in my 'Modes of Representation and Likeness to God', in Kenneth Surin (ed.), *Christ, Ethics and Tragedy: Essays in Honour of Donald MacKinnon* (Cambridge, 1989), 34–48.

[27] *Eruditionis Didascalicae*, bk. 7 (*PL* 176: 814b).

[28] i (Oxford, 1827), 83, poem for Septuagesima Sunday. I think that although Hilary Fraser is right to see Keble as extending the sacramental principle to nature, this verse (which she quotes in *Beauty and Belief: Aesthetics and Religion in Victorian Literature* (Cambridge, 1986), 40) does not quite exemplify it, for the reason suggested in the text. A more natural comparison might be with the idea that the Holy Spirit opens the reader's mind to the significance of Scripture.

[29] It is worth noting again that Christ is described both as Word and as Image.

LIKENESS TO GOD

The claim that the beauty of the created world reflects that of God may be regarded as an extension of the statement made in Gen. 1: 26–7 that we are created in God's image and likeness. It is an extension, because the text refers only to human beings, whereas our claim embraces all creation. Such an extension is suggested both by biblical texts which speak of the magnificance of nature as revealing God's power and glory (e.g. Ps. 19: 1–6 and Ps. 104) and by theologians' claims that the Creator shares his qualities with his creation. Of course, it does not always seem plausible, for often nature shows a hostile visage, which arouses fear and dismay and suggests a dark side in its Creator: Kenneth Clark contrasts the optimistic attitude to nature of Wordsworth and Constable with the pessimism of Turner and Géricault, both of whom convey its destructive aspect.[30] But there is a more serious philosophical problem, one already raised by the text from Genesis: how can a corporeal being be like God, who has no body or matter?

This difficulty was perceived by the early Christian Fathers, and indeed by Jewish thinkers like Philo. We find that the text from Genesis came to be taken in two different ways: some interpreted it as meaning that the image of God is to be found only in the soul or mind, because they thought it could be found only in what is immaterial, whilst others said that it is to be found in the whole person. The former group was much influenced by Platonic Dualism, and it includes theologians like Origen and Cyril of Alexandria. Origen finds the image of God in the rational soul, the inner man, which is invisible, incorporeal, incorruptible, and immortal.[31] The soul has a capacity for virtue; and when it is decked out in the virtues which constitute our true beauty, it is an authentic portrait of God. He accuses those who say that corporeal man was made in God's image and likeness of representing God himself as corporeal.[32] Similarly, Cyril finds the image of God

---

[30] Kenneth Clark, *The Romantic Rebellion* (London, 1973), 226, 265.
[31] *Against Celsus*, vii. 66 (*PG* 11: 1513b–1516a), viii. 17 (*PG* 11: 1544a–1545a); *Homilies on Ezekiel*, vii. 7 (*PG* 13: 724b–725a).
[32] *Homilies on Genesis*, i. 13 (*PG* 12: 155c–156a).

in the soul.[33] On the other hand, Irenaeus states that the whole human person is created in God's image[34]—an important claim for us, for if we can see God's image in a corporeal person, the way is open to look for some reflection of God's beauty in His whole creation. Augustine has a middle position: he says that we are made in the image of God in our minds, not our bodies, though he allows that there is some likeness in the latter.[35] Similarly, Aquinas says that in intensity and concentration there is more of a likeness to divine perfection in intellectual creatures, though there may also be some likeness in the whole universe (*ST* 1a. xciii. 2 ad 3; he goes on to say (in article 7), following Augustine, that there is a specifically Trinitarian image in the mind). Augustine also says that our inner beauty is more in the image of God than our bodily beauty,[36] a comment which exemplifies something which we saw in earlier chapters, the 'spiritualizing' of the concept of beauty. But it needs to be noted again that one can regard spiritual beauty as more important than physical without being a Dualist, just as, more generally, one can value intellectual, spiritual, and moral considerations over material ones without espousing metaphysical Dualism.

The Dualist position on this issue owes more to Platonism than to Jewish tradition, since the latter regarded persons as psycho-physical unities, and so would have found the idea that only a part of them is in God's image and likeness alien (a Christian might add here that we are not told that *only* our souls are being changed into the likeness of the Lord from one degree of glory to another (2 Cor. 3: 18) or will be transformed by God when 'we shall be like him' (1 John 3: 2); and that the whole Christ was glorified at the Transfiguration, that he appeared bodily at the Resurrection, and that icons of him are regarded as representing his one person

---

[33] e.g. in *In Ps.* xxxii. 9 (*PG* 69: 876c). For other references see Walter J. Burghardt, *The Image of God in Man according to Cyril of Alexandria* (Woodstock, MD, 1957), ch. 2. That chapter contains a valuable survey of patristic literature on this point.

[34] *Adv. Haer.* v. 6. 1; 16. 1. Irenaeus is attacking Gnosticism here.

[35] *Tractatus in Evangelium Ioannis*, xxiii. 10 (*PL* 35: 1589); *On Eighty-three Questions*, no. 51 (*PL* 40: 33).

[36] *Letter* 120 (*PL* 33: 462).

with its two natures[37]). But, in any case, Judaism understood Gen. 1: 26–7 mainly in terms of certain *capacities* given by God in the likeness of His own power, particularly human sovereignty over the rest of creation. This point is true also of many early Christian Fathers, even those who were Dualists: Cyril of Alexandria, for instance, whilst denying that our bodily shape is made in God's image and likeness, finds the area of likeness in our being capable of being good, just, and fitted for all virtue.[38] The philosophical point at issue then becomes one of whether the relevant capacities are located in the soul alone (using the body as its instrument) or in the whole person. But Judaism would not have accepted, or even understood (at least before Greek philosophical influences percolated through), the first alternative.

One particular capacity germane to our enquiry is that for creative work in the arts. Many Christian theologians have described God not just as Creator, but as an artist: St Bonaventure, for example, commenting on the text 'Consider the lilies . . .', describes God as the supreme artist and nature as His *opus*.[39] So it is not surprising that some of them have seen a human artist as imitating not only God's beauty but also His creativity. Thus Dorothy Sayers says that the 'idea of Art as *creation* is the one important contribution that Christianity has made to aesthetics', for the true work of art is the creation of something *new*;[40] and David Jones sees the gratuitousness in the operations of the Creator as being reflected in the art of the creature.[41] Thus we are confronted

[37] See Evdokimov, *L'Art de l'icône: Théologie de la beauté* (Paris, 1970), 178–9, and Aidan Nichols, *The Art of God Incarnate: Theology and Image in Christian Tradition* (London, 1980), ch. 5. Nichols draws attention to the importance of the doctrine of the Incarnation for the development of Christian aesthetics.

[38] See Burghardt, *The Image of God*, ch. 2.

[39] *Comment. in Lk.* xii. 39 (Quaracchi edn., vii. 321). In his discussion of the concept of glory in the Old Testament von Balthasar notes how Gen. 2: 7–8, 19 and many later texts use the terms *yoṣer* (modeller) and *yaṣar* (to model) of God in Creation (*Herrlichkeit: Eine theologische Ästhetik*, iii. 2: *Theologie*, pt. 1. *Alter Bund* (Einsiedeln, 1967), ch. 2).

[40] 'Towards a Christian Aesthetic', in *Christian Letters to a Post-Christian World*, ed. R. Jellema (Grand Rapids, 1969), 77.

[41] David Jones, 'Art and Sacrament', in Nathan A. Scott (ed.), *The New Orpheus: Essays toward a Christian Poetic* (New York, 1964), 27, 32. Maritain sees the artist's creativity as reflecting not only God's creation of the world but also the Father's begetting of the Son (*Art and Scholasticism*, trans. J. W. Evans (New York, 1962), app. 1).

now with two forms of likeness: that of the created product to divine beauty, and that of the artist's imagination and creativity to God's Creation.

Not all theologians, however, approve of the comparison between artist and Creator. It might be argued that no artist, not even a poet, creates out of nothing, for he or she depends on inspiration and imagination, and on a background of inherited forms. But others would attack the comparison more strongly. Wolterstorff thinks that it reeks of a 'Promethean vision' of man as the maker of his own world, a vision exemplified in Romantic and 'élitist' views of art and of the artist's autonomy. It privatizes the artist's role, and ignores both the social context of art and the artist's role of service to others—not to mention underestimating the sheer hard work of most artistic creation.[42]

I think that this criticism arises out of a wider reluctance to speculate about the relationship between aesthetic qualities in the world and divine perfections, a reluctance which would query most of the views discussed so far in this chapter as far as the question of divine likeness is concerned, though Wolterstorff could allow that works of art may be inspired by the Holy Spirit and may even convey a divine message (for instance, about the coming of a future *shalom*). I have already commented that Wolterstorff's view is a very chastened one, compared with the main thrust of this book, for it is one which acknowledges the arts and natural beauty as gifts of God, but does not assign them any sacramental role. It may be compared with Calvin's view of marriage: he allows that it is a good and holy ordinance of God, but, he says, so also are agriculture, architecture, shoemaking, and barbering, yet they are not sacraments; he denies, therefore, that it is a sacrament in the sense understood by the Catholic Church and he questions her reading of Eph. 5: 21–33, which sees the relationship between husband and wife as a sign of Christ's love for His Church, and instead says that St Paul is simply

---

[42] Nicholas Wolterstorff, *Art in Action: Toward a Christian Aesthetic* (Grand Rapids, 1980), pt. 2, §§13–14. See also C. Seerveld, *Rainbows for the Fallen World* (Toronto, 1980), 26, for a similar point, though he allows that an artist may have a priestly role with regard to the richness of creation.

using a similitude (*Inst.* iv. 19. 34–7). I have also suggested already that Wolterstorff's view ignores much of Christian tradition, especially its ascription of beauty to God. This ascription is grounded in Scripture, and cannot therefore be dismissed as a Platonic interpolation in Christianity. It is natural, then, to go on to ask what the relationship is between divine beauty and worldly beauty, both in nature and in art. But this brings us back to the question which I have raised already, but not answered, of how there can be a likeness between the beauty of God, who is invisible and immaterial, and the aesthetic qualities of a visible world. There is, then, a much wider and deeper issue at stake here, which we must pursue further.

This issue, however, is in turn part of the wider question of likeness between the world and God, a question which has been discussed traditionally more with regard to assessing how human moral and intellectual qualities may reflect God's nature than with regard to aesthetics. Here I am thinking again of the statement that we were made in God's image and likeness; but since the doctrine of the Fall, as it has developed in much Christian theology, asserts that the image and likeness have been at least marred by sin (though Paul says that by sin we forfeited God's *glory*, rather than the image and likeness: cf. Rom. 3: 23), I am also thinking of the Christian teaching that the image is being restored in those who are being remade through the Holy Spirit in the likeness of Christ, the perfect image and expression of God (cf. Rom. 8: 29; 2 Cor. 3: 18). Some Christian traditions see the saints as those in whom the likeness is being restored in an outstanding way, and indeed compare them to works of art.[43] The problem of how there can be a likeness between God and creation in these human cases is less severe than in aesthetics, because moral and intellectual characteristics can be analysed

---

[43] Maritain quotes a remark made by Ambrose Gardeil, 'If you must have works of art, will not they be preferred to Phidias who model in human clay the likeness of the face of God?' (*Art and Scholasticism*, 155). Other writers who pursue a similar theme are: G. Florovsky, *Creation and Redemption* (Belmont, Mass., 1976), 204–5; L. Ouspensky, *Theology of the Icon* (Crestwood, NY, 1978), 195–6; and H. Huvelin, *Some Spiritual Guides of the Seventeenth Century* (New York, 1927), p. lxxvi. The last of these writers specifically compares saints to portraits of Christ.

in terms of capacities and actions which are also ascribed to God. If we are told that human wisdom is somewhat like divine wisdom, then we may seek to gain some purchase on such a claim by trying to discern divine actions which manifest God's wisdom and providence. Likewise, we gain some understanding of God's righteousness and love by being told that He secures justice for the orphan and widow, and loves the stranger (Deut. 10: 18). Moreover, we are told to follow him in so doing, and to be merciful and forgiving as He is (Matt. 6: 12, 14f.; Luke. 6: 36). Here again Christianity goes a step further in its claim that God's perfections are manifested in Christ, who is the image of the invisible God, reflecting His glory (Col. 1: 15, Heb. 1: 3, John 1: 14), and whom we are enjoined to follow and to imitate (1 Thess. 1: 6, 1 Cor. 11: 1); and indeed in the doctrine of the Incarnation Christianity offers a bold answer to our question of how the visible can represent the invisible or the divine. But in the case of divine beauty we do not seem to have anything comparable to actions which we can try to discern, apart from the moral and spiritual beauty of Christ. Thus God's incorporeality is more of a difficulty here than it is in the case of qualities like love and justice, both for our understanding what the divine beauty is and for our seeing how there might be a likeness between it and created beauty. This factor perhaps contributes towards the 'spiritualization' of beauty which we noted earlier.

Some early Christian writers were content to leave the matter a mystery. Thus the ninth-century Irish writer, John Scotus Eriugena, said that God manifests Himself in creation in a wondrous and ineffable manner, so that, although 'being without form and species', He 'makes himself beautiful [*formosum et speciosum*]'.[44] But many of them adapted Plato's philosophy and wrote of there being degrees of likeness between created things and divine beauty according to the extent of their participation in it, their archetype.[45] Now such a solution raises questions similar to those raised by Aristotle

---

[44] *Periphyseon*, iii. 17 (*PL* 122: 678c), trans. I. P. Sheldon-Williams. There is a play on words in the Latin.
[45] e.g. Gregory of Nyssa, *On the Making of Man*, xii. 9 (*PG* 44: 161c).

in his critique of Plato's Theory of Forms, and also by Plato himself in the *Parmenides*, questions about, for instance, how things can be said to 'participate' in patterns and how particulars can resemble Forms—it must be a different kind of resemblance from that of particulars to each other, otherwise we would need to appeal to some further entity to explain the resemblance of the particulars to the Forms, and so we would be caught in an infinite regress (the so-called Third Man argument).[46] In his *Nicomachean Ethics* Aristotle objects specifically to the idea that the Form of the Good may explain different kinds of goodness; he asks how things which we regard as good in themselves, like intelligence, sight, honour, and certain pleasures, can come under a single Form. His own conclusion is that goodness is an analogical concept, a position which he illustrates with the example 'as sight is in the body, so is rationality in the mind'.[47] Such an argument seems plausible in the case of beauty, too. For a single Form of the beautiful raises questions analogous to those suggested by Aristotle about the Form of the Good: what is the value of an explanation which regards a sunset, a painting, a symphony, a human character, a scientific theory, and a mathematical proof as participating in a single Form of beauty? The difficulty is compounded if we widen our perspective and take account of other, more particular aesthetic concepts like elegance, delicacy, picturesqueness, and complexity, not to mention other critical concepts like profundity, subtlety, poignancy, and being life-enhancing. What is the relationship supposed to be between all these different qualities and the divine nature?

Several early Christian writers drew on Aristotle as well as Plato, though it is the former's teaching on the different kinds of cause rather than his teaching on analogy that was influential earlier on. Thus Pseudo-Dionysius says that the Super-Essential Beautiful, or Beauty, like the Good, is that from which things are and the pre-existent cause of all that is beautiful; is that unto which and for the sake of which things

---

[46] See Aristotle, *Metaphysics* i. 9. 990b 17 *ff.*, 991a 20 *ff.*, xiii. 5. 1079a 4–13, 1079b 24–6; and Plato, *Parmenides*, 132d–133a.
[47] *Nic. Eth.* i. 6. 1096b 29–30.

are, their goal, final cause, and their Beloved; and is that in which things are, their exemplar and formal cause.[48] It is the last of these kinds of causality, formal or exemplar, which is most relevant to aesthetics and which is appealed to by later writers in their discussions of divine beauty. Dionysius himself, in his *Celestial Hierarchy*, describes the beauty of God as the source of perfection and as reaching out 'to grant every being according to merit, a share of light and then through a divine sacrament, in harmony and peace, it bestows on each of those being perfected its own form'.[49] Thus things are shaped according to divine beauty.

Aquinas follows Pseudo-Dionysius' discussion of the different kinds of cause. In his commentary on *The Divine Names* he says that God is the effective cause of beauty, for He wishes to multiply the beauty that is His own by communicating His likeness; He is the final cause of things because they were made to imitate divine beauty; and He is the exemplary cause because all things are distinguished according to divine beauty, as is shown by the fact that no one cares to make an effigy or representation except with regard to the beautiful (§§352–4). Elsewhere he prefers to associate the good with final causality and the beautiful with formal, for he says that the former answers to appetite but beauty answers to knowledge and pertains to the nature of a formal cause (*ST* 1a. v. 4 ad 1). We find similar treatments of the different kinds of cause in other medieval writers' discussions of aesthetics.[50]

---

⁴⁸ *Div. Nom.* iv. 7, 10 (*PG* 3: 704b, 705d). The term 'exemplar' is derived from Aristotle's use of the word *paradeigma* when describing formal causality in *Metaphysics*, v. 2. 1013a 7 (a word also used by Plato in the *Timaeus* of the pattern used by the creator; and also of the pattern which the philosopher sees when trying to model a state on justice, in *Republic*, 500e).

⁴⁹ iii. 1 (*PG* 3: 164d), trans. C. Luibheid.

⁵⁰ Alexander of Hales's *Summa* says that beauty is based on formal causality (Quaracchi edn., i, n. 103, *contra* 1). Likewise, Ulric of Strasburg says that God is the efficient, exemplary, and final cause of beauty, which he defines as the spreading out of form in matter caused by the divine light; and St Albert, who defines beauty in terms of 'splendour of form', lists the three kinds of cause and identifies the exemplars of beautiful forms with God's nature. It will be seen that the concept of form plays an important role in these writers' notions of beauty. See further von Balthasar, *The Glory of the Lord: A Theological Aesthetics*, iv, trans. B. McNeil *et al.* (Edinburgh, 1989), 381–92; E. de Bruyne, *Études d'esthétique médiévale*, iii, 125–7, 175–80; W. Tatarkiewicz, *History of Aesthetics*, ii (The Hague 1970), 223 ff.

In modern philosophy final and formal causality have tended to drop out of sight. Yet we still occasionally explain what something is by describing its form or its purpose: thus a certain stone may have a hole in its centre because it is a millstone, and a statue may lack an arm because it is of Lord Nelson; and parts of the body and of mechanisms (e.g. a pendulum) are often described in terms of what they are *for*.[51] In theology, too, these two kinds of cause do not attract the same attention that was devoted to them in medieval times. Recently, however, Karl Rahner has used the concept of formal causality in his theology of grace: he says that in grace God communicates Himself to us by means of quasi-formal causality.[52] David Coffey builds on Rahner's work when, in his *Grace: The Gift of the Holy Spirit*, he construes grace as being that gift which consists of the Holy Spirit himself, and sees it as an example of divine formal causality. In such causality a worldly reality is drawn into the Trinity and made receptive, in union with the Son or with the Holy Spirit, to the Father's self-communication. Coffey treats grace as an exercise of divine formal causality by the Holy Spirit, though of course the Spirit draws the other two Persons with him.[53] In view of the meaning of *charis*, which covers both physical gracefulness and theological grace, it would be interesting to extend Coffey's treatment to aesthetics. Beauty, like grace, is given gratuitously and is transformative. Indeed, perhaps they are two varieties of the same thing, for we have seen already that many Christian theologians construe the Spirit's work of sanctification in terms of the restoration of spiritual

---

[51] See Max Hocutt, 'Aristotle's Four Becauses', *Philosophy*, 49 (1974), 385–99; and Peter Geach, *Providence and Evil* (Cambridge, 1977), 35–6, 72–4.

[52] Karl Rahner, 'Some Implications of the Scholastic Concept of Uncreated Grace', *Theological Investigations*, i, ch. 9, 330; 'Nature and Grace', ibid. iv, ch. 7, 175, 177. Rahner uses the phrase 'quasi-formal causality', to distinguish it from the formal causality which takes place wholly within the world.

[53] D. M. Coffey, *Grace: The Gift of the Holy Spirit* (Sydney, 1979), pt. 2, ch. 5. He is anticipated, as he realizes, by St Basil, who compares the Holy Spirit's presence in rational beings to that of a form, making them conformed to the image of the Son (*On the Holy Spirit*, xxvi. 61 (*PG* 32: 180bc); and also by Aquinas in i *Sent*. xviii. 1. 5, where he describes God as, through His wisdom, the 'exemplary formal cause' of our wisdom (Mandonnet edn., i. 445), and in the ensuing exposition of text (Mandonnet edn., i. 447) says that through charity, which is modelled on love, which is the Holy Spirit, we are made holy as by a form.

beauty. Thus both sanctification and aesthetic beauty might be subsumed under a wider concept of beauty.

In such theological uses of the concept of a formal cause, and in their possible extension to aesthetics, we have, however, come a long way from Aristotle (as Rahner indicates by his preference for the phrase 'quasi-formal causality'), who used the term of what makes particular kinds of entity in the world what they are, e.g. a man, a house, an eclipse, or a musical octave.[54] We seem to be much closer to Platonism and its vision of earthly realities as resembling and participating in the world of Forms; and indeed the frequent use of this term 'participation' by Aquinas[55] and others suggests this. Now there is no reason why we should regard 'Platonism' as a dirty word: Stephen Clark has recently recommended a version of Christian Neoplatonism which sees the phenomenal universe as the actualization in time of an ideal image or project grasped by the Christian community.[56] Nor is there any reason why we should not extend the concept of a formal cause beyond Aristotle's use. The trouble is, however, that in so extending it to theological aesthetics we raise certain questions which Aristotle himself did not have to face in his use of the term. In particular we face a problem similar to that raised in the case of the Form of the Beautiful, of how so many very different things could have the divine beauty of the Holy Spirit as their formal cause. A more natural use of Aristotle here would have been to develop his teaching on analogy, rather than on formal causes, and to relate the different kinds of worldly beauty to what later Thomists called the 'prime analogate' of divine beauty.

A MINIMAL SOLUTION

In view of these difficulties let us now go back to our original problem, and see if we can find a solution which will steer

---

[54] See *Metaphysics*, v. 2. 1013a 26–9; vii. 9. 1034a 7, 24; viii. 4. 1044b 13–15.

[55] Though Aquinas goes well beyond Plato in linking his concept of participation with that of *esse*, which is for him the first perfection and act of all acts: see Cornelius Fabro, 'Participation', *The New Catholic Encyclopedia*, x (New York, 1967), 1042–6; and von Balthasar, *The Glory of the Lord*, iv, 401–4.

[56] Stephen Clark, *The Mysteries of Religion* (Oxford, 1986), ch. 14. See also his Gifford Lectures, *From Athens to Jerusalem* (Oxford, 1984).

round some of them. The key question is: how can the beauty of God, who lacks body and matter, be reflected not only in people's 'spiritual' beauty but in their physical beauty, and indeed in the beauty and other aesthetic qualities of nature and art (here we must remember again not to confine ourselves to the visual, whether in nature or in art; those who feel God's presence in music are more likely to speak of His voice than His likeness)? We want any proposed answer to preserve a certain minimum of theological claims: that God has created the world and is present in it, that its beauty is therefore His creation, and that this beauty is like divine beauty. In using the word 'like' I am using the simplest and most widely used term, without forgetting that there is believed to be a causal priority between God and creation which is captured in more specific terms like 'image' or 'archetype', and in metaphors like 'mirror' and 'reflection', and that the likeness is created by the very presence of God in things: Aquinas wrote of beauty as caused by the indwelling of God (*In Ps.* xxv. 5), and more recent writers like Hopkins and Weil see it as a manifestation of the divine presence.

I have already discussed, in previous chapters, the reasons for ascribing beauty to God, an ascription presupposed in the belief that worldly beauty reflects divine beauty, and I have also made the point that we do not attribute beauty only to material entities but also to scientific theories, mathematical proofs, the plots of novels, and so forth. So God's invisibility, immateriality, and incorporeality are not the obstacle which they seem at first to ascribing beauty to Him. But how can we *compare* creation with God, the visible with the invisible? Again, we can go part of the way simply by pointing to what we do already. We often make what are called cross-categorial comparisons, in which, for example, dispositions and abstract entities are compared with physical beings. A stout heart may be said to be worth more than all the gold of Croesus, and mathematics may come to be more interesting than a collection of stamps. Many similes and metaphors are of this nature. Thus Shakespeare compares pity to 'a naked new-born babe' in *Macbeth*, and tells us that 'the quality of mercy is not strain'd, it droppeth as the gentle rain from heaven', in *The Merchant of Venice*. Such comparisons are common in evaluations of works of art: one may say, for example, that the plot of *Our Mutual Friend* is more convoluted than a Chinese puzzle, or that the development of a theme in a piece of music is heavy-footed or leaden. This is an area in which people make many kinds of cross-categorial comparisons: they speak of colourful music and harmonious designs, ascribe balance or sweetness to various kinds of art or to human personality, compare the development of a theme in music to that of a character in a novel, and match outstanding figures from different branches of art with other, e.g. Beethoven and Rembrandt or Michelangelo, Raphael and Mozart, and Berlioz and Delacroix. People also make cross-categorial comparisons of different kinds of beauty, and we have seen a good example of such a comparison in the work of Jonathan Edwards, when he says of the world that 'the sweetest and most charming beauty of it is its resemblance of spiritual beauties . . . How great a resemblance of a holy and virtuous soul is a calm serene day.'[57] It would, of course, be strange to say that one of these is more beautiful than the other; but then it would be strange to say that the 'Eroica' Symphony is more beautiful than Rembrandt's *Night Watch* or than Miss World. What we can do, however, is to compare things within certain categories with each other, and then to cross the boundaries of these categories and say that one thing has a higher degree of that beauty which is appropriate to its category than another one has of the beauty appropriate to its category. Thus Beethoven's music may have outstanding aesthetic merit amongst all music, whereas Perugino may occupy only the middle rank of painters, somewhat in the way that a gardener's roses may be worthy of a prize at a show whilst his tomatoes are undistinguished; yet we would be reluctant to say simply that one is better than the other.

Another kind of cross-categorial relationship is that in which a thing in one category is taken as *representing* one in another category. We are familiar with the idea that a map may be said to represent a particular terrain, and that such a representation is very different from that of a landscape

---

[57] *Images or Shadows of Divine Things*, 135–6.

painting. Here we have two different ways of representing a
material entity. But sometimes the material is taken as representing the immaterial or abstract. The most familiar
examples of such representations are found in iconography:
one thinks of depictions of Sacred and Profane Love in
Renaissance painting, or of the use of the symbol of a dove to
represent the Holy Spirit. But here again the point must be
made that a representation, like a sign, need not involve a
relation of likeness, for the representation may depend on a
system of symbols and so be more akin to linguistic denotation.[58] Our concern now is only with cases where the representation involves a likeness.

In God's case certain factors rule out any straightforward
comparison: He is believed to be infinite, the source of all
perfections including beauty, which, as Creator, he diffuses
in the world, and so not a member of any creaturely category.
Some theologians claim, too, that His nature is simple, for He
is not composed of matter and form, and His essence and
existence are the same. Aquinas makes these claims; and then
when he comes to discuss analogical predication, he warns us
that although a creature may represent and resemble God to
the extent that it has some perfection, it does not represent
Him as it might something else in the same species or genus,
but as a transcendent principle, somewhat as the forms of
physical objects represent the power of the sun; moreover, he
says, the perfections which pre-exist in God in a unified and
simple way are represented in creatures in a diverse and
manifold way (*ST* 1a. xiii. 2, 4). Nevertheless, as his words
indicate, he does allow that creatures represent and resemble
God. This is hardly surprising, not only because of his
theology of Creation but also because of his acceptance of the
philosophical principles that a cause must have the perfections
of its effect and that an agent makes a product to his own
likeness, principles which lead him to say that in a sense all
created things are images of God.[59] It seems, then, that
Aquinas felt it possible to speak of creation's likeness to
God without treating Him as one being alongside others or

---

[58] See again Goodman, *Languages of Art*.
[59] *ST* 1a. iv. 2; *Summa contra Gentiles*, iii. 19. 4, iii. 41. 1.

reducing Him to what Matthew Arnold called an 'infinitely magnified and improved Lord Shaftesbury',[60] and without losing sight of the religious requirement that the object of worship far surpass any other reality.

If we stress only the differences between the divine nature and other things, we are liable to end up in agnosticism about the former, and also perhaps in what Antony Flew calls 'death by a thousand qualifications', that is, the tendency to reduce language about God to vacuity by introducing too many qualifications in it.[61] It was in counterpoise to Flew that Ian Ramsey called for 'life by a thousand enrichments', that is, an approach which seeks rather to draw out the infinite richness of the divine nature in comparison with created things.[62] If indeed God's being is of surpassing splendour, then it will be refracted and reflected in His creation in a countless variety of ways. His wisdom is believed to be reflected in human intelligence and wisdom (though perhaps we should follow Prov. 6: 6 and look also to the ant, and maybe the fox and the bee, too). In the case of His beauty we have a vastly wider range of possible reflections to consider, because of the manifoldness of divine and human imagination. Thus seeking a likeness to God in the world is somewhat similar to asking the question of what England is like. Such a question requires us to consider several kinds of relation. We might reflect on England's likeness to Holland, France, and other countries in certain respects, and perhaps look then at some maps, photographs, and paintings. But a deeper answer would require us to consider how a national spirit is reflected in institutions, history, personal character and temperament, music and literature, and so forth, and to look at parallel reflections in other nations. If there are so many facets to the expression of a single nation's identity, then we can expect the richness and splendour of the divine nature to be mirrored in countless ways. Moreover, a Trinitarian account of God introduces a further factor, which not only posits relatedness in the deity

---

[60] Matthew Arnold, *Literature and Dogma* (London, 1873), 306–7.

[61] Antony Flew, 'Theology and Falsification', in Antony Flew and Alasdair MacIntyre (eds.), *New Essays in Philosophical Theology* (London, 1955), 96–9, 106–8. I quote from 97.

[62] Ian Ramsey, *Models and Mystery* (London, 1964), 60.

itself but also spells out the relation between God and creation in terms of the missions of each Person.

What I have suggested is a minimal account of how we can allow for a likeness between creatures and God, adequate to cover the essential theological points at stake. I have tried to spell out this account in terms of the idea of a cross-categorial comparison, rather than getting involved in theological versions of theories of universals. Of course, one may be led on from here to such theories, and indeed we find a very metaphysically ambitious one in some early Christian Fathers who adapt Plato's Theory of Forms. Such more ambitious accounts, however, start from the kind of considerations which I have put forward, even if they go far beyond them (thereby raising many difficulties). Moreover, without such a minimal account we cannot make sense of, or justify, the deep religious conviction that worldly beauty has a sacramental character because it reflects God's glory.

7

Anticipating the Final Transfiguration of Things

AT the beginning of this study I quoted some of Barth's tributes to Mozart. He held that the composer had a place in theology, especially in the doctrine of Creation and in eschatology, for he hymned the goodness of creation and transported his listener 'to the threshold of a world which in sunlight and storm, by day and by night, is a good and ordered world'.[1] Mozart, said Barth, 'had heard, and causes those who have ears to hear, even today, what we shall not see until the end of time—the whole context of providence'.[2] Here Barth was approaching an idea that constantly recurs in Christian theology and aesthetics, that beauty has an eschatological significance, that in it we glimpse the future transfiguration of the cosmos which is symbolized in the New Jerusalem and the new heaven and earth prophesied in the Book of Revelation (anticipated by Isa. 65: 17). He was writing about art, but one might also see outstanding natural beauty as a sign of what is to come.

The particular aspect of this subject which concerns us here is the role of the Holy Spirit: we have seen that some early Christian Fathers conveyed the eschatological role of the Spirit by referred to him as the 'Perfecter'. We shall see now that many theologians go on to assign the Spirit a role in the final transfiguration of the cosmos, giving an eschatological sense to the verse 'When thou sendest forth thy Spirit, they are created; and thou renewest the face of the earth' (Ps. 104: 30) by seeing this transfiguration as the completion of his work of renewal. More specifically, some theologians again

[1] Karl Barth, *Wolfgang Amadeus Mozart*, trans. Clarence K. Pott (Grand Rapids, 1986), 22.
[2] Karl Barth, *Church Dogmatics*, iii, pt. 3, p. 298.

link beauty and the Holy Spirit: Leonid Ouspensky, for example, says that 'true beauty is the radiance of the Holy Spirit, the holiness of and the participation in the life of the world to come'.[3]

The idea that the final transfiguration of things is already being anticipated now is an extension to the whole cosmos of the doctrine of redemption, somewhat in the way that the idea that the world reflects God's glory, discussed in the last chapter, is related to the claim that human beings were created in God's image and likeness. In both instances we move out from the human to the cosmic; in the present case we look for a new creation not only of the human person but of God's whole cosmos, which is regarded either as having been marred by the Fall or as incomplete because still evolving. Recent treatments of this theme have been presented more from a scientific than an aesthetic point of view, and they have usually been influenced by evolutionary theories (I am thinking here particularly of Teilhard de Chardin's work). They also have far more of a Christological than a pneumatological emphasis, e.g. in regarding Christ as the crowning glory of the cosmos (again, Teilhard is typical).

The main biblical warrants for such an extension of the concept of redemption are, besides the Book of Revelation, Rom. 8: 20–2, where St Paul, writing of the revelation of future glory and using the common biblical image of a woman in labour, says that the whole creation has been groaning in travail until now, for it was subjected to futility, and prophesies that it will be set free from its bondage to decay so as to obtain the freedom of the glory of the children of God; and Col. 1 : 20, where he proclaims that Christ made peace on the Cross, so that everything in heaven and on earth should be reconciled. In commenting on the first of these Pauline passages, Stanislas Lyonnet points out that it should be related to several texts in the Old Testament, including the early chapters of Genesis: just as the first covenant, that with

---

[3] Leonid Ouspensky, *Theology of the Icon* (Crestwood NY, 1978), 190. Ouspensky goes on to say that icons of the saints remind us of their holiness and so serve as 'a revelation of the holiness of the world to come, a plan and a project of the cosmic transfiguration.' (p. 228).

Noah, had cosmic implications, so the eschatological alliance (the coming of the Messiah) will necessarily have its impact on all creation; similarly, just as the earth was cursed through the sin of Adam and Eve (Gen. 3: 17), so it will be redeemed as a consequence of our redemption—including the redemption of our bodies, which Paul has mentioned earlier in the chapter (v. 11), saying that God will give life to them through the indwelling of his Spirit. Paul is rejecting the Stoic idea of a final conflagration of all things, and instead preaching that the universe will, like the human body, be transformed and glorified in its own way, though we are not told the 'how' of this transformation.[4] Lyonnet's concern is with eschatology, but other writers have extended the argument backwards by looking for a restoration of the beauty of Paradise before the Fall: thus Irenaeus says that the righteous will rise again to behold God in a renewed creation, restored to its original state (*Adv. Haer.* v. 32. 1; he too appeals to Rom. 8: 19–21), and Abraham Kuyper extends the point to art when he remarks that Calvinism has a stronger sense of the Fall than Roman Catholicism has, yet it too honours art as a gift of the Holy Spirit and as a consolation in our present life: 'art has the mystical task of reminding us in its productions of the beautiful that was lost and of anticipating its perfect coming lustre'.[5]

In this chapter I shall look at a few versions of the idea which I have sketched, bringing out both the role of the Holy Spirit and the connection with the Transfiguration and Resurrection of Christ, and then assess whether the parallel between it and the resurrection of the dead enables us to develop it further.

THE HOLY SPIRIT, TRANSFIGURATION, AND GLORY

The anticipated transfiguration of the cosmos is a favourite theme of many Russian theologians, who emphasize also the

---

[4] 'The Redemption of the Universe', in G. Weigel *et al.* (edd.), *The Church: Readings in Theology* (New York, 1963), 136–56.
[5] 'Calvinism and Art', ch. 5 of his *Lectures on Calvinism* (Grand Rapids, 1953), 155. Cf. John W. Dixon, *Nature and Grace in Art*, (Chapel Hill, 1964), 73; and Paul Tillich, 'Nature, also, mourns for the Lost Good', in *The Shaking of the Foundations* (London, 1949), 76–86.

role of the Holy Spirit in this work. In the last century Vladimir Solovyov put forward a very exalted view of beauty (and also of sexuality). He defined beauty as 'The transfiguration of matter through the incarnation in it of another, a supernatural principle'.[6] Whilst history continues, there can be only partial and fragmentary anticipations of perfect beauty. The arts, in their highest achievements, glimpse eternal beauty, and anticipate and give a foretaste of the reality beyond, which is to come. Thus they have a prophetic function, and the final task of perfect art 'is to realize the absolute ideal, not in imagination only but in very deed—to spiritualize and transfigure our actual life'.[7]

In this century Nicholas Berdyaev is the best-known Russian writer to have touched on such themes. He too saw human creativity in the arts as anticipating the final transfiguration of the world, foreshadowing a new Heaven and a new earth. In *The Meaning of the Creative Act*[8] he describes the artist's function as being to contribute to the actual transformation of the world-as-it-is into the world-as-it-shall-be, and to the realization of the Kingdom of God. It was this stress on the eschatological significance of art which led Berdyaev to dislike classicism, which, he thought, wrongly sought perfection in this limited and fallen world, and to prefer romanticism, with its 'pervading sense of the insufficiency of all achievement within the finite', and its longing for and aspiration to the trans-finite.[9]

We find, however, the fullest treatment, and one which brings out the role of the Holy Spirit, in the work of Sergius Bulgakov. In a festival sermon 'Pentecost and the Descent of the Spirit' he says that the Pentecost described in Acts 2 was anticipated by the first moment of Creation when the Spirit of God moved upon the face of the waters, which he calls 'the first cosmic Pentecost by anticipation', and by the creation of man when God breathed into his nostrils the breath of life,[10]

[6] Vladimir Solovyov, 'Beauty, Sexuality and Love', in Alexander Schmemann (ed.), *Ultimate Questions* (New York, 1965), 75.
[7] Ibid. 98.
[8] Nicholas Berdyaev, *The Meaning of the Creative Act* (London, 1955).
[9] Id., *Dream and Reality* (London, 1950), 215.
[10] In *A Bulgakov Anthology*, ed. J. Pain and N. Zernov (London, 1976), 183.

which he also describes as a Pentecost. Bulgakov hopes for a further cosmic Pentecost, for he thinks that the *whole* of creation is to be redeemed. This Pentecost will come after the universal resurrection, and then 'the image of God shall be reflected in all creation and God shall be all in all.'[11]

Bulgakov gives a fuller development of the subject in his book on the Holy Spirit. There he describes nature as having followed man in the Fall, but as not abandoned by the good angels, for it still bears the indelible image of God, 'not yet reborn but being born'.[12] Like Lyonnet he cites Rom. 8 in this connection (p. 202), and also as supporting the claim that all creation is to be redeemed, through the salvation of man (p. 292). There will be a transfiguration of the world, a new heaven and a new earth, which will be the culmination of the work of the Holy Spirit begun in Creation as described in Gen. 1 : 2, for the Spirit's work of giving life at the beginning of the world is parallelled by his role in bringing it to a new being (pp. 202, 327). Such a transfiguration will not be the work of the Holy Spirit alone, for he does nothing in the world without Christ: if revelation tells us that the Holy Spirit was involved in Christ's resurrection, then it will be the same with the end of the world and its transfiguration, which is linked with Christ's second coming, for which the Spirit is preparing in history (pp. 337 *f*. In any case, as we saw in Chapter 4, Bulgakov links the work of the Son closely with that of the Spirit, even before the Incarnation and Pentecost, in the 'dyad' of divine wisdom). Bulgakov concludes that the Holy Spirit's action goes on beyond the grave and indeed beyond history (he cites John 14: 16), and that 'Pentecost has no limits, neither in depth nor extension. It is an event as universal as the incarnation of Christ' (p. 338).

Elsewhere Bulgakov extends his thinking about the eschatological significance of beauty to art. He says that the divine source of objective Beauty is also the source of the human

---

[11] Ibid., 186. The cosmic aspect of Pentecost is represented in the Eastern liturgy of Pentecost and in icons: cf. Evdokimov, *L'Art de l'icône: Théologie de la beauté* (Paris, 1970), 287 *ff.*; id., 'Nature', *Scottish Journal of Theology* 18 (1965), 1–22; and José Comblin, *The Holy Spirit and Liberation* (New York, 1989), ch. 2.

[12] Sergius Bulgakov, *Le Paraclet* (Paris, 1946), 199. There is a play on words here, depending on the derivation of *natura* from *nasci* (to be born).

creation of beauty in art, for when God created us in His image, He gave us three gifts: a will directed to the good, reason or wisdom, and aesthetic appreciation. Hence we are called to create as well as to contemplate beauty, and artistic creativity helps to bring about the 'transfiguration of the world and renders it conformable to its true image'.[13] He does not discuss whether the Incarnation or Pentecost have made any difference to art as such—an interesting question and one germane to Bulgakov's work, because though he allows that there were sendings of the Holy Spirit in the ancient world and that he was present through Wisdom, he restricts the Spirit's hypostatic presence to the time after Pentecost.[14]

We find briefer expressions of these views among some Western theologians. Aquinas ends his *Summa contra Gentiles* by saying that since men will be clothed with glory, so also will bodily creation achieve its kind of splendour in its own way (iv. 97; he cites Rev. 21: 1 and Isa. 65: 17 *f.*); and elsewhere he says that the heavenly bodies will be more radiant when the world is renewed.[15] Among his followers, Gilson brings out the role of art here: 'Thanks to the fine arts, matter enters by anticipation into something like the state of glory promised to it by theologians at the end of the time, when it will be thoroughly spiritualized'.[16] Von Balthasar too, who often draws attention to the way in which overwhelming beauty points beyond itself, describes beauty as 'hidden eschatological transfiguration'.[17] Wolterstorff, like Kuyper, sees art as an instrument in our struggle to overcome the fallenness of our existence, and, by the delight which it affords, anticipating the *shalom* that is to come; he calls on Christian artists to share in the task of witnessing to God's work of renewal and to work for the greater glory of God: 'Paradise is forever behind us. But the City of God, full of

---

[13] 'Religion and Art', in E. L. Mascall (ed.), *The Church of God: An Anglo-Russian Symposium* (London, 1934), 177.
[14] Bulgakov, *Le Paraclet*, 220–4, 234–7.
[15] iv *Sent*. xlviii. 2. 3.
[16] Étienne Gilson, *The Arts of the Beautiful* (New York, 1965), 33.
[17] Hans Urs von Balthasar, *The Glory of the Lord*, iii, *Studies in Theological Style: Lay Styles*, trans. Andrew Louth *et al.* (Edinburgh, 1986), 277 (with reference to Hamann); cf. 341.

song and image, remains to be built.'[18] Few of these and other Western writers, however, give much consideration to the role of the Holy Spirit when discussing eschatology. Conversely, the many recent works on the Holy Spirit have little to say about the transfiguration of the world in beauty. But an article by Robert Faricy on art as a charism in the Church makes exactly the point that we have found in some Orthodox writers.

The Spirit that inspires art is the eschatological Spirit, the Holy Spirit who breaks through into the present from God's promised future. The Kingdom of God is to come, and yet it is here already, breaking in on us through the Holy Spirit as the pledge of future glory, and making all things new now. The Holy Spirit renews us toward the future. Partly, the Spirit renews through inspired art.[19]

Such theological accounts do not, I think, arise solely from religious considerations, for they also have their roots in certain common human experiences. People often talk of the 'other-worldly' character of beauty and intense aesthetic experience. Sometimes this conveys the conviction that they are, as it were, irruptions from another world, and I have noted how talk of inspiration fits in here. But often what is meant is that we have already glimpsed *this* world, transfigured. Such glimpses may give rise to a desire for redemption, in the weak sense of wanting to be free of evil and ugliness. Intense aesthetic experiences may also be the occasion of great peace and joy, and many people have drawn attention to the sense of timelessness which may be enjoyed then, and which can be regarded as an anticipation of some greater, timeless joy, say that of the Beatific Vision. Others, however, have drawn attention to the sense of discontent, perhaps of unfulfilled longing, that such experiences may engender. Their elusiveness and transiency may give rise to frustration and to a yearning for something more which would fulfil what has been given already. Such experiences, too, can

[18] Nicholas Wolterstorff, *Art in Action: Toward a Christian Aesthetic* (Grand Rapids, 1980), 199; cf. 84, 169.
[19] Robert Faricy, 'Art as a Charism in the Church', *Thought*, 57 (1982), 98. Cf. Walter Kasper, *The God of Jesus Christ*, trans. M. J. O'Connell (London, 1984), 200.

be interpreted in religious terms. Thus John F. Haught says 'that ultimately satisfying beauty for which we long but which continues to elude us is what the word "God" means', and suggests that God may be thought of as the horizon of ultimate beauty towards which we are irresistibly drawn.²⁰ Of course, none of these experiences of frustration or yearning shows that there *will be* a timeless state of bliss, a transfigured world or an intense experience of divine beauty which would satisfy them. But they indicate an area of human life in which people have thought both that our fulfilment demands eternal life and that such fulfilment is anticipated or glimpsed here and now.

There are also two Christological themes which need to be mentioned at this point: the Transfiguration and the Resurrection, both of which are *bodily* manifestations of Christ, in the former case in a visibly glorified form, and both are regarded by some as having a cosmic significance, because they are taken as anticipating a final restoration of all things. The Transfiguration looks both backwards and forwards. The details of the story in the Synoptic Gospels indicate that the writers wished to suggest a parallel between the manifestation of Christ's glory on Mount Tabor and the theophany to Moses on Mount Sinai, described in Exodus. But Luke's account, in particular, also looks forward: it describes Peter and his companions as seeing the 'glory' of Christ, when the appearance of his face changed and his clothing became dazzling.²¹ This glory can be regarded as anticipating that of Christ's second coming, for Luke has used the word a few verses earlier (v. 26), of the Son of Man coming in glory. But the second coming presupposes the Resurrection, so the Transfiguration has been taken too as an anticipation of the latter, which in turn is regarded as an anticipation of our resurrection, for St Paul describes the Resurrection as 'first-fruits'

---

²⁰ John F. Haught, *What is God?* (New York, 1986), 70. Cf. von Balthasar, *The Glory of the Lord*, i, 320–1 and, more generally, iii, 50. Bonaventure says that since God alone is goodness itself and beauty, only in Him is there perfect delight (i *Sent.* i. 3. 2; Quaracchi edn., i. 41).

²¹ Luke 9: 32. 2 Pet. 1: 16 uses the word *megalaiotēs* (majesty). In this context some Eastern Orthodox writers (e.g. Evdokimov, *L'Art de l'icône*, 30–1) adduce the transfiguration of St Seraphim of Sarov in the presence of his disciple Motovilov. The latter's account can be found in G. P. Fedotov (ed.), *A Treasury of Russian Spirituality* (Gloucester, Mass., 1969), 266–79.

(1 Cor. 15: 20, 23) and the risen Christ as the first-born among many brethren (Rom. 8: 29). Thus the Transfiguration can be regarded, through the intermediary of the Resurrection, as an anticipation of our transfiguration in the life to come; and therefore, according to the interpretation of Rom. 8, which we have already discussed, as an anticipation of a cosmic transfiguration. But in any case, that chapter goes in sequence from the Resurrection of Christ (v. 11) and our enlivening by the Holy Spirit (vv. 11, 13–16) to the glorification of Christ and us (vv. 17–18), to the redemption of the whole creation (vv. 19–22). St Paul evidently regards the Resurrection as the hinge on which all turns, and elsewhere he ascribes a cosmic role to the risen Christ, telling us that in him all things hold together (Col. 1: 17) and that everything is subject to him (Phil. 2: 9 f., 3: 21; Eph. 1: 10, 20–3). Hence St Ambrose regards the Resurrection of Christ as the resurrection of the whole universe, not just that of man;[22] and Teilhard de Chardin sees the risen Christ as inaugurating a new stage in the evolution of the universe, involving the spiritualization of matter and the development of consciousness.[23]

The theme of our future glory is expounded elsewhere by Paul, when he says that Christ will change our lowly bodies to be like his glorious body (Phil. 3: 21), and that those who have been raised with Christ will appear with him in glory (Col. 3: 4).[24] But Paul does not refer elsewhere to the transfiguration of the cosmos, so the other main biblical source usually quoted in this connection is the Book of Revelation, which prophesies that a new and glorified Jerusalem and a new heaven and earth will come, and that all things will be

---

[22] *De Fide Resurrectionis*, §102 (*PL* 16: 1403a). The cosmic nature of the Resurrection is also expressed in many Eastern icons.

[23] See e.g. 'The Christic', in *The Heart of Matter*, trans. R. Hague (London, 1978), 80–102.

[24] Commenting on the words 'Then the righteous will shine like the sun in the kingdom of their Father' (Matt. 13: 43), Bonaventure says that Christ's most glorious risen body offers 'an exemplary beauty of the human bodies to be raised up' (*Lignum Vitae*, 35; Quaracchi edn., viii. 81b). Aquinas says (following Augustine, *The City of God*, xxii. 19) that since the risen Christ had wounds, so risen martyrs may perhaps have them too, for the beauty of virtue rather than of body may shine out from them (*ST* 3a. liv. 4). This suggests, tenuously, an interesting question: need we expect the glorified cosmos to be uniformly beautiful?

made new (21: 1–5; cf. Matt. 19: 28). The first of these is
described as radiant, filled with light, and adorned with gold,
jewels, and precious stones (21: 11, 18–21, 23), a description
which aims to convey the splendour of what is to come.

BEAUTY AND SANCTITY AS FIRST-FRUITS

I mentioned at the beginning of this chapter that the idea that
the final transfiguration of things is being anticipated now is
an extension to the cosmos of the doctrine of redemption. It
is worth taking this point a little further, since this extension
may throw light on the work of the Holy Spirit as 'Perfecter'.
The claim that the transfiguration of the cosmos is being
anticipated now in the Spirit's work of creating beauty is
similar to the claim that the Spirit's present work of sanctification is an anticipation of our future glorification and life of
holiness. Again, there is a parallel between beauty and sanctification, a parallel which we have come across before and
which in the present case involves their eschatological character. Likewise, there is a parallel between the raising of the
dead to glory, and cosmic transfiguration, for they are both
seen as the fulfilment of creation and perhaps the overcoming
of the Fall—I say 'perhaps' because I think that Gen. 3 refers
only to the earth and I am not sure that Rom. 8 licenses talk
of a 'fallen' cosmos. Moreover, in both cases the Holy Spirit
is given a central role, for Christian tradition appeals to him
both as the sanctifier and as the one who renews the face of
the earth. But far more attention has been given to the former
role, so let us look first at the connection between sanctity and
the world to come, and then see how far we can push the
parallel which I have sketched out.

There are some passages in the New Testament which
associate the Holy Spirit with sanctification, e.g. Rom. 15:
16, 1 Pet. 1: 2, and others which associate the Spirit with the
Christian's hope, e.g. Rom. 15: 13. But there are a few texts
which link the two: St Paul writes of those who sow to the
Spirit reaping eternal life thereby (Gal. 6: 8) and of sancti-
cation having eternal life as its end (Rom. 6: 22 *f.*); and in
Rom. 8 (a crucial text for the present chapter!) he says: 'If
the Spirit of him who raised Jesus from the dead dwells in

you, he who raised Christ Jesus from the dead will give life to your mortal bodies also through his Spirit which dwells in you.'[25] He uses the metaphors of 'first-fruits' and 'earnest': the Spirit is the first-fruits of our adoption as sons and of the redemption of our bodies (Rom. 8: 23), an earnest of our heavenly dwelling and of the swallowing up of what is mortal by life (2 Cor. 5: 5; cf. 1: 22); and the seal of the Holy Spirit is the earnest of our inheritance (Eph. 1: 13 *f.*; cf. 4: 30). Similarly, the Epistle to the Hebrews uses the metaphor of a foretaste, of those who 'have become partakers of the Holy Spirit, and have tasted the goodness of the word of God and the powers of the age to come' (6: 4 *f.*).

A variation on this theme is the belief that the Spirit has a role in the raising of the dead. This belief is not commonly expressed, perhaps because John 5: 21 and 6: 40 *ff.* mention only the Father and Son in this connection. But if the raising of the dead is an external work of the Trinity, then we would expect the maxim that such works are undivided to apply here too. And indeed St Paul writes of God giving life through His Spirit, in Rom. 8: 11 (already quoted). Hence some Christian writers, both early and late, assign a central role to the Holy Spirit in the raising of the dead. St Basil, for example, says that the Spirit causes both our renewal in this life and our resurrection from the dead,[26] whilst the Macarian homilies teach that the risen saints will be clothed in external glory through the work of the Holy Spirit now within them (Homily 5, §9). There is an interesting Rabbinic teaching which both offers a parallel with the Christian position being considered and reveals an unusual angle on an Old Testament text which we have found used often by Christian writers on aesthetic questions. The text is Exod. 35: 31, in which Bezalel is described as being filled with the spirit of God and

---

[25] v. 11. I follow Augustine and Chrysostom in taking Paul as referring here to the final resurrection rather than to the continual operation of the Spirit in us here and now. See C. E. B. Cranfield, *A Critical and Exegetical Commentary on the Epistle to the Romans*, i (Edinburgh, 1975), 391; and Geerhardus Vos, *The Pauline Eschatology* (Grand Rapids, 1961), 163–4.

[26] *On the Holy Spirit*, xix. 49 (*PG* 32: 157ac). See my *Spirit, Saints and Immortality* (London, 1984), 52 *f.* for some other texts. Ch. 4 of that book, and also my 'A Neglected Argument for Immortality' (*Religious Studies*, 19 (1983), 13–24) gives a fuller version of the argument being considered.

endowed with skill, perception, and knowledge; the commentary says 'In this world, my spirit hath given you wisdom, but in the time to come it will give you new life', and it quotes Ezek. 37: 14, 'And I will put my spirit in you, and ye shall live.'[27] Here we move from the Spirit's inspiration of art, not to the final transfiguration of reality, but to the raising of the dead.

Some Christian writers have gone a step further and have seen the Holy Spirit's sanctifying power revealed in this life as *evidence* for his power in the life to come. Thus St Irenaeus, after quoting St Paul's remarks in 2 Cor. 3: 3 about the Spirit writing on the tablets of the human heart, asks: 'If, therefore, in the present time, fleshly hearts are made partakers of the Spirit, what is astonishing if, in the resurrection, they receive that life which is granted by the Spirit?'[28] Earlier in the same book, though in a different context, Irenaeus appeals not only to God's power, but also to His promises and His fidelity as grounds for his belief in immortality. He instances the translation of Elijah and the preservation of Jonah and of the men cast into the fiery furnace by Nebuchadnezzar, and sees these as demonstrating God's power, promise, and fidelity, and therefore as confuting those who cannot believe that God can and will raise up their bodies to eternal life (*Adv. Haer.* v. 5. 2).

If indeed God has promised both to bestow His sanctifying Spirit and to raise the dead by this Spirit, then His fulfilling His first promise provides evidence of His power and fidelity, and therefore gives us further grounds for trusting that He can and will fulfil His second promise. So Irenaeus has presented us with a good evidential argument, though it is one which depends on certain general theological assumptions and on the particular claim that we can identify the relevant divine promises. Moreover, St Paul's metaphors of 'firstfruits' and 'earnest' suggest not only God's fidelity to His promises but also that the sanctification effected by the Holy Spirit now is an anticipation as well as a preparation for the

---

[27] *Midrash Rabbah*, iii *Exodus*, ed. H. Freedman and M. Simon, trans. S. M. Lehrman (London, 1939), 551.
[28] *Adv. Haer*, v. 13. 4, trans. Roberts and Rambaut.

life of the resurrection, that there is a relationship of fulfilment as well as of succession. An earnest is something more than a pledge or a guarantee, for the Greek term used, *arrabōn*, differs from the term *enechuron* (pledge) in that it denotes what is actually a small part of the whole that is promised, for instance a portion of the purchase-money given to ratify a contract.[29] The phrases 'down payment' or 'first instalment' are probably closer in meaning to the original than 'pledge' or 'guarantee' used in many modern translations (though some people may dislike their connotations of buying washing-machines and so on). Of course, we must be chary about inferring too much from the use of metaphors; and in any case we do not want to suggest that the future life will be just 'more of the same', for some of the other analogies used by St Paul, for instance the seed in 1 Cor. 15: 36 *ff.* and the tent and the house in 2 Cor. 5: 1, suggest that there will be a great change within the continuity. A seed or a tent is not quite a first instalment of a plant or a building.

The argument I have sketched out moves from moral beauty or saintliness to the life of the resurrection. Can we construct a similar argument whereby we might go from physical beauty in the world now, whether in nature or in art, to the eschatological transfiguration of the universe, appealing to the claim that both beautifying and sanctifying are ways in which the Spirit perfects creation? There are some differences between the two cases: for example, there is nothing quite corresponding to death in the case of the cosmos except perhaps for the great natural disasters and cosmic catastrophes prophesied in much apocalyptic literature (e.g. Mark 13, 2 Pet. 3: 10 and Augustine, *The City of God*, xx. 16); and sanctity is a perfection only of rational beings, whereas beauty can be possessed by inanimate nature and artefacts. Still, we can imagine how such an argument might go: God has promised to beautify the world through the Holy Spirit; He has also promised to transfigure the cosmos in glory at the end of time; He is already fulfilling His first promise, in natural beauty and in art; therefore, since He has the requisite power and is always faithful to His promises, He can be trusted to

[29] J. B. Lightfoot, *Notes on the Epistles of St Paul* (London, 1895), 323 *f.*

fulfil His second promise. The trouble is, however, that we lack biblical support for the premisses of the argument. We admitted that the argument adumbrated by Irenaeus depends on certain theological premisses. In his case, however, the premisses are supported by the biblical texts about the Holy Spirit, the life to come, and the connection between them, whereas in the case of the argument about cosmic transfiguration we lack such a biblical base, particularly the relevant divine promises. Although this transfiguration is perhaps prophesied by Rom. 8 and the Book of Revelation, it is not linked there with the Holy Spirit in the way that sanctification and the raising of the dead are by Paul. Conversely, although there is some biblical warrant for linking both natural beauty and artistic skill with the Holy Spirit, as we saw in Chapter 1, still they are not *promised* in the way that sanctification and the raising of the dead are, nor are we told that they are the first-fruits or an earnest of what is to come. Thus we cannot simply extend to the cosmos the kind of argument which Irenaeus suggested, an argument which expresses what is implicit in Paul's metaphors.

We can, however, go part of the way on the basis of what we have already established. From what has been said in this and previous chapters, we can put forward the following three propositions:

i If there is to be a final transfiguration and glorification of all things through the power of God, then the Holy Spirit will participate in this, as being a work of the Trinity.

ii Moreover, the Spirit will have a special affinity with this work because of his particular connection with beauty.

iii Hence we can say that his work in creating and inspiring earthly beauty is an anticipation of what is to come.

Moreover, we can boost the argument by appealing to a further consideration, one I have already discussed, the Resurrection (in which the Holy Spirit has a role), if we understand it as having a cosmic significance, as symbolizing and anticipating God's transfiguration of all nature in His new and final Creation.

THE LIFE TO COME

It remains for me to touch on a few other issues. Since the term 'cosmos' refers to the whole universe and not just the earth, and since we now know it to be far larger than the ancients believed (to put it mildly), the thought of its transfiguration makes one dizzy. We can imagine, perhaps, the 'redemption' of our planet through the restoration of a damaged ecology, but we find it difficult to grasp the idea of a cosmic transformation. And does not such an idea fly in the face of contemporary cosmology? A recent work of popular science suggests a very different outcome from the one we have envisaged:

It is very hard to realize that all this [the earth] is just a tiny part of an overwhelmingly hostile universe. It is even harder to realize that this present universe has evolved from an unspeakably familiar early condition, and faces a future extinction of endless cold or intolerable heat. The more the universe seems incomprehensible, the more it also seems pointless.[30]

It is important, however, that we do not allow ourselves to be bullied here, for such views may be as much a projection as the kind of picture we are considering. I do not think that the size of the universe is a theological problem: for if the whole universe, however vast, is God's creation, then does it not all come within His purposes, unimaginable though they are to us? Who are we to say that it is already fully 'formed', and may not be glorified by Him? What is perhaps more difficult for people today than for earlier generations is the Christian belief that this little corner of it, planet earth, is of such great significance for the whole. But, of course, it is certain events which have happened here, rather than the earth itself, which are held to be significant; and again, we must be careful about our setting a priori limits to the ways in which God may choose to work. In any case, our concern now is not so much with the role of the earth within the whole as with the evolution of the whole. The point at stake is the belief that God has a goal for the universe, so that its

---

[30] Steven Weinberg, *The First Three Minutes* (London, 1983), 148–9.

history will not culminate in universal destruction or continue as cyclical repetition, and that part of this goal is its glorification.

It is probably unprofitable, even if interesting, to speculate on the nature of the transfigured cosmos, or on the life of the resurrection. Of course, literal-minded questions press in upon us: will extinct volcanoes become alive again? But then similar questions can be asked about the resurrection of the dead: will those who rise again have to cut their toe-nails? It may, however, be worth bearing in mind now Oscar Cullmann's observation that art is the most suggestive medium for conveying eschatological ideas, avoiding the banality of putative descriptions of the afterlife. He instances Grünewald's picture of the Resurrection in his Isenheim altar-piece, the Credo in Bach's B Minor Mass, and the last part of Handel's *Messiah*.[31] I would single out also Gluck's 'Dance of the Blessed Spirits' in his opera *Orpheus and Eurydice*, as conveying a yearning for an everlasting peace, for a kingdom beyond suffering and disharmony; and Mozart's Masonic Funeral Music, as suggesting nobility, hope, and a sense of divine splendour. In so far as a sense of redemption or transfiguration of the world can be conveyed, it is by such works rather than by speculative descriptions (or by quasi-realistic paintings of Heaven and Hell). Of course, there are many attitudes to death and to the life to come besides Christian hope: there may be acceptance, fear, protest, and despair, and there may be corresponding expressions of these in art.[32] One might ask where Brahms's *A German Requiem*, Strauss's *Four Last Songs*, and Dylan Thomas's poem 'Do not go gentle into that good night' belong on a spectrum of such attitudes. One might also ask whether there can be anticipations of Hell in art (apart from attempted depictions of it), for example, in some of Francis Bacon's paintings.

Otherwise, I think, one must be satisfied with some minimal comments, indicating certain logical requirements and

---

[31] At the end of his 'Immortality of the Soul or Resurrection of the Dead', in K. Stendahl (ed.), *Immortality and Resurrection* (New York, 1965), 53.

[32] I have been helped to see this by Geoffrey Turner, 'The Music of Death and Resurrection', *The Month* (1988), 589–96.

limits. Presumably the transfigured cosmos will be spatial, at least in the sense of involving perceived relationships between things. We can, however, say nothing, from a theological basis, about its material nature; though those who assume that the present laws of physics and chemistry will continue to hold sway and who therefore predict the running-down of the universe from the Second Law of Thermodynamics may, again, be making an unwarranted projection. Possibly there is a parallel here with the doctrine of the resurrection of the body, which states that the life of the resurrection will be a bodily one, though the bodies concerned with be 'spiritual' ones—a term which St Paul probably used in 1 Cor. 15: 44 to indicate the relationship of such bodies to the Holy Spirit rather than their composition, though he also says that they are imperishable (1 Cor. 15: 42).[33] Will the transfigured universe be in time? Aquinas argues that it will be incorruptible (and therefore lacking animals, plants, and 'mixed bodies'), without motion, and not in time (*Summa contra Gentiles*, iv. 97); and many, likewise, have said that the life of the resurrection will be eternal in the sense of timeless. Some have seen mystical experience or intense aesthetic pleasure as anticipating such a life.[34] There is, however, an alternative tradition which sees the life to come as occurring in time, in the sense that it is a life of continued development. This tradition has, not surprisingly, been more concerned with the development of persons than with that of the cosmos as a whole. Thus the Marburg neo-Kantian Hermann Cohen, for instance, following Kant's view of the acquisition of holiness as an infinite progress, described holiness as an 'infinite task', which 'consists in self-sanctification, which, however, can have no termination, therefore cannot be per-

---

[33] See R. J. Sider, 'The Pauline Conception of the Resurrection Body in I Cor. xv. 35–54', *New Testament Studies*, 21 (1975), 428–39, and C. F. D. Moule, 'St Paul and Dualism: The Pauline Conception of Resurrection', *New Testament Studies*, 12 (1965–6), 106–23.

[34] Ronald Hepburn questions whether aesthetic time-transcendence is an 'earnest' of a wholly non-successive eternal life hereafter; for although in music and poetry there is a synoptic grasping, it is from *time*, the temporally spread-out, that the non-temporal structure emerges ('Time-Transcendence and Some Related Phenomena in the Arts', in *'Wonder' and Other Essays* (Edinburgh, 1984), 113 ff.).

manent but only infinite striving and becoming'.[35] More generally, Miguel de Unamuno argued that our highest aspirations are dynamic rather than static, so that an eternity which was an eternal timeless present would allow no scope for creation or progression.[36] Their view is anticipated in St Gregory of Nyssa's concept of *epektasis* (straining forward), which he uses of the soul's constant stretching out towards perfection, a process which Gregory regards as continuing beyond the grave, for in one of his sermons he says 'The graces that we receive at every point are indeed great, but the path that lies beyond our immediate grasp is infinite . . . those who thus share in the divine Goodness . . . will always enjoy a greater and greater participation in grace throughout all eternity.'[37]

Gregory is concerned not merely with our growth in holiness but also with our awareness of the inexhaustible splendour of God; for elsewhere he applies his concept of *epektasis* to the contemplation of divine beauty. In the passage from his *Life of Moses* which I quoted in Chapter 3 he writes of the constant desire of the lover of beauty to go beyond perceived beauty and 'to be filled with the very stamp of the archetype . . . to enjoy the Beauty not in mirrors and reflections, but face to face'.[38] This passage echoes Plato's *Symposium*, but also 2 Cor. 13: 12, so presumably Gregory is thinking of what has come to be called the Beatific Vision. This vision has often been conceived of in terms of a solitary disembodied soul immediately present to God, without reference to body or community. But the Christian doctrines of the Resurrection of the Body and the Communion of Saints suggest that the life to come will be both bodily and communal (note that the context of 1 Cor. 13: 12 is Paul's hymn on love, which says that love will continue forever). The Vision has

---

[35] Hermann Cohen, *Religion of Reason out of the Sources of Judaism*, trans. S. Kaplan (New York, 1972), 111.

[36] Miguel de Unamuno, *The Tragic Sense of Life* (London, 1967), ch. 10.

[37] *Sermon* 8 (*PG* 44: 940 f.), trans. H. Musurillo.

[38] ii, §§231–2 (*PG* 44: 401d–404a), trans. A. Malherbe and E. Ferguson. Likewise, Cyril of Alexandria, citing 1 John 3: 2 ('we shall see him as he is'), says that then we shall understand the divine beauty as we contemplate the glory shining from God (*In Jn*. xi, commenting on John 16: 25, *PG* 74: 464b).

often been regarded too as eternal in the sense of timeless. But if God's nature is a mystery in Rahner's sense of a reality of unfathomable depth,[39] then it may be, again, that there is a development in the Beatific Vision, in that those who enjoy it are led ever onwards to penetrate more deeply into God's inexhaustible splendour. Finally, the Vision has often been regarded in terms of the divine essence, without reference to the doctrine of the Trinity. Again, there seem to be grounds for questioning such an interpretation, grounds suggested by what we have said in this book about the work of the Trinity and the role of the Holy Spirit in it. In his book on the Holy Spirit Paul Evdokimov says that the Eastern Church does not see the future beatitude as a vision of the divine essence, but rather in terms of deification, participation in the divine life and vision of the Trinitarian glory through the glorified humanity of Christ.[40] Likewise, David Coffey concludes his study of grace, conducted in Trinitarian terms, by writing of its fulfilment in the Beatific Vision in a similar way. He argues that the work of Christ and the Holy Spirit, far from being discontinued in Heaven, reach their completion there. For the vision of God spoken of in the New Testament is precisely a vision of the *Father* (Coffey cites Matt. 18: 10 and 1 John 3: 2). Hence Coffey argues that the Beatific Vision is mediated to the just in heaven by the Incarnate Son, and that in Heaven we receive the Holy Spirit in fullness. He concludes 'In this view God is everlastingly Trinitarian, not just in himself but in his dealings with men . . . If grace, then, is truly Trinitarian . . . glory too must be the same.'[41]

Coffey goes on from there to consider the world (which he notes correctly is more than the earth), to which we are related through our bodies. Although he acknowledges, citing Rom. 8: 21–3, that the whole world shares in the redemption, he

[39] Karl Rahner, 'The Concept of Mystery in Catholic Theology', *Theological Investigations*, iv, ch. 2, 36–73.

[40] Paul Evdokimov, *L'Esprit Saint dans la tradition Orthodoxe* (Paris, 1969), pt. 1, ch. 5.

[41] D. M. Coffey, *Grace: The Gift of the Holy Spirit* (Sydney, 1979), 257. Rahner ascribes to the humanity of Christ a place in the immediacy of the Beatific Vision: see 'The Theology of the Symbol', in his *Theological Investigations*, iv, trans. K. Smyth (London, 1974) ch. 9, 221–52, esp. 244.

confines his further discussion of the question (p. 259) to pointing out that we should love both the world and our neighbour, and therefore that we should work with the latter to perfect the world through our skills and to resist violence (which he takes to include pollution, thus relating his theme to a theology of the environment). He does not then extend what he has said about the future life of the Beatific Vision to our other topic, the transfiguration of the whole cosmos. And there, perhaps, he is prudent, for the theologian has very little to go on here. It would indeed be nice to invent a new branch of theology, perhaps to be called eschatological aesthetics, which could speculate further upon the matter. But there is the obvious danger of lapsing into fantasy and wish-fulfilment. If, however, Coffey is right in arguing that the life of the Beatific Vision is a Trinitarian one, then perhaps by analogy we can argue likewise for the transfiguration of the cosmos, as I have sought to do with special reference to the role of the Holy Spirit. If so, then the theologian may not be too imprudent in accepting the propositions which I put forward earlier: that if there is to be a final transfiguration of the universe through God's power, then the Holy Spirit will participate in it; that the Spirit will have a special affinity with this work; and that the Spirit's creation and inspiration of earthly beauty may be regarded as an anticipation of what is to come.

8

Conclusion

IN the middle of the sixteenth century one of the theologians associated with the Council of Trent, Melchior Cano, wrote a work, *On the Sources of Theology*, in which he attempted to give an account of the sources available to theologians. He found ten: the main ones listed were Scripture, Church tradition, and the statements of Councils. He did not mention the beauty of the world nor art (for that matter, he also omitted prayer, liturgy, and personal experience). Yet three centuries later Dostoevsky could say 'Beauty will save the world', and many others have spoken of the revelatory character of great art and of the 'other-worldly' character of beauty, both in the sense of being a sign of a higher world now and of anticipating a future transformation. We see an enormous chasm, both spiritually and intellectually, between these two mentalities. In this work I have attempted to do something to bridge it, by looking at the religious significance of natural beauty and of art in terms of the doctrine of the Holy Spirit, exploring a connection made first by St Irenaeus among Christian theologians, though anticipated in the Old Testament. The thesis I have looked at is that the divine beauty is to be explained in Trinitarian terms, for the Father's glory is reflected in the Son, his perfect image, and diffused through the Holy Spirit; that the Spirit has the mission of communicating God's beauty to the world, both through Creation, in the case of natural beauty, and through inspiration, in that of artistic beauty; that earthly beauty is thus a reflection of divine glory and a sign of the way in which the Spirit is perfecting creation; and that beauty has an eschatological significance, in that it is an anticipation of the restored and transfigured world which will be the fullness of God's kingdom. It remains for me to say a little more about some particular difficulties we have encountered, and to point a few morals.

RETROSPECT

Clearly I have assumed that a concern with natural beauty and art is a serious one. It is not merely a luxury; still less is it to be dismissed with the derogatory term 'aestheticism' (it would be interesting to speculate on how both 'theological' and 'aesthetic' have tended to become derogatory terms, especially considering that their parents, religion and art, are both supposed to be concerned with what is profound and moving in human life). Theologically, such a concern arises both out of one's own experience and out of an acceptance of the doctrine of Creation. John W. Dixon points out that an artist cannot hate his material, and that for a Christian artist physical material is glorified both through Creation and through the new creation which proceeds from the Incarnation.[1] If indeed the world has been created by God, then the qualities in it which delight us (or disturb us too, sometimes) have been put there by Him, perhaps with this purpose[2]— which is not to say that they must affect everyone in the same way at the same time. Likewise, our creative powers and faculties of appreciation are gifts of God; and although they may be abused (for a lack of grace can contaminate them as much as any other human powers), they may also be infused and guided by His spirit. Thus both worldly beauty and our creative powers may be described as a 'grace'. Indeed, there are some grounds for going still further, if we accept that our creative powers are part of the image and likeness of God with which we are endowed, and if we accept also that God's glory shines through His creation. In exercising their creative powers in the production of things of worth, men and women may become channels of God's creativity; and the beauty of what they create may, like natural beauty, have a sacramental significance, in that by it the material may convey the spiritual and indeed, some would say, serve as a sign of God's presence and activity.

[1] John W. Dixon, *Nature and Grace in Art* (Chapel Hill, 1964), 197.

[2] Thomas Reid conjoins the claims that the beauty which God has diffused is not our fancy but a real excellence in His work, expressing His perfections, and that the faculties which He has given us are not fallacious. See his essay, 'Of Taste', ch. 4, in *Essays on the Intellectual Powers of Man* (Edinburgh, 1785), esp. 741.

Here we are approaching one of the most difficult subjects discussed in this work, the divine beauty and the way it is reflected in the world. Although it is true that a lot of Christian thinking on the matter is much influenced by Plato and his successors, especially Pseudo-Dionysius, there is nevertheless good biblical warrant for ascribing beauty to God and for treating worldly beauty as a reflection of His glory. In any case, it is hardly likely that He would choose to disguise this particular attribute, though most theologians may have given this impression by their neglect of the topic. If, however, this part of the argument is still unacceptable, the reader can simply ignore Chapters 3 and 6 of this work, for the thesis which it presents can be presented either in a full-strength version, or in various diluted ones. Many Protestant theologians (though not Jonathan Edwards) are unhappy with what they regard as speculations about God's beauty, and are content to claim simply that natural beauty and artistic talents are divine gifts, particularly associated with the Holy Spirit. This position is not one which I accept, because I think that it disregards much Christian tradition and fails to do justice to the religious character of beauty and other aesthetic properties (just as I find Calvin's view of marriage limited) but it must be treated seriously. The same is also true of positions which reject a Trinitarian analysis of the Holy Spirit or Spirit of God, and prefer to treat these terms as ways of describing God's outreach to the world, particularly the human heart. Here I am thinking of liberal Christian theologians like Lampe, who favour a unitarian account of God and reject traditional Trinitarian formulations; but also Jewish theologians who have no difficulty in accepting the divine beauty and its manifestations, and also the particular association of artistic gifts with the divine spirit, but who reject later Christian doctrines, especially the hypostasization of the Word and the Spirit into Persons in the Trinity. Such people would have difficulty rather with Chapter 4. But, again, a weaker version of the argument is possible, which associates beauty with the Holy Spirit, but simply regards the latter term as a way of describing certain modes of God's power and presence.

I have often had occasion to point to parallels between

claims about the Holy Spirit's association with beauty and similar claims about sanctity. Some of the early Fathers indeed treated sanctity as a form of beauty, and as the most important one; and theologians have developed the view which we have been considering much more commonly with reference to sanctification than to other kinds of beauty (it must be admitted that the relation between the Son and the Spirit is more easily seen in the former case: the invisible Holy Spirit renews us in the likeness of the holiness of Christ, who is the visible image of the Father). We found too in the last chapter that both beauty and holiness have often been regarded as having an eschatological significance; we have found, also, that both have been regarded as forms of likeness to God, and have been associated particularly with the work of the Holy Spirit, in that he is believed to restore the image of God in the fallen human race and to adorn things as likenesses or reflections of God's glory. But there is a more general parallel: in both cases we are concerned with what we *perceive*, and in both cases there may be a sense of God's shining through the world. Thus George Steiner says: 'Be it in a specifically religious, for us Judaeo-Christian sense, or in the more general Platonic-mythological guise, the aesthetic is the making formal of epiphany. There is a "shining through".'[3] Likewise, many people have witnessed to the power of saintly people in drawing others to religion, not so much by what they say as by what they *are* (perhaps they too should be listed in Cano's list of theological sources), hence a consideration of them must be part of any theological aesthetic, in von Balthasar's wider sense of that phrase, as including any concern to perceive revelations of the divine glory.

Philosophically, the main problems in this work are suggested by the commonly quoted remark that 'beauty is in the eye of the beholder' and by the claim that beauty is no longer a central concept in aesthetics. It is indeed true that many of the ideas which we have considered were set out originally in an intellectual milieu very different from today's. Writing of the ancient belief that all worldly beauty is the epiphany of divine glory, von Balthasar remarks:

[3] George Steiner, *Real Presences* (London, 1989), 226.

The Renaissance and the Reformation destroyed this unreflected configuration from opposing directions: the former, with its enthusiasm for Antiquity, dissolved the Christian glory into an all-embracing cosmic revelation (which was then perfected in the Enlightenment), while the latter so stressed the distinctiveness of the biblical glory that by comparison all cosmic beauty faded and was submerged.[4]

The intellectual difficulties are reinforced by the confusion occasioned in many people's minds by some modern artistic movements, especially in painting and music. But perhaps the difficulties are not quite as severe as they appear at first sight. Beauty is indeed subjective, in the sense that it is a matter of our reactions to the perceived properties of things, and people may disagree about this as about so many other matters. But it does not follow that these properties are unreal or our perceptions illusory.[5] Likewise, although it is true that beauty is not as central a concept in modern aesthetics as it was in much ancient and medieval aesthetics, and also, more generally, that critical evaluation is regarded today as only one part of aesthetics, it is still an important concept and one which attracts a lot of attention. What is true is that modern aesthetics tries to 'place' the concept of beauty logically by elucidating the relationship between it and other aesthetic concepts, showing that it is part of a network of such concepts. But this development is all to the good, since there is no reason why we should confine our treatment to a single concept; and other aspects of nature and of works of art may have a pneumatological significance besides beauty. Modern aesthetics offers us all sorts of possibilities here, and not just with regard to aesthetic evaluation. There is also the nature of symbolic systems in art to be considered, and the analogy which they suggest with languages; and there is the investigation of the social and economic factors which influence artists. The latter investigation is often suspect to religious people

---

[4] Hans Urs von Balthasar, *The Glory of the Lord: A Theological Aesthetics*, iv. *The Realm of Metaphysics in Antiquity*, trans. B. McNeil *et al.* (Edinburgh, 1989), 323. Of course, von Balthasar himself raises the question of whether these developments may not really be an impoverishment of aesthetics as he understands it, and much of the following volume of the work can be regarded as a treatment of that question.

[5] See again Guy Sircello, *A New Theory of Beauty* (Princeton, NJ, 1975), §33.

and regarded as materialistic, perhaps because of its connection with Marxism. But if God can work through secondary causes (as I have argued in my discussion of inspiration), there is no good reason for excluding the factors which I have mentioned from a theological aesthetics. Modern aesthetics may well make a positive contribution to our investigation, rather than blocking it off or hindering it.

OPENNESS TO THE SPIRIT

The argument which we have examined has a disturbing consequence: those who destroy the beauty of God's creation or who create ugliness may be sinning against the Holy Spirit. Such a conclusion is likely to seem unwelcome and strange to most people, because we have got used to the ideas that beauty is a luxury, that a concern with natural beauty or with art is only one among many things which may occupy people's leisure hours, and that such a concern has little to do with religion. Occasionally such assumptions are shattered, as in the scene in Heinrich Böll's powerful novella, *And where were you, Adam?*, in which the concentration-camp commandant shoots the Christian Jewess, Ilona, because he cannot bear the beauty of her singing of a Latin motet, when she is being auditioned for the choir which is his great pride and which he subsequently orders to be destroyed; the commandant's action is depicted by Böll as something like a sin against the Holy Spirit. But perhaps these assumptions are themselves a sign of the disastrous divorce between religion and a sense of beauty in our time, a divorce which is a far more serious problem than the pagan nature of much modern art, and which is manifested in many different ways, for instance in the toleration of drab or makeshift liturgies and in the failure to follow up Ruskin's denunciation of the squalor of industrial towns and cities (often the squalid has simply been replaced by the dreary). But if indeed the argument of this book is correct, then a failure to create beauty, and a lack of appreciation of it, are both signs of an absence of the Holy Spirit. Either the Spirit has not been given, or else there has been what St Paul calls a quenching or suppression of the Spirit (1 Thess. 5: 19). If the Spirit has not been given, we have to ask whether this is simply a matter of divine freedom ('The wind/ spirit blows where it wills'), resulting in the lack of inspiration so familiar to artists in their dry periods, or whether there has also been a lack of openness to the Spirit, and a failure to pray for and to eagerly await his promptings.

All this, however, sounds rather grim and condemnatory (though it has to be said). Let us be more positive and turn the argument round. Aquinas, as we have seen, said that all truth is from the Holy Spirit, and Calvin followed him in saying that the Spirit of God is the only fountain of truth, even that of profane writers. Now, again, if the argument of this book is correct, it would seem that the Holy Spirit is the source of all real beauty and aesthetic merit, both because of his work in Creation and because of his freedom to inspire whomsoever he wills, often, it seems, without much regard to the recipient's moral character or religious orthodoxy. So the argument has also a more tolerant and wide-embracing aspect.

Even this more positive note, however, is still too solemn and moralistic to end on. The Book of Proverbs describes wisdom as delighting God at Creation and playing joyfully in His presence, and as at play everywhere in the world, delighting to be with the sons of men (8: 30 *f.*); and the Book of Job describes all the stars of the morning as singing with joy at the Creation (38: 7). Barth too brought in an element of play in his tribute to Mozart from which I quoted at the beginning of this work, when he said 'it may be that when the angels go about their task of praising God, they play only Bach. I am sure, however, that when they are together *en famille*, they play Mozart and that then too our dear Lord listens with special pleasure.'[6] That is a better note on which to end. The important thing is that we look (or listen), rejoice, and give thanks.

---

[6] Karl Barth, *Wolfgang Amadeus Mozart*, trans. Clarence K. Pott (Grand Rapids, 1986), 23.

SELECT BIBLIOGRAPHY

WORKS LINKING THE HOLY SPIRIT AND AESTHETICS

ASHTON, PETER D., 'The Holy Spirit and the Gifts of Art', *Theological Renewal*, 21 (July 1982), 12–23.

BALTHASAR, HANS URS VON *The Glory of the Lord: A Theological Aesthetics*, trans. John Riches *et al.* (7 vols.; Edinburgh, 1982–), esp. vol. i. *Seeing the Form*, trans. Erasmo Leiva-Merikakis (Edinburgh, 1982).

BULGAKOV, SERGIUS, *Le Paraclet* (Paris, 1946).

—— 'Religion and Art', in E. L. Mascall (ed.), *The Church of God: An Anglo-Russian Symposium* (London, 1934).

DELATTRE, ROLAND A., *Beauty and Sensibility in the Thought of Jonathan Edwards* (New Haven, 1968).

EDWARDS, JONATHAN, *Essay on the Trinity*, ed. George P. Fisher (New York, 1903).

—— *The Mind*, in *The Works of Jonathan Edwards*, vi. *Scientific and Philosophical Writings*, ed. Wallace E. Anderson (New Haven, 1980).

—— *Miscellanies*, in *The Philosophy of Jonathan Edwards, from His Private Notebooks*, ed. Harvey G. Townsend (Westport, Conn., 1972).

EVDOKIMOV, PAUL, *L'Art de l'icône: Théologie de la beauté* (Paris, 1970).

FARICY, ROBERT, 'Art as a Charism in the Church', *Thought*, 57 (1982), 94–9.

KUYPER, ABRAHAM, *Lectures on Calvinism* (Grand Rapids, 1953).

—— *The Work of the Holy Spirit*, trans. H. de Vries (Grand Rapids, 1975).

SHAFFER, PETER, *Amadeus* (London, 1980).

WEIL, LOUIS, 'The Arts: Language of the Spirit', in Gerard Austin *et al.*, *Called to Prayer: Liturgical Spirituality Today* (Collegeville, Minn., 1986).

WORKS ON THE HOLY SPIRIT

ALÈS, ADHÉMAR D', 'La doctrine de l'Esprit en Saint Irénée', *Recherches de science religieuse*, 14 (1924) 497–538.

184   *Select Bibliography*

BALTHASAR, HANS URS VON, *Spiritus Creator: Skizzen zur Theologie*, iii (Einsiedeln, 1967).
—— *Theologik, iii. Der Geist der Wahrheit* (Einsiedeln, 1987).
BERKHOF, HENDRIKUS, *The Doctrine of the Holy Spirit* (London, 1965).
BOUYER, LOUIS, *Le Consolateur: Esprit-Saint et vie de Grâce* (Paris, 1980).
BULGAKOV, SERGIUS, 'Pentecost and the Descent of the Spirit', in J. Pain and N. Zernov (eds.), *A Bulgakov Anthology* (London, 1976).
COFFEY, DAVID M., *Grace: The Gift of the Holy Spirit* (Sydney, 1979).
—— 'A Proper Mission of the Holy Spirit', *Theological Studies*, 47 (1986), 227–50.
COLERIDGE, SAMUEL TAYLOR, *Confessions of an Enquiring Spirit*, ed. H. St J. Hart (London, 1956).
COMBLIN, JOSÉ, *The Holy Spirit and Liberation* (New York, 1989).
CONGAR, YVES, *I Believe in the Holy Spirit*, trans. David Smith (3 vols.; London, 1983).
—— *Word and Spirit*, trans. David Smith (London, 1986).
EVDOKIMOV, PAUL, *L'Esprit Saint dans la tradition Orthodoxe* (Paris, 1969).
FEDOTOV, G., 'De L'Esprit Saint dans la nature et dans la culture', *Contacts*, 28 (1976), 212–28.
FLORENSKY, PAVEL, 'On the Holy Spirit', in Alexander Schmemann (ed.) *Ultimate Questions: An Anthology of Modern Russian Religious Thought* (New York, 1965).
HENDRY, GEORGE S., *The Holy Spirit in Christian Theology* (London, 1957).
ISAACS, MARIE, *The Concept of Spirit: A Study of Pneuma in Hellenistic Judaism and its Bearing on the New Testament* (London, 1976).
LAMPE, GEOFFREY, *God as Spirit* (Oxford 1977).
MACDONALD, GEORGE, *A Dish of Orts* (London, 1908).
MCDONNELL, KILIAN, 'The Determinative Doctrine of the Holy Spirit', *Theology Today*, 39 (1982), 142–61.
—— 'A Trinitarian Theology of the Holy Spirit', *Theological Studies*, 46 (1985), 191–227.
MARMION, COLUMBA, *Fire of Love* (London, 1964).
MEYENDORFF, JOHN, *Byzantine Theology* (New York, 1984).
MOLTMANN, JÜRGEN, *God in Creation: An Ecological Doctrine of Creation* (London, 1985).
MÜHLEN, HERIBERT, *Der Heilige Geist als Person in der Trinität,*

bei der Inkarnation und im Gnadenbund: Ich—du—wir (Münster, 1969).
PANNENBERG, WOLFHART, 'The Doctrine of the Spirit and the Task of a Theology of Nature', *Theology*, 75 (1972), 8–21.
RAVEN, CHARLES E., *The Creator Spirit* (London, 1927).
STREETER, BURNETT H. (ed.), *The Spirit* (London, 1928).
TAYLOR, JOHN V., *The Go-Between God* (London, 1972).
TORRANCE, THOMAS F., *Theology in Reconstruction* (London, 1965).

MORE GENERAL WORKS

ABRAHAMS, ISRAEL, *The Glory of God* (Oxford, 1925; reprinted in his *Foundations of Jewish Life: Three Studies*, New York, 1973).
APOSTOLOS-CAPPADONA, D., (ed.), *Art, Creativity and the Sacred* (New York, 1984).
BALTHASAR, HANS URS VON, 'Revelation and the Beautiful', in *Word and Revelation*, trans. A. V. Littledale (New York, 1964).
BARTH, KARL, *Wolfgang Amadeus Mozart*, trans. Clarence K. Pott (Grand Rapids, 1986).
BERDYAEV, NICHOLAS, *The Meaning of the Creative Act* (London, 1955).
BRUYNE, EDGAR DE, *Études d'esthétique médiévale*, ii, iii, (Bruges, 1946).
DAVIES, OLIVER, *Living Beauty: Ways of Mystical Prayer* (London, 1990).
DILLENBERGER, JOHN, *A Theology of Artistic Sensibilities: The Visual Arts and the Church* (New York, 1986).
DRURY, JOHN, 'God, Ugliness and Beauty', *Theology*, 76 (1973), 531–5.
ECO, UMBERTO, *The Aesthetics of Thomas Aquinas*, trans. H. Bredin (London, 1988).
—— *Art and Beauty in the Middle Ages*, trans. H. Bredin (New Haven, Conn., 1986).
FARRER, AUSTIN, *The Glass of Vision* (Westminster, 1948).
FRASER, HILARY, *Beauty and Belief: Aesthetics and Religion in Victorian Literature* (Cambridge, 1986).
GILSON, ÉTIENNE, *The Arts of the Beautiful* (New York, 1965).
—— *L'École des Muses* (Paris, 1951).
GUTMANN, JOSEPH, *Beauty in Holiness: Studies in Jewish Customs and Ceremonial Art* (New York, 1970).
HAZELTON, ROGER, *Ascending Flame, Descending Dove: An Essay on Creative Transcendence* (Philadelphia, 1975).

HEGEL, GEORG WILHELM FRIEDRICH, *Aesthetics: Lectures on Fine Art*, trans. T. M. Knox (Oxford, 1975).

HEPBURN, RONALD, *'Wonder' and Other Essays* (Edinburgh, 1984).

JONES, DAVID, 'Art and Sacrament', in Nathan A. Scott (ed.), *The New Orpheus: Essays toward a Christian Poetic* (New York, 1964).

KRUG, HEINRICH, *De Pulchritudine Divina* (Freiburg im Breisgau, 1902).

LEEUW, GERARDUS VAN DER, *Sacred and Profane Beauty*, trans. D. E. Green (London, 1963).

McINTYRE, JOHN, *Faith, Theology and Imagination* (Edinburgh, 1987).

MARITAIN, JACQUES, *Art and Scholasticism*, trans. J. W. Evans (New York, 1962).

MARTIN, JAMES A., *Beauty and Holiness: The Dialogue between Aesthetics and Religion* (Princeton, 1990).

MAURER, ARMAND, *About Beauty* (Houston, 1983).

MOLTMANN, JÜRGEN, *Theology of Play*, trans. R. Ulrich (New York, 1972).

MOTHERSILL, MARY, *Beauty Restored* (Oxford, 1984).

NICHOLS, AIDAN, *The Art of God Incarnate: Theology and Image in Christian Tradition* (London, 1980).

OSBORNE, HAROLD, 'Revelatory Theories of Art', *British Journal of Aesthetics*, 4 (1964), 332–47.

OUSPENSKY, LEONID, *Theology of the Icon* (Crestwood NY, 1978).

PELIKAN, JAROSLAV, *Fools for Christ: Essays on the True, the Good and the Beautiful* (Philadelphia, 1955).

REINES, CHAIM, 'Beauty in the Bible and the Talmud', *Judaism*, 24 (1975), 100–7.

SAYERS, DOROTHY, *Christian Letters to a Post-Christian World*, ed. R. Jellema (Grand Rapids, 1969).

—— *The Mind of the Maker* (London, 1941).

SEERVELD, CALVIN, *Rainbows for the Fallen World* (Toronto, 1980).

SIRCELLO, GUY, *A New Theory of Beauty* (Princeton, 1975).

SPARGO, EMMA J. M., *The Category of the Aesthetic in the Philosophy of St Bonaventure* (New York, 1953).

STEINER, GEORGE, *Real Presences* (London, 1989).

TATARKIEWICZ, WLADYSLAW, *History of Aesthetics*, ii, iii (The Hague, 1970, 1974).

WEIL, SIMONE, *First and Last Notebooks*, trans. R. Rees (Oxford, 1970).

—— *On Science, Necessity and the Love of God*, trans. R. Rees (Oxford, 1968).

WEIL, SIMONE, *Waiting on God*, trans. Emma Craufurd (Fontana edn., London, 1959).

WILSON, JOHN, *One of the Richest Gifts: An Introductory Study of the Arts from a Christian World-view* (Edinburgh, 1981).

WOLTERSTORFF, NICHOLAS, *Art in Action: Toward a Christian Aesthetic* (Grand Rapids, 1980).

INDEX